Mudlark River

—ɯ—

Down the Thames with a Victorian Map

Simon Wilcox

MUDLARK RIVER
Published by Simon Wilcox
Copyright © Simon Wilcox, 2014

Printed by CreateSpace

ISBN: 978-0-9930163-0-1
ISBN 0993016308

About the Author

Simon Wilcox worked as a journalist for magazines and newspapers in the UK and Singapore, popped up as a reporter on BBC local radio and went all digital for a while as a website editor for an NGO before finally deciding to sit down in the quiet solitude of his study to write this book. He is based in Warwickshire, England.

For Fiona

A Note from the Author

MUDLARK RIVER is based on a journey down the River Thames that I undertook in the spring and summer of 2013. I tackled the task in three parts, walking along the upper reaches of the Thames Path in early spring, the middle reaches in late spring and the lower reaches in the summer, staying at riverside pubs and small hotels along the way.

Whatever my progress along the way, I could always rely on my wife Fiona to offer me the utmost support in my efforts to become an author. The encouraging noises made by my sister Sally, other members of my family and friends were much appreciated too.

I am also grateful to independent editor, writer and agent Jennifer Barclay who read the book, liked it and gave me some invaluable advice.

Thanks too to the staff at the British Library, the British Newspaper Library, the National Archives at Kew and the libraries at the Royal Geographical Society and the University of Warwick who, unbeknown to them, assisted me in my research as I delved into newspapers, memoirs, letters, directories and other sources to unearth the history of the Thames and the story of the Victorian mapmaker, Edward Weller. As far as possible the details from the past I present in this book are historically accurate – Weller really did live at 34 Red Lion Square, he really was a producing a series of maps for the *Weekly Dispatch* in 1863 and public gas lamps really were installed in the riverside village of Pangbourne in November the same year.

Finally, I must express my appreciation to the people I met in the Thames valley who put me up for the night in their lovely pubs and guest houses, passed the time of day with me, and pointed me in the right direction when I got lost, including the walker who guided me to the source of the river shortly before I started my journey in earnest – I included him in my final travelogue.

While I'm on the subject of the people I met, I would like to add that, as this is a true story, I have tried to be discreet about people's identities, offering only first names in some instances and also changing a name here and there.

Simon Wilcox

September 2014

Contents

An extract from Edward Weller's map

"Antiquities are history defaced, or some remnants of history which have casually escaped the shipwreck of time."

Francis Bacon, The Advancement of Learning, 1605

LONDON, 1863

A short walk away from the rolling brown of the Thames – not far away, either, from the mudlarks scrabbling on its muddy shoreline in search of some strange treasure that might have been dropped from one of the great trading ships coming into the port – Edward Weller sits, bent over his drawing board.

I can see him now. Outside his window, London's belching chimneys, the sooty fog; but inside the velvety warmth of his studio at 34 Red Lion Square, through the cold winter of 1863, his little yellow, smoky gas light burning, the coal in the fireplace crackling, he is tracing the line of the river.

First, it is the humble beginnings in a field near Cirencester and the slow trickle of the upper reaches through Cricklade and Lechlade. Then it's the twists and turns of a waterway snaking past ancient towns and melancholic hills towards London. Finally, the majestic roll through the capital city as England's major artery seeks its muddy destiny in the swirl of the sea beyond.

Weller's pen lingers over the bends of the river between Henley and Marlow. The 41-year old map engraver has been busy of late, producing a series of maps for *Cassell's Weekly Dispatch Atlas*. It all seemed to start with his charts of Sir Richard Burton's expedition to find a lost lake in east Africa. These charts produced a gale of publicity for the cartographer that his previous map showing "the temperature of the air and the distribution of constant, periodical and variable winds over the globe" had never been able to conjure up.

And then there was his chart of a journey to the Tian Shan Mountains of Kazakhstan, his portrayal of Japan and his plan of Syria showing all its ancient Roman sites. Not a week goes by before Weller is asked by a publishing house such as Longman or the Royal Geographical Society, of which he is a member, to produce another chart.

But now it is the commission for Cassell's that has been occupying most of Weller's time. Since 1855 or thereabouts, he has been etching out maps for *Cassell's Atlas*, published in monthly segments for readers of the *Weekly Dispatch*, the well-known Sunday newspaper based in Fleet Street. At the beginning of the year it was his map of Egypt and the Red Sea; then it was a series on the Far East, the borderlands of Siam and Burma and the Indian Archipelago in all its mazy entirety, covering the Dutch East Indies, Borneo, the Philippines and the Malay peninsula; and finally the map he is working on now – a chart of the River Thames, from its source to the sea. This map, along with many others in the Weller collection, will make up the *Dispatch Atlas* to be published towards the end of 1863.

Occasionally, in my mind's eye, the map engraver allows himself a brief respite from his work to accept a regular invitation from the editor of the *Weekly Dispatch*, Thomas Serle, to update him on the progress of the drawings.

I can imagine that the routine is always the same. At about 12 noon, Weller looks out of the grimy window of his studio at the grey outside, puts on his frock coat and top hat and ventures out into the London imbroglio. In the sooty fog he can barely see the little gated garden in the centre of the square, still less the house across the square at No 17 where the radical artists William Morris and Edward Burne-Jones have recently set up a design company.

It matters little, however, because the cartographer knows his well-worn route. Turning left into the mist, he heads towards Red Lion Street. At No 35, there is Mansell Joseph, the stationer, and at 36, Owen & Stodart, the piano makers. Next door is home to Perry Jas & Co, which manufactures the ink for the copper plates on which the *Dispatch* maps are finally engraved; and next door again is the engineering firm of Frederick Hahn & Co.

Frederick Hahn heralds the beginning of Lambs Conduit Passage that will take the London mapmaker through to Red Lion Street. At the end of the passage, he can see the dim gas lights of The Grapes run by William King pointing the way. Down Red Lion Street now and past William Edwards, the grocer, and John Taylor, the cheesemonger; past the newsagents Elijah Cornish and Charles Cook and then the looking glass manufacturer Francis Stoppani. Weller stops to look in at Mr Stoppani's, spying his old friend at his counter through the smeary windows. Stoppani's magnifiers – together with the mathematical instruments made by Francis Huddy at 34 Red Lion Street – have helped the draughtsman fix the exact locations of rivers and mountains over many years.

Leather shoes drumming smartly on the cold stone: Miss Martha Brown, the milliner at No 26 who makes hats for his wife, Mary Ann; and Mrs Maria Burn, at the same address, who runs the favourite toy shop of his sons Edward, Francis and Alfred, and his daughters Mary, Margaret and Agnes. But he must hurry on, past makers of umbrellas and watches and wooden cabinets, until he reaches Frederick Griffin's coffee rooms.

It is here that the relative gentility of Red Lion Street gives way to the cacophony of street hawkers on the busy thoroughfare of High Holborn: newspaper sellers dodging between clattering carriages and cabs making their chaotic way between Cheapside and Oxford Street; pack-men peddling their cotton and linen goods; and the wandering costermongers pushing everything from herrings and oysters to wild rabbits and turnips.

Weller rushes on through the discord, past a shabby gathering of people keeping warm around the fiery charcoal pan of a street coffee stall, until he is turning into Chancery Lane, either side of which, hiding in their cloisters, the smartly waist-coated lawyers of Victorian London – the likes of Cyrus Slater, Wyndham Holgate and Spencer Perceval – are pondering over their cases.

It's a bit of a walk through the stench of technicalities and loopholes, but finally Edward Weller makes it. He turns left into Fleet Street. *Bradshaw's British and Continental Guide of Railways* on his right hand side at No 59, *Bell's Weekly Messenger* at No 91 and the *Sunday Times Weekly* at No 103. The *Daily Telegraph* offices at No 135.

Then, finally, at No 138, the home of the *Weekly Dispatch*.

The map-maker climbs the stairs to the floor where Thomas Serle's office is located. There, in the ageing journalist's musty centre of operations at the end of a long corridor, his story is usually the same. Yes, sir, he has been making excellent progress.

I
The Map

"It's by Edward Weller," said the tall man with grey hair hovering over my shoulder. "He was a Victorian mapmaker."

The panels of lighting above our heads – in defiance, seemingly, of the cold dark winter night outside – were throwing a waxy glow over the ageing illustration that I had just picked out of a stack of antique maps. In the fragile luminosity, I could make out the title of the work – *The River Thames from its source to the sea* – and below it in smaller and more spidery capital letters the words: By Edward Weller, FRGS.

Above the title and the by-line was an image of a half globe with a sash tied around it upon which was written rather grandly, *The Dispatch Atlas*. Floating above it was the winged god of travel and commerce, Mercury, carrying his trademark staff entwined with two serpents.

From top to bottom, the map was divided into three sections, as explained by a legend: the upper reaches showing the course of the river from its source to Abingdon; the middle reaches from Abingdon to London, and at the bottom, the lower reaches from London to the sea. The result was a strange amalgamation of towns and country lanes and escarpments hanging over one another in places where they should not really have been – Lechlade hovering somewhere north of Marlow, Regents Park propping up the Oxfordshire plains, Chertsey suspended over the Southend mud flats and Southend Pier. The one constant, though, was the river itself, the flood plain of which was picked out brightly throughout the chart in pinks and blues and greens.

I had been navigating around this antique shop near St Martin's Lane for about half an hour, lingering over the large number of maps and pictures that seemed to fill every available space on the walls around me.

It was an eclectic collection: old English county charts, a chart of the Mississippi in 1912 and one of Tripoli in 1932 as well as some beautiful illustrations. There was a particularly striking one drawn in 1859 of Victorian steamers and sailing ships moored by London Bridge. You could almost hear the creaking timber and the shouts of the dock workers as they unloaded exotic cargoes from the East on the quayside – tea, perhaps, from Ceylon, or lacquer from China, or spices from the Moluccas. Another drawing depicted the rooftops of London as seen from the top of St Paul's – thousands of chimneys caught in the light of a blue dusk.

I also spent some time leafing through a group of maps plotting the Sahara. Some seemed to be the work of medieval Arab scholars who had travelled with the caravans that once criss-crossed the desert, rising with the traders and their mewing camels in an orange, dusty dawn and then trekking through the day under an unforgiving sun before they reached another oasis just before nightfall. Others might have been charted by some intrepid Victorian explorer about to meet his destiny in the great desert, men like Mungo Park who drowned in the Bussa rapids while tracing the course of

the Niger or John Davidson who was murdered on his way
to Timbuktu.

But, in the end, there was something about this map of
the Thames by Edward Weller that caught me in its spell.

Perhaps it was the intricate outlines in pen and ink of
the meandering river and its ragged estuary or the fragile
Baskerville typography of the hundreds of place-names that
must have taken hours of painstaking work: familiar places
such as London where I had spent much of my working life,
but also obscure spots such as Medmenham Abbey or corners where danger lurked for people who strayed from the
path such as Maplin Sands.

Or was it the scramble of meandering needle-thin lines
denoting the hundreds of country lanes that joined up all
these places in a time before motorways and A-Roads, or
the powdery grey folds that indicated the hills and escarpments of the Home Counties – produced in the days before
Edinburgh firm John Bartholemew & Co invented a spec-
trum of greens and ever darker hues of brown to denote the
changing contours?

The map fixed my gaze. I had liked maps ever since my
father had shown me an Ordnance Survey map of the area
around the run-down beach chalet our family used to rent
out on a spit of land in Wales each summer in the sixties and
seventies, and then a little later when he drew my attention
to the River Dove on a chart of the Peak District squeezing
itself through the narrow gorge between the Twelve Apostles

and the Tissington Spires. This map many years later gave me the same kind of thrill. Unlike a map of faraway Timbuktu on the edges of the River Niger, this old illustration of the Thames seemed to offer me a firm possibility of exploration. I could easily imagine myself running my finger along the course of the river one day, just as I had done with the River Dove many years ago, and the next find myself clambering over a country stile with a view of a great river valley appearing before me.

Edward Weller's name was reprinted in the right hand corner of his Thames vision. And in the other corner, the name of his publisher, the *Weekly Dispatch Atlas* of 138 Fleet Street. On the back, there was a little sticker telling me that this work had been produced in 1863. Maybe it was Edward Weller himself who intrigued. Who was he? I caught a whiff of the era in the antique smell of the scroll and in the ghostly, whimsical translucence of its ageing paper.

"It's a lovely map, isn't it?" said the dealer, who was now circling around me ready for a sale. "He was a London cartographer. Produced a lot of beautiful maps."

"I'll take it," I said.

—◊—

What was happening in 1863? Who was Edward Weller? Who or what did he love? I spent the lengthening days of the spring and summer that followed delving into books, trying to find out.

Things were changing fast in Weller's Britain. You could tell as much by all the railways running busily in and out of London on his map of the Thames – the London Tilbury & Southend Railway for instance, the North & South Western Junction Railway, and the most prestigious of them all, the Great Western.

In 1863, London was at the fulcrum of Britain's industrial revolution, the first of its kind in the world, and international trade was booming. Coal exports had risen from £750,000 a year to £3 million in the space of a few years; iron and steel exports had increased from about £3 million to well over £13 million, driven in large part by Britain's huge railway construction programme in its most important imperial possession, India.

On the back of the wealth that all this generated, the city was being transformed. It had not been long since Weller had produced for Cassell's a coloured plan of London showing the "railways and street improvements projected and in progress in the City of London". Now, in 1863, work had begun on the much-anticipated Holborn Viaduct, which, when completed, would link Holborn with the City. Even more momentously, the world's first underground railway, the Metropolitan Line, had just opened, carrying 26,000 passengers a day between Paddington and Farringdon Street.

Somewhere, also, not far underneath Weller's feet, navvies were laying 1,300 miles of brick tunnels that, when finished, would whisk nine and a half million cubic feet of foul waste now collecting in stinking cesspools in the middle of the city to a new pumping station in unsuspecting Beckton, a few miles downriver. A grand embankment on the shore of the Thames would be built over the tunnels as part of Joseph Bazalgette's ambitious scheme.

"The history of England is emphatically the history of Progress," the Victorian historian, Thomas Babington Macaulay, had written. From his attic window at 34 Red Lion Square – where he lived with his wife, his six children, his servant, 29-year old Eliza Turner, and the children's nurse, 20-year old Eliza Warbank – the map engraver would have watched it all unfold.

But while Macaulay was thunderous in his approval, others had reservations. The *Daily Telegraph* – then a Liberal sort of Fleet Street paper based next door to the *Weekly Dispatch* – ran a column on 23 January 1863 lamenting the destruction of London's old neighbourhoods under the developer's hammer. "Metropolitan improvements have played sad havoc" with "the old London landmarks of the romantic and the mysterious" which have "nearly all disappeared", the column commented. "Dark deeds may have been done in the old time in Exeter Changes, but that dingy arcade has been swept away. Alsatia is full of printing offices, the sanctuary of Westminster no longer shelters rogues, St Giles proper is a thing of the past, the Strand Hotel company has made short work of Lyons Inn."

"Ranges of princely villas and stately rows of shops" had now replaced "tumbledown tenements", it continued.

"A smirking uniformity" had replaced "the scowling yet picturesque vagabondage of the past".

Once tumbledown tenements, now a sparking residential and shopping complex. Once labyrinthine passages leading down to the river, now a commercial warehouse and a smart new jetty. It had all started with the filling in of the canals on Jacob's Island in Bermondsey, that pestilent nest of slums linked by a web of rotten, rickety bridges and a maze of alleyways that led into the darkest rooms of the poor, a world created by industrialisation yet left untouched by its benefits – all swept aside to make way for the loading loopholes and iron catwalks of the New Concordia Wharf, built to supply tea, coffee and other vital commodities to the florid drawing rooms of Richmond and Twickenham upriver.

Then it was Bluegate Fields, near the East London docks and the infamous taverns of Field Lane, the labyrinth of slums behind Westminster and the impoverished alleyways of St Giles near Covent Garden – secret worlds of ruffians and scoundrels and debtors and hawkers and beggar boys, and laughter in some hidden drinking den, and deals and murders committed behind closed doors and rats running along timber beams, all now vanishing under the iron fist of the railway companies and the newly-formed Metropolitan

Board of Works which had commissioned so much of the new work.

Once run-down taverns, now one of the new London railway stations made of iron and glass. Once dark streets where lovers and conspirators met under the veil of the night; now a city of 360,000 public gas lamps, consuming 13 million cubic feet of gas a day. Although nests of poverty still abounded in narrow alleyways and the big old houses gone to seed, and the poor and marginalised still gathered under low lamps in low-ceilinged rooms in the neighbourhood of St Giles, London was undoubtedly changing.

Yet, writers like Charles Dickens and his even more popular contemporary, George WM Reynolds, drew much of their inspiration from the dark side of London now beginning to disappear under the developer's hammer. Dickens wrote *Bleak House* and *Great Expectations*, while Reynolds kept London's growing middle and lower class readership entertained with two very popular fictional series, *The Mysteries of London* and *The Mysteries of the Court of London*, in which the author revelled in the gothic romance and mystery of the old capital.

Not for him, the new railway viaduct or the new street lights. No, Reynolds' lurid tales were more about dark deeds carried out on Jacob's Island or a treasure trove found in a subterranean vault underneath the streets or a cobra from a ruined temple in India turning up in a church vault in Notting Hill.

It was the sort of London in which a scavenger on the shore of the Thames might accidentally find a jewel case containing a string of pearls. Elegising further in the winter of 1863, the Daily Telegraph columnist, probably the famous Victorian journalist George Augustus Sala, tapped playfully into a rich vein of sentiment when he wrote:

"The main drainage works [for London's new sewerage system] are in continual progress, but no herds of wild hogs are discovered in the sewers, nor, so far as we have been enabled to ascertain, have the mudlarks come upon any caskets of Oriental Pearl.

"The Metropolitan Railway Company have driven their tunnels through the bowels of Marylebone," he added, "but the engineers discovered no subterranean vaults full of dead man's bones or hidden treasure."

—◊—

But, for me, that summer nearly one and a half centuries later, it was as if I had stumbled by chance upon a romantic, mysterious something in the heart of London, a treasure trove of sorts found in a subterranean world of antique maps that lay just beneath the surface of the bustling, modern metropolis. I had found my chart.

One evening in September when the ailing sun was turning everyone's face in the city to gold, I decided to walk down to the grey forbidding promenade beside the Thames that the Victorians had built in the 1860s and named the Embankment, and from there onto one of my favourite spots in the great metropolis: Charing Cross Bridge. There, I knew I would find the gritty splendour of the London waterfront ready to welcome me in the evening dusk.

The lights were coming on when I reached the middle of the wobbling footbridge, caught in its daily embrace with the commuter trains shuddering across the adjacent railway bridge. To my right were the shimmering blues and indigos of the South Bank – the silky legacy of the Festival of Britain in the summer of 1951.

On the north bank, the ribbon of lights suspended above the hard granite of the Embankment led as far as I could see from the soft glow of the American Bar at the Savoy Hotel – where in the 1920s the Savoy Orpheans would entertain well-heeled guests with the latest dance numbers – to Blackfriars Bridge, which hovered silently in the sepulchral radiance of St Paul's Cathedral standing just a few streets away. Beyond Blackfriars, I could just make out the slatted glare of 1970s office blocks before the skyline erupted into the constellation of lights of the financial district and the silvery-green lustre of the Gherkin. All of these lights, of buildings old and new, were reflected in the frothy darkness of the water flowing below them. Layer upon layer of London history lamented, regretted, celebrated in the phosphorous sorrow of its great river.

Of course, I was not alone on the walkway. Visitors from Tokyo and Taipei stopped and took photographs;

young couples lingered by the iron railings; people in suits now alone at the end of the day pressed the numbers of loved ones on their mobiles – all of us, just a microcosm of the daily cascade of people who had poured across the bridge since it opened in 1845. Broadcasters on their way from Waterloo Station to the World Service building on the Strand; jazz fans on a Monday night in 1933 heading to see Duke Ellington play at the Astoria Ballroom. Tailors, hairdressers, estate agents pounding their regular beat across the river to their shops around Covent Garden; opticians, boot makers, milliners, drapers, jewellers, all making their way home in the orange grey glare of a Charing Cross sunset before the First World War, in-between the wars, after the Second.

And then – in my mind's eye – there was Edward Weller, in 1863, gazing downriver towards the West India and Royal Victoria docks, down Britain's great imperial stream and out onto the wide oceans of Victorian idealism.

I imagined that the map-maker would regularly make his way down to the bridge – it is, after all, only a short walk down the Kingsway and across the Strand from Red Lion Square – and here, he would ponder all the mysteries of a world that he and his engraving tool were opening up for the readers of the Weekly Dispatch: the Nile, India and Ceylon, the borderlands of Siam and Burma, the Indian archipelago, and, of course, the meandering loops of the River Thames.

The river below the bridge would have been in ceaseless movement: barges chugging in and out of the Belvedere coal depot on the south bank, drowsy barrel-laden tubs puffing out of the riverside Lion Brewery, fuming cargo vessels plying the waters between the scores of docks and wharves reeking of mud and salt and smoke lining the banks.

A little downriver, ragged mudlarks wading through the mud left by a receding tide around Arundel Stairs near Temple Pier or the Paris Garden Stairs near Blackfriars Bridge would be foraging amongst the multitude of artefacts washed up from London's past and present – Roman coins, Elizabethan costume jewellery, Victorian coal – for anything they could sell on. Pieces of coal, bits of old-iron, usually, but if they were lucky, copper nails dropped from a ship under repair at a dock somewhere. Children in rags as young as six and old women bent double: slum-dwellers of the river scattered along the shoreline amongst the barges and the boats, their hats and baskets filled with bones and coals and the distant hope that they might one day find that casket of Oriental Pearl washed up from a shipwreck out in the Essex marshes.

Further on still, at the Victoria Docks, a rag-tag army of Victorian adventurers would be milling in front of the Marine Hotel and the Tidal Basin Tavern, rushing porters off their feet in their hurry to get to their allocated berth. A trader headed for Hong Kong, a reporter with a letter of appointment from the *Bombay Gazette*, a railway engineer timetabled for Ooty – restless souls riding the tide of a booming age.

Edward Weller had read all about them. He would have known that David Livingstone was lost somewhere on the Zambezi, but had got further than Richard Burton in the search for the lost lake of east Africa. He would have read in the newspapers, too, that Sir James Brooke was bringing sure and steady 'Progress' to the jungles of Borneo, revenues for the last year having hit an all-time high of £23,000.

The map engraver might have regarded himself as an important cog in all this industry. After all, he had brought scientific enquiry to the crashing surf of the Indian Ocean and every contrary twist and turn of the Thames, so that every Victorian household could navigate their way around the furthest-flung outposts of the Empire or recognise every changing feature of their great English waterway.

Perhaps, for a moment, though, particularly when he was standing here on the bridge watching the water-hyacinths float past on the currents of the river, he dreamt that he was not in his studio in Red Lion Square or his offices on Duke Street in Bloomsbury hunched over another chart under the shadow of another deadline; but out there on the open water, piloting his boat between the jetties and docks of the old river, or drifting out on the open sea, with no compass or lights to guide him, drifting among the nutmeg rocks and emerald isles of the Orient.

—ⱳ—

The faces in the glaring light of the railway carriages scraping and sparking past me on the Charing Cross Rail and Foot Bridge looked pale and weary. Trade was not booming in 2012; instead, unemployment was at an 18-year high, and the tired faces in the carriage windows carrying the weight of the office day in their eyes were the lucky ones.

Nevertheless, London was continuing to modernise itself. Metropolitan improvement was still in progress. Giant diggers had started preparing the ground for a much-needed overflow tunnel for the Victorian-built sewerage system, which would take excess effluent down to the Beckton sewage plant. The Shard at London Bridge, the tallest building in Europe, had recently opened. The newly-built extension to the Docklands Light Railway now took Londoners all the way to the enormous Westfield shopping centre at Stratford International, which had been the disembarkation point that summer for the London Olympics.

It was time for a beer. I made my way down the stone steps back onto the Embankment, and after passing through Embankment Underground station with its chessboard floor and green District Line signs, and then along Villiers Terrace past all the pubs and bars that hide in the subterranean vaults underneath Charing Cross Station, I reached the Strand. From there, I cut through the side roads to Covent Garden, eventually finding the alleyway that led to an old drinking haunt of mine, the Lamb and Flag.

My favourite seat by the window was waiting for me when I got to the top of the flight of wooden stairs that led to the first floor bar.

For a few moments after I had settled down with my pint, I watched the evening drinkers through the open window milling in the alley outside. A loud businessman in a pin-striped suit was telling his admiring friends that Asia was now the place to invest.

But then the image that had lodged itself in my head all summer popped up again – the mazy lines of the country lanes, the serpentine swagger of the river, the perilous sands and spits of the estuary. Like a fragment from a sooty gas-lit London in 1863, like a vagabond from a world we have lost, Edward Weller's chart of the River Thames offered me something, and, at first, I could not tell what it was.

Gradually, almost imperceptibly, however, as the beer began to take hold, the realisation crept upon me.

It offered me a journey, a journey away from modern Britain, away from economic recession and weary faces in train windows, away from upgrades and road works and gigantic shopping malls pretending to offer freedom.

Yes, the decision was made. I would free myself from the fetter of modern life, the shackles of petty politics, financial scandals and reality shows; and, instead, follow the old river chart.

The plan was simple. I would amble down the Thames, following Weller's map, from Kemble to Putney Bridge and onto Southend Pier, searching out church vaults and run-down taverns, and old neighbourhoods gone to seed. I would roam through dingy alleyways, and over time-hallowed hills and antique lands, crossing crumbling bridges, following in the footsteps of people long gone, losing myself in the mysteries of the past. I would explore an older Thames that lurked underneath the veneer of the modern river, and peel back layers of time never quite erased by the shopping malls of Reading or the skyscrapers of modern London. The Thames that Weller drew up in 1863, the Thames of the Celts and the Saxons.

Everywhere I went, though, I would not be alone. He would always be there, armed with his compass and his set of dividers, fixing my position. Edward Weller, the mapmaker, would be there with me, as my guide.

His map fell into my hand; and slowly, gingerly, like a mudlark looking for a casket of Oriental pearl, I opened it up.

The Upper Reaches

II

Trewsbury Mead

The man from the Loire Valley had told me that I might
lose my way a few times, and now there was no doubt about
it: I had lost the trail that should have been leading me to
the source of the River Thames. Follow the signpost to the
left and then hope for the best, the young man with big
walking boots who divided his time between his girlfriend
in Bath and the lush wine region of France had said; and,
initially, it had all gone very well, the shallow stream full of
green weed on my right hand side – the kind of stream in
which a drowned Ophelia might float by at any moment –
apparently pointing me in the right direction.

This thin thread of hope, however, had soon petered
out. The waterway suddenly dried up in a coppice of fallen
trees and wild brambles, and that seemed to be that. To my
right there was a gate and a driveway that led up to some
farm buildings; to my left, field upon field of green pasture
rolling into the grey mizzle of winter. There was no sign at all
of the beginnings of the great river, a river that would later
force itself through the Goring Gap, loop through Berkshire
and sweep past Richmond into London – a river quite capable of bursting its banks, washing away bridges and destroying homes if it were not for the 45 locks taming its flow all
the way to Teddington Locks; a river, moreover, which, if left
undefended by the Woolwich Barrier, could invite the sort
of tidal surge from the North Sea that in 1928 sent a wall of
water over the Chelsea Embankment, drowning 14 people
in their basement flats in Pimlico.

There was no sign either of the other face of the Thames,
the lifeline for Roman, Saxon and Norman settlements and

the millions of other migrants who have lived beside it for centuries, working in the power stations and gas works and shipyards that have lined its banks, drawing on its hydraulic powers.

No sign at all. I turned around and started to retrace my steps.

But then, suddenly, I saw him. He was standing by the stream: a tall man decked out in blue waterproofs struggling slightly under the weight of a very large rucksack and using one of those modern aluminium walking poles to aid his progress. "I was looking for the start of the Thames," I shouted over to him, holding my hands up in bafflement. "But now I'm lost".

He looked up and smiled. A big wide smile that lit up a pleasant, ageing face crowned by a mop of silver grey hair. "Well, I'd better show you then, hadn't I?" he said. "I was at this spot a few years back. Hopefully I can still remember."

We left the marshy banks of the stream that led nowhere and headed upwards through the bitter stillness of winter fields. "So, what brings you here?" I asked my new-found guide.

"I got off at London Bridge three weeks ago," he answered.

"You've walked all the way up the Thames from London Bridge?" I was suddenly interested.

"Yes, I had to get to this point to pick up the path to Swanage. My sister lives there, you see."

I didn't really see, but let him continue.

"My friends said, 'why don't you catch the fast train from London to Kemble just up the road from here, and then walk?', but I thought that as the Thames Path was heading this way, it seemed silly not to take it."

His friends had got a point, I thought, but then the man flashed me a smile again. "You see, I've been walking for 20 years," he explained. "I woke up one morning and decided I didn't want to work anymore. Didn't want to work in an office to the end of my days."

The lock gates on our conversation now opened up and our little vessel of companionship chugged through the gaping timber into the wide channel beyond. I told him about Edward Weller's map of the River Thames and how I was now following its route from the source to the sea; my fellow trekker, whose name I regrettably never learnt, told me about all the walks he had undertaken over the years. He had caught a bus to the Algarve and walked the length of Portugal; he had walked through the deep valleys and across the high peaks of the Alps when the Via Alpina opened in 2005; he had crossed the Yorkshire Moors. But his best walk, he told me, was the one that had started in a tent in a bed of nettles opposite Tower Bridge and had ended at the Eiffel Tower. He had caught a ferry across the

Channel to Calais and then walked along the Normandy coast before turning left for Paris.

"'Je marche à Paris,' I would say to passers-by. That's about all the French I knew," he laughed.

"One day, a couple of nuns driving in a little Renault, actually travelling in the opposite direction towards Le Havre, offered to turn their car around and take me to Paris. I politely refused their offer. But ten minutes later, they returned, now travelling in the right direction and offering me a lift again. I still said 'No'!"

We were now crossing a country lane, looking for a stile that would take us into the next field. "Have you ever written about your experiences?" I wondered. "It sounds like you've had some interesting ones."

"No, not as such," my fellow explorer said. "But I have kept diaries since I was 14, and I've spent the last decade or so building them into the walls of my house in Tunbridge Wells.

"One day, someone will find them all. You know, like how some people find dead bodies under the floorboards."

We walked on through the next field, stopping at a cattle trough for the man to fill up his water bottles from the tin container of clean water set aside for ramblers. He took them out of his backpack with some difficulty – the pack looked very heavy and its owner looked as if he was in his early seventies.

I felt that both our spirits were beginning to lift now, though, and at first it was difficult to know quite why given the chill in the air, and for my companion, the weight of his backpack. But as we climbed over the next stile into the final stage of our journey the reason became apparent. The greyness was beginning to lift and a sort of brightness taking its place. By the time we reached the stone marking the source of the Thames, the sun was out.

"This is it," my companion said.

A withered ash tree, a dried up limestone well and a clump of white snowdrops apologetically defying the cold weather – it seemed an unlikely spot for a river that, as far as Dorchester eight miles south of Oxford, is referred to by Edward Weller's map and most maps before and since as 'Isis', after the Egyptian goddess of fertility. It seemed an unlikely spot too for a flow of water that had fed the fertile imaginations of generations of poets, writers and artists, the likes of Turner, Shelley and Lewis Carroll.

But my companion was right. This was it. The memorial stone told us so. "The conservation of the River Thames 1857-1974," it read. "This stone was placed here to mark the source of the River Thames."

"Of course, the source of the river is disputed, you know," the man added suddenly, after taking a couple of photographs of the stone. "Some people say the real beginning is at a place called Seven Springs, ten miles north of here."

With that, he took his leave. He was headed for a campsite over the next hill, where he would recuperate overnight before embarking on the next stage of his journey – heading south on the Macmillan Way through Wiltshire and Dorset to join his sister in Swanage. I wished him well and watched him – a lone figure with his walking pole and backpack – disappear slowly into the horizon. A clump of trees and suddenly he was gone. I wondered whether one day someone would find his diaries in the walls of his home in Tunbridge Wells, and if so, what they would find inside.

He was right about the origins of the Thames. Some do indeed place it at Seven Springs, north of Cirencester, although the historical consensus is firmly in favour of the field I was now standing in – Trewsbury Mead. Curiously, though, Edward Weller's map hedges its bets. The Victorian mapmaker scrawled the words 'Thames Head' in his fragile mapmakers' font in a field next to the Roman Fosse Way, near to the village of Kemble – in other words in this very field. But follow the spidery black line he used to denote the river and it will lead you up beyond the Thames Head, into the next field, underneath the Cheltenham & Great Western Union Line which was built during the great railway boom of the 1840s and onto a place called Tunnel House at the edge of a coppice of trees called Hayley Wood. I had walked past a sign for the Tunnel Inn the day before on a lonely road just north of this spot. The road to the inn, leading away under the shadow of wintry trees growing over it, had looked dark and forbidding.

But now I was here on Trewsbury Mead beneath a sign-post that told me this was the true beginning of Thames Path and I was happy to believe it. "Thames Barrier London, 184 miles, 294 km," it read.

Whatever the true origins of the river, the course was now set. I was going to walk the whole length of the River Thames, all 184 miles of it. Well, perhaps I would catch the occasional boat or two, but I would walk most of it from its source to the sea, following Weller's 1863 map.

I have never been a serious walker like my new-found friend from Tunbridge Wells. To be honest, I am always the one straggling at the back of the pack on a Sunday family walk. I am more like a serious dawdler, really.

But I had an idea that this particular journey would do me good, get the trivialities of modern life out of my hair, you know, shake me up a bit. Yes, I would do the whole thing, do the distance and get to Southend, the last point on the estuary. In the meantime, I would get to know the old river, explore its treasures, get to know its twists and turns until one fine, fair day I finally reached the sea.

III

Somerford Keynes

It was difficult to appreciate at that cold dry spot at Trewsbury Mead, but the Thames was actually with us – it was just underground, bubbling out of a spring beneath the surface. Sometimes in periods of heavy rain it emerges from its subterranean vaults into the light of day. Usually, though, it does not make its first real appearance until further downhill in a pool called Lyd Well, the spot where I had met my fellow rambler.

From Lyd Well, the small stream that will eventually grow into a great metropolitan river trickles through the folds of a Cotswold hill down to a very straight road, the A433. This was once the Fosse Way, an important Roman road which linked Lincoln in the north-east to Exeter in the south-west, via Leicester and Cirencester, in an almost perfect arrow-like trajectory.

It was the first sign that I was ambling through a landscape imbued with the patina and grain of the past, and others would soon follow. A short tramp over grey fields took me to the outskirts of Kemble, a honeycomb of cottages congregated around a Victorian church steeple and the tidy timetables of the Victorian railway station where I had disembarked that morning; but sitting, according to various guides I had read, on the site of something even more antiquarian – a Roman burial chamber. After that, a scramble along a rough path on the brown fringes of a field under the plough and over a crossing called Parker's Bridge brought me to a little place called Ewen, another village of sagging amber-stoned cottages which, while not quite of Roman stock, still traces its roots back to Saxon times. The name Ewen is derived from the Saxon word for 'river source' or 'spring'.

It was here that I had scheduled in my first night's stay, at a sixteenth-century pub called The Wild Duck, which stood at the far end of the village. From the photographs on its website a few days before, it had looked a cosy, warm place; and opening the sturdy oak door that cold grey afternoon I was not disappointed. A crackling inglenook fire welcomed me in, and then a young woman popped her head over the bar. Moments later I had the keys to my room.

I spent the evening in the flickering shadows of the inglenook flames, grazing over a couple of beers and a dinner of chicken in a marsala wine sauce, and gazing at the paraphernalia that littered the old pub's warm crimson interior: here a couple of stuffed stags' heads and a stuffed cockerel in a glass case, there a painting of Princess Di and dozens of portraits of eminent Victorians looking stern and disapproving. It was not until around 10 o'clock, sufficiently fortified, that I retired back to my room.

In contrast to the fussy old English feel of the bar, which probably wouldn't have looked out of place in Edward Weller's local hostelry in 1863, my room was decked out like a hotel in the Orient. A Buddha's head greeted me on the dressing table, looking like one of those strange Buddhist effigies French explorer Henri Mouhot had discovered at Angkor Wat in the jungles of Cambodia in the early 1860s, and another peered over my bed from an oil painting on the wall.

Opening a drawer in the dressing table, I was not that surprised, therefore, to find not only a copy of the Bible, but also a glossy orange-coloured book called *The Teaching of Buddha.*

Idly, I flicked it open to one of the pages. "In the sky there is no distinction of east and west," it read. "People create the distinctions out of their own minds and then believe them to be true."

It continued: "Buddha keeps away from these discriminations and looks upon the world as upon a passing cloud."

A few pages on and more words of wisdom caught my eye. "Suppose a log is floating in a river. If the log does not become grounded, or sink, or is not taken out by a man, or does not decay, ultimately it will reach the sea.

"Life is like this log caught in the current of a great river."

I slipped into bed and flicked the television on to watch the late night current affairs programme, but I was almost asleep when the latest images from the Syrian civil war beamed over the airwaves. That night, I dreamt about floating down a swelling river towards a wide estuary.

—⚏—

This cosy overnight break galvanised me for the bleak late winter trek under greying skies that followed. From Ewen, a flooded Thames Path forced me to take a slight detour on a country lane before I returned to the stream trickling through a broad expanse of sallow fields, the eerie hush of the winter weighing heavily upon them.

When sounds did finally puncture this wintry cocoon, they weren't welcome ones. I had heard the barking a few hundred yards away and suspected there might be a confrontation of some kind. Sure enough, as I passed over a wooden bridge by the pretty Kemble Mill and clambered over a turnstile beside it, it was there waiting for me, snarling and crouching low as if ready to attack: half sheep dog, half something else, I'm not sure, but definitely a dark patch over one eye, guarding his owner's mill with full-bloodied menace.

Fortunately, the Thames ran between him and me and it ran quite deep, deep enough for me to leave him snapping on the opposite shoreline and move on hurriedly; startled, ruffled, certainly, but working hard to maintain a look of ambling nonchalance.

Gradually, though, the barking fell out of earshot behind me and as it did so, the fledgling river began to dance and weave its way through a wild tangle of brittle winter wood, soothing my nerves and lifting my mood. One moment, it was right beside me; the next, it had slipped off behind a dying tree choking in the stranglehold of creeping ivy, wiggling amongst the ancient undergrowth, caressing banks of dead leaves and pale rushes, only to reappear seconds later alongside the path.

For the first time in my journey, the river felt friendly, amiable, playful even. Five minutes later, it deposited me into the welcoming arms of a pretty wooden bridge with a view of a lake beyond.

I had reached the edge of the Cotswold Water Park, a large area of wetlands created by the large scale extraction of sand and gravel from the Thames floodplain. The mining companies had arrived in the 1960s to take advantage of these mineral deposits laid down in the last couple of Ice Ages, their giant metal diggers creating gaping holes in the earth that immediately filled up with water.

There are now more than 150 lakes stretching from the village of Somerford Keynes in the west to the river town of Lechlade in the east, a haven for nightingales, bats and orchids as well as families down from London and other crowded English cities who come to sit on their private decking at the water's edge with their binoculars, searching for the Cotswold nature experience.

The Cotswold experience in 1863 was very different. According to Edward Weller's map, the area was full of hard-working mills then – Somerford, Skillings and Kemble (where I had met the snarling dog) as well as Washburns and Pool – drawing on the waters of the Thames. Grinding the grain produced by local farmers with a series of gears and drive shafts running from a large dripping water wheel to the millstone, the grain mills of mid-Victorian Britain were part of a flourishing agricultural scene.

Flourishing for the landowners and the farmers, that is. The low wages and cramped living conditions which had been the lot of ploughmen, shepherds and farm labourers ever since the enclosure acts in the previous century robbed them of the bits of common land they used to till persisted; and by Weller's time they were looking for a way out.

They found it in the emerging industrial cities created by the new railways now puncturing England's green pastures with viaducts and cuttings. At one end of the Cheltenham & Great Western Union scything through the countryside on Weller's illustration of the upper Thames were the Midlands conurbations; at the other end, the boom towns of the Great Western Railway – Swindon, Reading and ultimately London.

Nearly half a million English rural workers left the countryside to find work in the towns between 1851 and 1881. For those leaving the upper Thames valley, their last view of the place where they grew up might have been from one of the penny-a-mile third class carriages puffing out of Minety station, just down the lane from Somerford Keynes.

—ฑฌ—

The Thames flows crystal clear along the northern edge of the Cotswold Water Park for a short while until it dips under a country lane on the outskirts of Somerford Keynes. Notwithstanding the beauty of the lakes that lay to my right, I now took another detour from the Thames Path and down the lane into the village. I had read somewhere that the church, which was built mainly under the patronage of the Keynes family between 1100 and 1300, still contained a megalithic doorway from the original Saxon place of worship built on the site in 695AD. I wanted to take a look.

The sun was struggling to come out again as I pushed open the thirteenth century oak door of All Saints and stepped inside. The feeling of quiet sanctuary was immediate. The weak sunlight oozed through the arched windows onto the rows of wooden pews in the nave. High above me, there was a vaulted ceiling framed by timber beams and, before me, a beautifully carved chancel screen that invited you quietly into the altar – everything elicited a sense of calm reflection, as if the door I had just shut behind me had shut out all the worries of the world.

A group of ladies had gathered around the pulpit in the far corner to hear a stern-looking woman wearing a tweed skirt and an expression of doctrinal authority explain the arcane art of flower arranging, and a few minutes after my arrival two elderly couples stepped over the threshold, the two men with their thick white wavy hair looking like brothers.

Otherwise, though, there was very little to break the contemplative hush as I roamed around the Victorian tiled floor, reading the inscriptions on some of the memorial plaques that adorned the walls.

About 300 years ago, a writer called John Aubrey did exactly the same thing for his county history of Wiltshire, which became part of a pantheon of works produced by a generation of English thinkers eager to revive the past after the wanton destruction by Oliver Cromwell's Puritan armies of all church artefacts they considered to be Popish and Catholic. Wall paintings, statues of saints, monuments and much else besides disappeared in the iconoclastic violence of Cromwell's followers during the English Civil War of the 1640s and the Protectorate in the 1650s. Fifty or so years later, Aubrey and other writers of the antiquarian movement were roaming the countryside in search of ancient remains and traces of anything, in fact, which smacked of Ancient Britain or Roman Britain or the nobility of past generations, anything that might speak to them over all those lost centuries before Cromwell's Year Zero.

Tucked in the corner of All Saints Church in Somerford Keynes, he found, like I did many centuries later, the reclining marble effigy of a man called Robert Strange, the last in the line of a noble family who were lords of the manor after the Keynes. It was the biggest and grandest monument in the church and yet, as Aubrey noted in his history of Wiltshire in 1691, this man had died in 1654 at the tender age of 23.

He also noted, as I did, the Greek inscription engraved below the effigy which read: "He whom God loves, dies young."

He would not have found the famous Saxon doorway, though. The opening, which sits opposite the Norman font, was blocked up and plastered over around 1500 and not re-opened until 1968.

And even if he had found it, would he have recognised it as Saxon? There was something about this tall, narrow, lop-sided entranceway carved from a single stone that seemed very un-Saxon to me. Absent was the squat sturdiness of the wide Saxon doorways that grace many of our parish churches. Instead, the doorway I now looked through – the opening glazed so I could see the graveyard outside – was crowned with curvaceous stone ruffles and interlacing as if it might belong to a more elaborate, romantic tradition. It had that decadent, sensual flavour of Celtic crosses and other pieces of jewellery that you might find in a craft shop in nearby Glastonbury.

Some lingering Celtic influence? I had no idea at the time, though I did find out later in a book about old English churches that the doorway at All Saints did in fact feature Celtic-style door lining. The Celts had been here, or at least their influence had.

So too, had the Vikings as I found out as I was making my way out of All Saints Church. To the right of the font, I suddenly noticed a plaque on the wall, featuring a drawing of what looked like two flying dragons fighting over a small, round sphere. There were a couple of paragraphs above the image explaining that the carving dated from the first half of the eleventh century AD when the Vikings held sway in Britain.

But there was no carving! I looked at the wall above the plaque, and then beneath it. There was nothing but empty space.

I carried on reading the explanatory notes. "The design is Scandinavian in style of the Ringerike type," it read. "Two beasts face each other, their mouths touching and holding a round ball between them. One is now only a snout but the other retains its mouth, eyes and a curving neck. The detail is very clear and the carving has survived damage from weathering."

"It was stolen in October last year," a voice behind me suddenly said. I turned round and found a man with white wavy hair, one of the gentlemen who had appeared with the elderly party in the church earlier, one of the two men I had assumed were brothers.

"Oh, really?" I said, now spotting a worn patch of stone-work above the plaque.

"Yes. They pulled it off the wall. Caused quite a lot of damage," the man said.

"It must have been worth something," I surmised.

"I suppose so, but more than anything it's been a shock to the village. They haven't caught the thieves. They haven't recovered the engraving."

The two of us passed the time of a day for a while, the elderly gentleman explaining that he had recently moved to the village to live in a house bequeathed to him many years ago by his parents; and I told him, in return, about my mission to walk the Thames Path.

"You know that field near Kemble isn't the real beginning of the Thames, don't you?" the man said gravely as he bade farewell.

"I know," I smiled, and we went our separate ways.

IV

Ashton Keynes

"We're off to a meeting now, our local twinning association, so just make yourself at home," the amiable landlady of my guest house in Ashton Keynes said breezily, her arms full of bright hats and ball gowns.

"I think my husband showed you the visitor's sitting room up in the attic, didn't he? Yes, well, why don't you make a nice cup of tea and relax up there in the warm."

After walking through the bitter greyness of an unseasonably cold March I was only too glad to take her advice. I had been expecting a pretty walk along the Thames from Somerford Keynes, where the route squeezes itself between the lakes of the Cotswold Water Park before reaching the next village, but instead it had been surprisingly dull, the lakes looking more like the gravel pits they truly were and my watery companion taking on the leaden hue of the sky above it. With the exception of a momentary flash of blue above the water at one point which turned out to be a kingfisher, my journey had been uneventful, and I had been relieved to reach the village of Ashton Keynes – a charming place of elegant stone houses and ponds and ditches spanned by tiny wooden bridges.

Now I was ascending the stairs with my cup of tea to the attic of an elegant house built in 1590, and putting my tea down on a small wooden table by the radiator to open up a copy of *Cotswold Life* I had found in my room.

Valerie, the landlady, was inside it, a good-looking woman with wavy hair peering out at me from the glossy pages of the magazine, her arms again full of bright hats and ball gowns. She was a costume historian, it transpired, and the house she ran as a guest house with her husband Roger was full of dresses, skirts, hats and shoes that she had acquired through a lifetime of collecting. The evidence was all around me in that attic room as I looked up from the magazine, a glass cupboard opposite me stuffed full of bowler hats and high-heeled shoes from the 1940s, a seamstress's mannequin in the far corner draped in a sequinned tea gown from the 1920s.

It was not only costumes though, according to *Cotswold Life*. There was also a Chinese room in the house, which featured furniture made of black lacquer and bamboo, Oriental wall embroideries and a bed canopy made of Chinese silk. Most of this, plus the pieces of dainty porcelain that inhabited every other nook and cranny of the house, were bought in local antique markets.

Meanwhile, outside in the garden there was a ghost called Henry, the magazine continued. This was the ghost of Henry Richmond, a Royalist in the English Civil War, who was accidentally shot by his brother John, a Parliamentarian follower of Cromwell, on the eve of the Battle of Newbury in 1643.

"Henry's brother mistook him for a Cavalier intruder and shot him dead with a musket," landlord Roger, a tall man with a rather patrician air about him, told me the next day in the kitchen as I ate the breakfast he had prepared for me. "That was the thing about the English civil war. It divided families right down the middle, tore them apart."

"So what happened to John?" I asked.

"He ran away to America where he started a Richmond clan. Every so often we get a knock on the door and we open it to an American looking for their ancestral home."

Valerie entered the kitchen at this moment. "We certainly do," she laughed. "We have to show them around and show them the garden too where Henry met his end."

"I was a bit worried I might meet him when I returned from the pub last night," I smiled. "Have you ever seen him?"

"No, we haven't, and we've been here 37 years," Roger now volunteered. "But neighbours say they have."

"But you know we have another ghost, don't you?" he added. "The ghost of a maid in the Blue Room, the Chinese Room. A guest saw her once.

"But again, we've never seen it."

I was beginning to wonder whether a moment the previous afternoon when the door of the attic sitting room had swung open inexplicably was perhaps due to forces other than the cold easterly wind outside lashing through the eaves as I had assumed at the time; but at that point Valerie changed the subject to my walk along the Thames.

"Terrible weather for it," she said. "Rained all last year, and now it's January temperatures in March."

"And I'm pretty sure you won't be able to walk on to Cricklade from here because of all the rain we've had. There is flooding all along the path."

I would soon realise that Valerie was right. Trying to pick my way through a sodden sports field just outside Ashton Keynes a little later on, I realised that another detour was necessary.

To continue my Thames journey, I abandoned the river path and, instead, walked along a country lane which runs parallel to the river for a time before crossing it at Waterhay Bridge. I picked up the route again there – which is a bridle-path at this point, running parallel to a waterway that has become half stream, half swamp, and is fenced off. Notices hammered into a couple of trees in the cordoned-off area bore a rather alarming notice: "Dangerous – Quicksand. Keep to the bridlepath."

I took heed and a couple of hours later, after weaving my way between more of the lakes that make up the Cotswold Water Park, and then picking up an old railway cutting for the last half-mile, I eventually arrived in Cricklade, the first town along the river's great journey towards the sea.

V

Cricklade and Beyond

If medieval chroniclers got it right, Cricklade hails back to around 1180 BC when Brutus, the fabled founder of Britain, turned up with a band of exiles from the Trojan War and founded a university there. The *History of the Kings of Britain* by the cleric Geoffrey of Monmouth, in particular, tells the story of the Greek goddess Diana appearing to Brutus in a dream, urging him to sail to an island beyond the setting of the sun, past the realms of Gaul, to build a second Troy.

With the winds behind them, the Trojans sailed through the treacherous Strait of Gibraltar, between the Pillars of Hercules, and, after many adventures in France, washed up in Totnes in Devon, venturing inland from that point in their efforts to realise Diana's vision.

Sitting in their sanctified cloisters, with their quills dipping into a palette of different inks – red from the Mediterranean turnsole plant; blue from lapis lazuli, a gemstone mined in the Kokcha Valley in Afghanistan and traded on the Silk Road – medieval monks tended to write obsessively of visitors from the East washing up on the shores of Albion sometime back in the mists of time, their pens not only etching out stories of Trojans and Greeks but also Scythians and other refugees from the edges of the Black Sea and beyond.

A little far-fetched you may think, but some contemporary historians are now saying they were probably correct. There were indeed mass migrations from central Asia due to widespread famine and conflict in the twelfth century

BC, these academics argue, and it was quite possible that some of these got as far as Britain.

Some even suggest that it explains why the muddy old Thames echoes the name of a tributary of the Ganges called the Tamasa, which in Sanskrit, the ancient Asian language, means 'dark'.

It would also explain why learned scholars in earlier ages thought 'Cricklade' was a corruption of 'Greeklade' where Brutus and his fellow Greeks tried to build a seat of learning, a second Troy. The belief was clearly still widespread in the eighteenth century when antiquarian Thomas Cox noted in his 'Magna Britannia et Hibernia, antique & nova' that the ancient Britons "began an University" at Cricklade, "which the Saxons removed to Oxford".

"Greek philosophers .... had schools here, and educated Youth in their Language and Science," he added.

A second Troy was not, however, what radical journalist William Cobbett saw in Cricklade when he rode into town nearly three thousand years later, amid Britain's Industrial Revolution of the 1820s. "I passed through that villainous hole, Cricklade ... and certainly a more rascally looking place I never set my eyes on," wrote the journalist, who had ridden out into the countryside on horseback to witness for himself the harsh living conditions of farm labourers. "Their dwellings are little better than pig-beds, and their looks indicate that their food is not nearly equal that of a pig."

Such conditions, which meant that farm workers lived in wretched hovels held together with rods and ropes on the roadside, were, Cobbett concluded, the result of an emerging industrial system, which he called rather darkly 'the thing'. It was 'the thing', he believed, that had not only robbed these people of access to land through a series of land enclosures but had now introduced a situation whereby the produce of agriculture in the upper Thames – wheat, barley, cheese, mutton, beef and so on – was whisked off by canal and river to middle class consumers in London, leaving the local workers to survive on cold potatoes. "I could broom-stick the fellow who would look me in the face and call this 'an improvement'," he wrote.

Things had not improved very much for the people of Cricklade by Weller's time. Those who had not escaped to find a new life in the boom towns of the Great Western Railway – Swindon, Reading, London – eked out a harsh living in the flat river valley surrounding this little Wiltshire town. William Woodward, a farm labourer living at No 23 on the High Street had to send his 13-year old son, James, onto the farms too; while Mary Habgood at No 45 was still working out in the fields at the age of 79.

For some, life became unbearable. In the summer of 1863, two local boys found the body of a man floating in the River Thames. A week or so later, the widow of Edmund Ricks of 44 Sadlers Lane, Cricklade, told an inquest that her husband, a sawyer, had been drinking heavily for three weeks before his death because he could not find work. In the end, the inquest decided, he had committed suicide by tying his hands together with a neckerchief and throwing himself into the river.

There were neither the confetti remnants of dreamy academic cloisters nor the shards of nineteenth century hardship, though, when I passed through Cricklade in the early spring of 2013. In their place was the pretty high street of a commuter town midway between Cirencester and Swindon, and a pretty pub with a welcoming log fire where I checked in for the night.

Later that evening, I ate Chicken Kerala, washed down with beer, amid the warm terracotta reds and saffrons of a trendy Indian restaurant at 47 High Street called The Ancient Raj, which in Weller's day was home to a cooper.

The Ancient Raj was, I guess, a little culinary outpost in a far-flung village of a very different kind of diaspora to the one from Troy which graced Cricklade in ancient times, one that emerged instead from colonial contact much later between Britain and India. Usually brought over in the service of the East India Company families, Asians started arriving in Britain as early as the 1600s; and by Edward Weller's time there was a small but significant population – about 40,000 – living in Britain, mainly servants and ayahs (nannies), and lascars (Indian sailors), but also travellers and students.

Working class Indians in nineteenth century London – Edward Weller's London – tended to congregate in the slums of the East End, where they ended up in cheap boarding houses or found refuge in the number of homes run by Victorian philanthropic organisations such as the Strangers' Home for Asiatics, Africans and South Sea Islanders, which opened in Limehouse in 1857. On the other side of the coin, an Indian professional called Federick Akbar Mahomed became a physician at Guy's Hospital at London Bridge in the 1870s. His grandfather, Dean Mohamed, had opened London's first Indian cafe in 1810 – the Hindostanee Coffee House in George Street, near Baker Street, where diners could smoke hookah pipes and recline on bamboo-cane sofas as they tucked into their curries.

This Asian presence in the heart of the capital plus a daily diet of news from India, the jewel of Britain's empire, dished out by the London press, fuelled a growing obsession with India, and with the Orient, in general. Victorian gentlemen took to sitting on curvaceous 'Hindoo' chairs in 'Oriental' smoking rooms at home which were decked out in all kinds of Eastern paraphernalia – from hanging Ottoman lamps and Persian carpets to intricate Jaipur cabinets peeping out from behind a tropical profusion of potted ferns. Meanwhile, Mrs Beeton's *Book of Household Management,* published in 1861, recommended numerous ways to curry fish, meat and eggs, and relished in the idea of 'Kidney toast, Madras style'. This was despite the shockwaves that the recent Indian Mutiny against British rule – particularly the rebels' massacre of 120 British women and children at a villa near the River Ganges – had sent through every polite Victorian household.

In fact, the horror of the Indian Mutiny – or was it the thrill? – increased the allure of mysterious India for many Victorians, including writers such as Wilkie Collins who, in the 1860s, was piecing together his famous detective story based on the theft of a sacred Hindu gem from an English country house. *The Moonstone* features three Indian characters lurking in the shadowy corners of London, intent on recovering the diamond that was stolen from their village by British troops during the Siege of Seringapatam in 1799.

Perhaps, who knows, Collins had discussed his ideas for the book with the fellow London scribes he used to meet regularly at the Albion Tavern near the Strand – authors Charles Dickens, Charles Reade (author of *The Cloister and the Hearth)* and George WM Reynolds of *Mysteries of London* fame, as well as the *Telegraph* journalist, George Augustus Sala.

There was very little mystery attached to my Indian restaurant in Cricklade 150 years later, at least as far as I could tell. The Ancient Raj was just one of the thousands of curry houses that now pepper the British culinary scene, symptomatic of the UK's sizeable Indian community and our continuing love affair with Indian food, and all its Eastern trappings.

Vindaloos, dhals, rogan josh – I love curry; so by the time I retired to bed that evening I felt I was set up well for another jaunt down the Thames.

—⟋⟍—

I left the Red Lion at about ten o'clock fully-armed with essential supplies for my survival of an 11 mile walk – a bottle of water and a Twix bar – and slipped full of hope down a lane opposite a church called St Mary's, a former Anglican church redenominated as a Catholic place of worship.

At the end of the lane, I found a gap in a hedge which led me onto a waterlogged rugby field, sodden with water from a point along the Thames which was bursting its banks. I reached the end of it where there was a concrete farm bridge, which led onto another field and then finally back to the river through a metal barrier.

The ground around the barrier, however, was a muddy swamp, and it took a good deal of leveraging between the adjacent fence and a foothold on a swing gate to progress. Eventually, though, I managed to haul myself through and swing myself onto the pathway beyond.

This is the joy of trekking along the Thames, I thought as I landed with a squelch underneath a low bridge belonging to the A419; and my optimism would have remained intact if I hadn't been required to repeat this difficult manoeuvre at three more gates beyond. Finally, after a few more muddy twists and turns, with my spirit waning fast, I came upon a bend in the river so deeply swampy that I could not see a way through it.

I turned around and headed back to Cricklade, where, somewhat disheartened, I ordered a taxi to take me onto the next town on the river: Lechlade.

My taxi driver explained the problem as we sped along a country lane that ran parallel to the river. "You can't really walk the Thames until after Lechlade," he said cheerily. "At least you haven't been able to for the last few years."

"The flooding started in that summer of 2007 and has never really gone away. The water levels are so high, you see, that it only takes a bit more rain and the river and all the fields around it are swamped."

"But it's been so cold and dry recently," I conjectured.

"Won't change things," the driver – his name was Terry, I think – said emphatically, his Cotswold lilt oozing softly out of a beard as tangled as a bird's nest. "You'd need a full month of dry hot weather before you could walk that path properly."

We went on to talk about the strangeness of the weather: the rain that had enveloped us all for most of 2012 after possibly the hottest March on record and the current cold snap. Climate change? Terry wasn't sure. After all, the winter of 1962-63 had been especially bad too. "I've lived here all my life and that was the worst winter," he said. "The snow was the height of the hedgerows."

"But you'll like Lechlade," he added, as if the pleasantness of the town was some sort of compensation for that winter and all the puzzling weather since. "It's a pretty town."

As it turned out, I wasn't so sure about Lechlade, walking about its streets after Terry had dropped me off. Maybe it was the weather, but the cold greyness of its stone buildings seemed to mirror the cold greyness of the skies above.

But I did appreciate the historical importance of the town, which was built on the Thames river trade. 'Commencement of the Thames Navigation', Edward Weller noted underneath the river at Lechlade on his 1863 map, thereafter changing the depiction of the waterway from a thin black thread to an ever widening blue; and that, in a nutshell, was the reason why Lechlade became a prosperous river port from the fifteenth century onwards. From here, all the way down to London and out to sea, the river, with the help of 45 locks, is navigable by boat. Wool and cheese was brought here from all over the Cotswolds, and salt was brought here from the Midlands, to be loaded onto barges bound for Oxford and London.

A little later, in 1789, the Thames and Severn Canal was completed, joining the Thames at Roundhouse Farm near Lechlade and opening up the way for the transport of goods from Bristol all the way to London.

But, in the end, the future of commercial transport lay with the railways. A series of well-attended town hall meetings during 1863 signalled the growing excitement local traders and farmers had for a new line connecting

Lechlade and nearby Bampton with the main railway network around Oxford. The East Gloucestershire Line opened in 1873, sounding the final death knell for the Lechlade barge business, a death already foretold by the coming of the Great Western Railway which unlocked the potential of towns like Swindon – only 12 miles to the south of Lechlade – as staging posts between Bristol and London.

The Thames-Severn Canal closed down in 1933 and Lechlade was left to decline gracefully as a pretty stopping off point for pleasure cruisers steaming up and down the river.

There was also the tourist legacy of an ode to its handsome church penned in 1815 by an itinerant poet called Percy Bysshe Shelley.

"Clothing in hues of heaven thy dim and distant spire," Shelley wrote of St Lawrence's distinctive steeple, which can be seen for miles down the Thames. "Around whose lessening and invisible height gather among the stars the clouds of night."

Tucked up in my room in a local pub that night, I turned out the light.

—⟋⟍⟍—

For a moment I couldn't see where it was coming from. A rhythmic beating overhead like the lonely sound of a wind turbine on the crest of a desolate hill. I looked up and saw two swans a few metres above me flapping their huge wings, coming into land like jumbo jets over west London on their approach into Heathrow.

Only this wasn't the Thames curling into west London; this was the Thames flowing eastwards from a little town called Lechlade. As the magnificent spire of St Lawrence began to disappear from the horizon behind me on my walk the next morning to my next stopping point in the village of Kelmscott, so too did all sounds of life. The last people I saw were a woman and two men on a boat at St John's Lock; the last swans I saw were the couple that passed above my head moments before.

After St John's, the first lock on the waterway, there was nothing. Just me, donned in the gear I had hastily assembled a few days before I set out on my epic trip: a pair of khaki trousers with big pockets on the side of them which I had bought from Marks & Spencer at the last minute; a pair of weathered hiking boots handed down through generation after generation of my Scottish wife's glen-walking family; and as many layers of clothing as I could muster on my top half – a T-shirt, a heavy blue cord shirt, a thick woollen jumper and a cagoule. Some people dress for hiking as if it was a form of dressage, striding out in their especially braided waterproofs; I was dressed for dawdling and plodding.

No, there was nothing. Just me in my dawdling livery. At least, it felt like it. I sauntered from field to field, round each twist and turn of the river, and as I did so the silence of the landscape seemed to grow and fill all the spaces around me: the hollows between the trunks of trees, the smudges of grey sky between the branches, the vast vapoury expanse of grey above me. An electric fence now separated the path and the river from fields on the other side, but there were no sheep, no cattle looking up as I tramped past, no sheep or cattle to contain with a short sharp shock of sizzling voltage.

I did have a new companion, though. A companion which would pop up at regular intervals during the rest of my sojourn to the sea. The problem was that it too was silent. It was the pillbox.

My walking friend from Tunbridge Wells who had shown me the way to the source of the Thames had told me about them. "You'll find them all along the river," he had exclaimed, "as if that would have deterred the Nazis!"

"If they'd have got as far as Henley the game would have been up anyway."

The pillboxes, those little forts made of concrete, had been built as a defence measure at the outset of the Second World War. On my walk to Kelmscott, they looked more like phantom medieval turrets erected by the Knights Templar to fight for some long forgotten cause.

I passed one, rotting and ghostly as I entered a field; then the river looped right round on itself and I was beside another one, just yards away from the first but ten minutes walk away from it because of the circuitous mean-der of the river. It was stained with 70 years of rain, sleet and snow and I couldn't help thinking as I passed it that there was someone or something slight menacing inside silently looking out at me, watching my slow progress over the damp grass.

There were probably many unseen eyes watching me, visible only to the kestrel now hovering overhead, its tail fanned out and wings flapping vigorously. It lingered there for a few minutes scanning the ground for mice and voles before catching a thermal and gliding to another spot above the fields.

At this point, I spotted another turret on the horizon, but this time of a more familiar and comforting nature than the pillbox. My ordnance survey map told me that this was the Saxon church steeple at Buscot and therefore I would soon be at Buscot Lock.

Ten minutes later, I was sitting on a bench amongst the typical furnishings of a Thames Lock. There is always a little wooden hut with slatted windows and a gabled roof, containing important information such as water levels in the vicinity and the number of boats which have passed through the lock in the past 28 days. There is always a lock-keeper's cottage constructed out of local stone with a bas-relief etched out under its eaves containing the emblem of the Thames Conservancy. This was the body responsible, from 1857 onwards, for managing the navigation of the Thames and maintaining its locks and weirs before it was taken over in 1974 by the Thames Water Authority, which itself was replaced by the Environment Agency in the 1990s.

There is always the machinery of the lock itself, those heavy timber sluice gates which hold a strange sort of mechanical power over water levels.

And there is usually a weir nearby, plastered with danger signs plucked from the very depths of our worst nightmares about being swept away in dangerous currents. The boarding at Buscot said: "Warning. Strong Stream Weir on right hand. Keep Away".

More soothingly, there is always a friendly tourist information board, usually near the wooden hut, telling stories about the history of the lock and the local area. Buscot was no exception. Built in 1790, it is the smallest of all the boat junctions on the Thames, a friendly board told me as I sipped from my water bottle. I read on.

The lock – together with Buscot Park, a stately home up on the hill overlooking the river – was bought up in 1859 by an Australian gold tycoon called Robert Tertius Campbell, who set about fitting it with a water-wheel-driven pump to help irrigate his estate which he was transforming into one of the most industrialised farms in nineteenth century England.

In 1863, as Edward Weller inscribed the word 'Workhouse' underneath the river at Buscot, Campbell built a single wheel at the lock and twin wheels downriver at Eaton Hastings to feed a 20-acre reservoir on the hillside to the west of his house. About one hundred navvies were employed on the project, which may account for Weller's inscription.

These were the first moves in an ambitious scheme to grow sugar beet on the estate to distil into alcohol. In 1869, a distillery was opened on an island adjacent to the lock – it is now a derelict Thames Water pumping station which may be pulled down to make way for a marina – and in the following year a narrow-gauge railway was built to collect the sugar beet from the farms on the estate. At the same time, with no expense seemingly spared, a telegraph system was installed so that farms at opposing ends of the Campbell's little fiefdom could communicate with each other.

In 1871, Campbell was still making a profit from his spirit, which was exported to France at nearly three shillings a gallon; but, gradually, after the outbreak of the Franco-Prussian War in 1870 his export trade slipped away.

Now a sick man, his health not helped by a sensational inquest into the poisoning of his eldest daughter's husband, Charles Bravo, at their home in Balham, which revealed his daughter Florence's love affair with prominent physician James Gully but found insufficient evidence to name a murderer, Campbell sold his distillery business.

Two years after his death in 1887, his estate was sold to a financier called Alexander Henderson and another chapter opened in the history of Buscot. Henderson became the 1st Lord Faringdon and started amassing an eclectic art collection, which included the *Legend of Briar Rose*, a series of paintings produced between 1885 and 1890 by a certain Pre-Raphaelite artist called Edward Burne-Jones, who had come a long way from those early days working in the design firm he founded in 1861 with William Morris opposite Edward Weller's house in Red Lion Square.

Gavin Henderson, the second Lord Faringdon, who succeeded his grandfather in 1934, carried on the tradition of art collecting, but added to it a strong interest in public affairs. This led to his keen support for the Republican cause on the Spanish Civil War and another significant episode in the history of Buscot – the arrival of child refugees from Guernica.

—⁂—

The story of Guernica – immortalised in a painting by Picasso – started as routinely as things could do in a small town in the Basque region of Spain which had been caught up for nearly a year in the desperate civil war between the country's Republican government and General Franco's Fascists and his Nazi allies. It was Monday, 26 April 1937, and it was a market day. The town was filling up with farmers and people from local villages coming into town to sell their produce.

But it soon became apparent that there was something different about this particular day. There had been more than the usual number of reconnaissance flights by the

Fascist forces over the town in the morning so when the church bells started ringing in the afternoon, the people of the town were mindful enough to make their way to the air-raid shelters.

It was to no avail. For the first time in the war, the Luftwaffe's Condor Legion employed experimental incendiary devices in tandem with their conventional aerial bombs. In the uncontrollable fires that burned until late into the next day as a result, air-raid shelters caught fire, houses caved in and around two thousand of Guernica's inhabitants were either killed or wounded. Thousands more spilled out onto the road heading for Bilbao, trying to flee the carnage.

Over the following weeks, as Franco's grip on the Basque region tightened and the international community began to awake to the gravity of the situation, a huge evacuation programme was mounted from the ports of Bilbao and Santander. About 120,000 people, a quarter of them children, who, just a week or so beforehand, had been terrorised by Franco's air raids, were now being whisked away on ships under the cover of night, tracer bullets from enemy aircraft whizzing overhead, to safe havens across Europe.

In late May, after an uncomfortable night on board the Habana, nearly 4,000 Basque children arrived at Southampton where, despite the opposition to the whole operation of the Hitler-appeasing government in Whitehall, they were welcomed by thousands of cheering people.

From a holding camp near Southampton, these hungry, traumatised, confused children were then dispersed by the efforts of church groups and trade unions to 'colonies' all over England, Scotland and Wales – Salvation Army homes, neo-gothic manor houses, Catholic orphanages and convents and one grand old house in poor repair in Kingston upon Thames.

One small group of young exiles under arrangements made by Lord Faringdon arrived at Buscot Park. There, sheltered by pretty walled gardens and cedar trees and lofty rooms filled with paintings by Edward Burne-Jones and Dante Gabriel Rossetti, but hundreds of miles away from their home and their families, if they still had families, the children of Guernica would, over time – possibly, hopefully – have picked up the pieces of their shattered lives.

In the wide valley below the ridge on which the house stood and the children played – a ridge that Edward Weller on his 1863 map shaded in grey – the River Thames did what it had always done. It slid quietly by.

—␊␊—

I cut myself loose from the moorings of Buscot Lock and followed after it on a bitterly cold and grey day in March 2013, and very quickly all the historical associations of the lock and its cosy lockkeeper's hut, filled with information about water levels and emergency numbers to call should you encounter any difficulties along your journey up or down the Thames, became a distant memory.

Now I was alone in the silence of the fields and the drift of the river again. At one point, I came across a pair of Canadian geese who trumpeted loudly as I approached; at another point I heard the tapping of a woodpecker in a far-off wood. But I saw no-one and heard no-one. Only an occasional farm building on the horizon hinted at a human presence in the area.

Yet, according to Weller's chart, there was a large wharf on the banks of the river here. It would have been Buscot wharf, rented out to London cheesemongers in the eighteenth and nineteenth centuries for the transport of thousands of tonnes of cheese each year from the farms of Gloucestershire, Oxfordshire and Wiltshire to the markets of London.

That was the thing about Weller's Thames chart, it occurred to me in the silence of the fields that followed the phantom wharf. His map was all bustle and business. It was all about railways and workhouses, wharfs and mills, and a canal that began its life on the River Severn and reached the Thames just outside the river port of Lechlade. Yet the river I had experienced was often about grey skies and a woodpecker tapping against a tree in a far-off wood.

On the other hand, I had already seen many things that had been invisible to the eye of the map-maker, not only Saxon churches containing the evidence of a dragon etching sculpted by a warrior people from the east, the Vikings, but also stories of other settlers and refugees who hailed from roughly the same direction: the rag-tag band of exiles from the windy plains of Troy who established a university in Cricklade, for instance, and the Scythians escaping famine and conflict on the edges of the Black Sea.

Of course, it was not the job of Edward Weller to record these, but it was beginning to strike me, as I compared his map with my modern Ordnance Survey, how much modern maps will point out places of historical and cultural interest – making a virtue out of old stones, dilapidated churches and the merest hint of a primitive fort – while Edward Weller concentrated on what mattered to people in 1863: towns and railways, trade and improvement. Unlike our generation, which suspects that all our hard-won progress might be just an illusion and the keys to Shangri-La actually may have been held by another people in another time, Weller drew up his maps within the co-ordinates of a more confident age, one that, by and large, believed in progress and trade and its own superiority. His map was the Victorian version of the River Thames. It was not the whole story.

But my modern map wasn't the whole story either, I realised. The Thames is much bigger than that. It is bigger than that because it is not only a line of water gliding through mellow English hills and meadows and settlements; it is also a river of history, a story – a very international story – about the people who have washed up on its shores over the centuries.

And not only that. It is a story about people leaving. In St Sampson's Church in Cricklade, I had found a memorial to a Joseph Nott who had died "at Madras in the East Indias" in 1769; and in the graveyard of Cricklade's smaller church of St Mary's, where I had tried to pick up the Thames Path heading eastwards, I had found the gravestone of a Mark Pike who had fought as a private in the Welsh Fusiliers in Spain and Portugal in the 1807-14 Peninsular War against Napoleon. This morning too, while wandering around the Church of St Lawrence in Lechlade, I had discovered another memorial: a brass plaque dedicated to the memory of a William Pitt Robbins, a major general in the Indian Army, who had died in Melbourne, Australia, in 1862. These characters were the first of many fragments of evidence I would discover along my journey of the men and women who had left their cosy firesides in riverside villages or warm summer evenings in riverside pubs to fight the wars of the British Empire, or to work for it, or to simply travel around it. Working in the city at the heart of this empire, with ships leaving every day for the far-flung destinations illustrated in his charts, Weller would have known what I meant.

People coming and going. Exotic lands. They were all part of the story, the world, of the Thames, I decided on that walk to Kelmscott.

It would need a new map to record it all. Weller's chart was a good starting point, but I would have to build on it, superimposing my observations, my textures and my tones over those of the Victorian mapmaker's, not erasing what he had laid down but filling in the pregnant spaces between his busy river towns and wharfs with the stories of those he had missed out. Like some sort of Victorian draughtsman bent over his drawing board in a warehouse drafting office, a large sheet of translucent parchment pinned to a frame over the original design, a pencil in hand to add more drawings and sketches.

Or to bring it all up to date, like the modern draughtsperson, sitting with a digital toolbox on their computer, adding layer upon layer of dimension, notation and detail to an original template which they can turn on and off with a click of their mouse.

For the moment, though, I was on the path to Kelmscott on a bitterly cold March day, looking forward to reaching a warm pub, and a warm room for the night, perhaps a Chinese room like the one they had at the guest house in Ashton Keynes or a room furnished with the Buddha like the one at The Wild Duck Inn. Who knows?

I passed an old weir-keeper's cottage and a wooden bridge which once made up the paraphernalia of Eaton Weir, dismantled in 1936 to alleviate local flooding. There had once been a pub here too called the Anchor Inn, which burnt down in a fire in 1980.

Somewhere overhead, a warm front from the mid-Atlantic was clashing with a bitter easterly blowing in from the Russian steppes.

VI

The Fireplace Reaches

At Eaton Weir, I had one of my first views of Kelmscott – a huddle of weathered stone houses which looked as if they hadn't been built by man at all but had just grown up naturally over the centuries amongst the hedgerows and trees around them.

Which is probably why William Morris, one of the founders of the Arts and Crafts movement, liked this Oxfordshire hamlet so much. It was about as remote as you could get in England from the fuming, belching metropolis in which he had spent so much of his career, starting off in shabby rooms with fellow Oxford graduate and fellow member of the Pre-Raphaelite Brotherhood, Edward Burne-Jones, in Red Lion Square, opposite the home of Edward Weller, before moving just up the road to Queen Square.

Morris and Burne-Jones were the brothers-in-arms of an artistic phenomenon which eschewed the ugly industrialisation of Victorian Britain in favour of something more romantic. At 17 Red Lion Square, Morris and Burne-Jones began to translate this way of looking at things into interior decor, developing a range of fabrics, furniture and stained glass windows which, among other things, told the heroic legends of medieval knights, St George and the dragon, and King Arthur and Guinevere.

Morris, Marshall, Faulkner & Co, or simply 'The Firm' as it was later known, was born in 1861. With the emphasis on the traditional craftsmanship and folksy, organic styles, Morris and his partners went on to produce wallpapers, chintzes, carpets and other furnishings that would soon inspire generations of artists, architects and designers – from Charles Rennie Mackintosh to Edwin Lutyens and Laura Ashley.

It was a decade later when William Morris, looking for a rural retreat away from the travails of London, found a Tudor farmhouse a minute's walk from these upper reaches of the Thames and took up a tenancy on it. The famous designer rarely resided more than a few days at a time there – though his beautiful wife Janey did spend a good deal of time there with the children and, rather controversially, with his business colleague, the Pre-Raphaelite artist Dante Gabriel Rossetti. Nevertheless, Kelmscott Manor would become a source of inspiration for the rest of the designer's life.

It was during the Kelmscott years that Morris developed his 'small is beautiful' ideal based on small rural communities living off the land, creating what they needed for their homes but also conserving the natural environment around them. It was also during these years that he launched the Kelmscott Press, which used traditional typography and calligraphy to produce a series of beautifully illuminated books, including his own – a utopian socialist fantasy set in the twenty-first century called *News from Nowhere*. As for Kelmscott itself, Morris described it as "a heaven on Earth".

It was certainly a pretty village, I thought, as I followed a sign for 'The Plough at Kelmscott' from the Thames Path. I passed Kelmscott Manor on my left hand side – a home brimming full with vivid home furnishings, as you might imagine, including a tapestry, embroidered by Morris in his Red Lion Square days, and also the 'must-have' for every well-to-do Victorian, a China room, which in Morris's case was full of blue and white Chinese ceramics patterned with willows and floating mountains.

Beyond the manor, there was a field and a row of neat cottages, one of them sporting a carved stone plaque depicting Morris sitting under a tree in a meadow; and then, on a bend in the road, the Plough Inn, which had been serving beers since the 1840s and was about to serve me one too.

It was idyllic. But the village was not without its problems as the young landlord told me at dinner that night.

"The whole of Kelmscott was under three feet of water," he said, referring to the 2007 floods. "The Plough itself was so badly damaged by the water it had to be closed for two years for renovations."

The remoteness of the hamlet would not have helped. No roads pass through here on the way to anywhere else. The country lane down from the Lechlade road stops here and then turns back. The only other way out is via the dark river, somewhere out there in the cold night.

So it was a good thing that there was a bed here for me – in a room called 1631 because that was when the building was first put up – and a cosy bar. I ordered a last beer and settled down in a corner seat next to the warm log fire.

—⚋—

A warm fireside. It was rapidly becoming my best friend on my journey along the Thames. One had welcomed me into The Wild Duck in Ewen, bringing feeling back to hands struck numb by the wintry blight outside; another had cocooned me in its warm glow in The Red Lion in Cricklade, bringing life back to weary feet; and another had lifted my mood in Lechlade as I stumbled into a pub from the stark greyness outside.

Now it was the dying embers of a wood stove in Kelmscott, igniting soft moments of memory after another day of walking the Thames. Turning my thoughts to another fireplace, in another time, another place.

I could feel these thoughts like I could feel the warmth from the stove beside me. The crackling and spitting in the stone hearth in the tumbling old house up there on the Northamptonshire escarpment. When I was young. Many years ago. In the village where my father grew up. Aunts, uncles, cousins, cousins of cousins, sisters, brothers, parents, the vicar, the verger, Aunt Edith in her nineties. Our incandescent faces lit up in the conviviality of the family Christmas party. The tree by the French window, crowned with a plastic angel. Logs in the coal bucket waiting to be thrown on the fire.

The next day. Christmas Day. The traditional family walk along the dismantled railway line. First the tramp across the muddy brown fields that led from the back of the church towards the Brackley Lane, then a meander through the coppice of trees to the precipice where the railway bridge had once been, and finally the march along the country road that took us back to the village via a steep hill, the top of which offered views down to the River Cherwell and the Oxfordshire floodplain.

Somewhere beyond that, beyond the trees and through the winter mist, the Thames slipped into Oxford.

Thinking about that mist many years after, it was as if the family parties and my father slowly disappeared into it. The family parties came to an end in the 1970s, my father passed away in the 1980s, and it was many years before I would return to the house.

When I did, in my late twenties, it was to open a battered tin chest that had been languishing in the corner of the attic at the top of the house for years.

It was packed with the stuff of my father's life, things he'd never got round to sorting out when he was alive. There were wartime letters from the 'Gold Coast' in West Africa and a large photograph album of African scenes: the piercing eyes of an Ashanti tribeswoman with her three children peering out of one page; a crowd drifting towards the spectators' enclosure at the Accra races on another; a solitary canoe skimming across a lake on another page, setting up gentle ripples in its wake.

There were also memoirs he had typed out on the portable Imperial typewriter he bought second-hand in 1938 and kept all his life, memories of growing up in the village before the Second World War, and of how, after leaving school at 15 in 1938, he had answered an advertisement for an apprentice reporter on the local newspaper at an initial salary of 10 shillings a week and got the job. This was a very lucky break for two reasons: firstly because it broke the mould of Wilcox men toiling in the fields – most of them had been tenant farmers or agricultural labourers; and secondly because the other job my father applied for was as a porter at a local railway station: the successful candidate was killed by a German bomb dropped on the station a few years later.

The first years as a newspaper apprentice were fun, my father recorded, in spite of the exceptionally long hours (from 9am to 9pm, often longer). District reporting was carried out in an old car (driven by one of the older journalists) which was so decrepit that, when ascending hills, the doors had to be held open to expel the blue fumes from under the dashboard. Later on, my father took to the road on one of the pool motorbikes, riding from village to village, town to town, covering council meetings, inquests, murders, suicides, fires, village fetes, garden parties, flower shows. More and more so, as the older reporters slipped off to war.

My father diligently kept scrapbooks of the articles he wrote during his subsequently lengthy career in newspaper and magazine journalism. I had seen a few of them. But there were more here –ageing dog-eared cuttings from the *Portsmouth Evening News*, the *Birmingham Gazette* and others.

My aunt brought me a cup of tea, and sitting back in the living room next to the fireside of all those childhood memories of family parties, I opened one of the scrapbooks.

—ᴡ—

It was the prospect of the next fireplace that kept me going as I trekked during the following days on the Thames through what seemed to be an endless patchwork of fields and trees. However tiring and cold my walk along the Thames Path got, there was always another warm pub to look forward to. After the Plough Inn, there was the roaring hearth in the Trout Inn at Tadpole Bridge, the ashen glow at the Talbot near the Swinford Toll Bridge and the burning coals in the grate at the White Hart in Wolvercote.

They were all very welcome, because in-between times, the walking could be bleak and lonely. This is the Thames at its most remote. No villages or farms come near the river. Very few ramblers seem to venture this way. Except for the occasional bridge or lock, there is little more than the caprice of the river meandering through a flat flood plain of Oxfordshire clay.

You only need to look at Weller's map to see it. From Kelmscott to Wolvercote downstream, there was very little in 1863 except for a series of weirs, many of which do not exist anymore because they were primitive wooden affairs called flash locks erected by local farmers and mill owners to hold up the water for their own specific purposes. With names to conjure with - Old Nan's Wear, Ten Foot Wear, Skinners Wear – the 11 weirs along this 25-mile stretch would have been pressed into the service of the occasional farmsteads dotted either side of the river, and the two mills: one at Newbridge and the other, a paper mill at Cassington. There was also the occasional village set back from the river on terraces of gravel, villages such as Duxford and Shifford; and the four bridges – Radcot, Tadpole, Newbridge and Swinford.

There have been a few changes since then, but nothing significant. In some ways, the area has become slightly more remote. The mills have gone and there are now only six weirs, one of which is now part of Grafton Lock and another which is part of Northmoor Lock; and there are still only four road crossings. There has been no sign, either, of any new settlements springing up in the intervening years.

Despite this, I began to assemble during my walk from Kelmscott a map of the river in my own mind that differed in nuance and degree to Weller's. The walking was still bleak and lonely, but gradually I managed to add my own sketching and drawings to the mapmaker's picture of the river.

Firstly, there was the vegetation along the waterway, something that is highlighted in a bright lime green on modern Ordnance Survey maps, but missing from Weller's map of a Victorian working river. This was the land of the crack willow, rows of them lining the waterside, their roots reaching into the waters below, their wispy winter branches rising high above their thick low stumps. It was also the land of the poplar, standing tall, slender and regimental along the banks, towering over the rag-tag thickets of aspen and hazel spilling into the river below them.

Leafless and stark, with only the occasional bud or catkin emerging from the prolonged embrace of winter, it was a desolate, sinister landscape. More sinister still were the occasional groves of broken and gnarled trees I came across that looked as if they had been severed and lashed in winter storms. I chanced upon one of these on the path between Tadpole Bridge and Tenfoot Bridge, the site of the old flash weir, an avenue of low twisting branches reaching out along the ground towards me. I found a similar grouping near a place called Bablock Hythe, but this time the low branches had spread over the river, throwing their tentacles mangrove-like into the water.

Nearby, I stumbled upon a clump of poisonous mistletoe sucking the life out of a silver birch. Overhead, the cawing of birds signalled the presence of rookeries. Looking up, I spotted them on the horizon crowning a colony of oak trees like the look-out posts of some unknown malice.

This stretch of the floodplain was also a landscape of things once important to people, but now lost to history. According to Weller's map, there was a ferry crossing at a village called Duxford, which on the other side of the river joined a path leading to the Chimney meadows. The ferry is long gone and there is now an artificial canal and pathway which cuts off the meander of the river that takes you down to Duxford, taking boaters and walkers down to Shifford Lock instead.

A concave bridge across the weir just beyond the lock took me onto the south bank of the river and around the fringes of a wide green expanse which seemed to be all that the landscape had to offer until something back on the other side of the water caught my eye. Two bells, exposed to the elements, hanging in an open belfry rising above a desolate looking church. This abandoned chapel, I had read somewhere, is all that remains of the lost town of Shifford, now just a name but once an important place where the Saxon king, Alfred, called a parliament – an assembly of nobles, bishops and other men of importance brought together to discuss the important issues of the day. What happened to Shifford no-one quite knows, but legends still swirl around King Alfred's rule: that the parliaments and the rule of law that the king who burnt the cakes adhered to were the beginning of some sort of democratic tradition in England.

Whatever the truth of the matter, the ghost town of Shifford gradually disappeared from my view and I carried on, past a man-made lake, through a smattering of trees and onto Newbridge. No more than two pubs now, Newbridge also once had its day in the historical limelight, being the scene in June 1644 of a fracas in the English Civil War as a Parliamentarian army commanded by William Waller clashed with Royalist soldiers trying to protect King Charles 1's military stronghold at Oxford. Two forces on either side of the Thames: one led by believers in the king's divine right to rule; the other, a vanguard of Puritan merchants and shopkeepers joined by a motley collection of revolutionaries – Levellers, Diggers, Fifth Monarchists, Ranters, Seekers and all manner of other political and religious heretics brought together in the common cause of political liberty.

The sombre tunics and metal helmets of the Roundheads prevailed over the frilly white shirts and the feathered hats of the Cavaliers, and Waller forced his way across the Thames. The following evening, however, the king gave the circling Roundheads the slip, taking his army out of Oxford under cover of darkness, marching that night towards Worcester.

Through it all, the Thames, no doubt, flowed unflinching, as it continues to flow unflinching, but ever changing. Sometimes as still as a mill pond, a watery mirror of the sky above and the trees around; sometimes flowing swiftly. Mainly muddy and green, but at moments suddenly crystal clear. At other moments, everything at once. Still and calm near the far bank, but swirling and spiralling on the near bank, currents and eddies bubbling up to the surface from unknown fathoms below.

I followed this ever changing river onto Bablock Hythe, where another lost ferry crossing awaited me. For more than a thousand years a ferry operated here; but in 2007, the floodwaters swept the boat onto the land where it has sat ever since. The landlord of the riverside Ferryman Inn has started a campaign to relaunch the service, so when I snuck in for a lunchtime drink I enquired.

"No, that's gone," the barmaid answered. "It's sink or swim now!"

I tramped on – on a route which diverted onto country lanes for a while before rejoining the river – past the Farmoor Reservoir and the ghost of Skinners Weir, and onto the Pinkhill Lock.

—w—

Mr Brown, the lockkeeper at Pinkhill, had been busy this month. Twenty eight boats had passed through Pinkhill in the past 28 days, a notice declared on the window of his lock hut; and another was passing through as I arrived.

But it was the flood levels recorded on a white stone above the steep wall of the lock that really caught my eye. There were three plaques, the lowest marking the flood level of January 2003, the middle one the levels in March 1947 and the uppermost recalling the bursting of the river banks in November 1894. Above them all, however, in makeshift red paint was another sign, recording the worst flooding of them all, in July 2007.

The Thames Conservancy kept detailed records of the changing tempers of the river. For November 1894, it recorded 32.44 inches of rainfall in the Thames watershed, which caused such devastation that the Conservancy was still referring to it when it came to report on the floods of 1947. The floods that year caused by snow followed by heavy rain were still only second in volume "to the great flood of 1894", the Conservancy noted.

The upper Thames and Oxford area took the brunt of both of these calamities, as they did again in July 2007 when record water levels were observed at Pinkhill Lock and in the area I had been walking through for the last day or so, the area where the Windrush and Evenlode rivers empty into the Thames. Interestingly, the amount of rainfall, at 121mm, was only a fraction of the amount that fell in November 1894, but as the Environment Agency, which is now responsible for managing the Thames, noted in its report on the floods, there were other factors at play – high moisture levels in the ground from the previous winter and the fact that most of the rain fell torrentially over just two days, the 19th and 20th of July. Four thousand homes up and down the river were flooded out as a result, the majority of them west of Oxford in villages like Kelmscott.

As I left Pinkhill Lock, I noticed for the first time the crest of the Thames Conservancy etched into the face of the lockkeeper's cottage – two white shields on a sky blue background; one depicting the cross of St George, the English flag; the other showing two ships on a choppy sea. For me, this was another reminder of the dichotomy at the heart of the river's personality: on the one hand, a very English river; on the other, a trading river, a river of ships and connections with the wider world.

But it was another side of the river's character that revealed itself to me over the last few miles to Wolvercote, a side I had glimpsed momentarily near the beginning of my journey, on my approach to Somerford Keynes, but not seen again as the gloom of a lingering winter descended once again on my trek: the river's amiable side.

The principal reason for this was the sun. It came out of hiding again over those last few miles leading to the outskirts of Oxford, and with it, all those lonely days in bleak fields were dispersed like dandelion seeds in a sudden breeze. The Thames was now a bright blue as it snaked from side to side through the flat Oxfordshire floodplain, eating away at the land around it on one bend, depositing little beaches of sand and silt on another. Wytham Hill, meanwhile, unfurled itself on its banks and the River Evenlode slipped shyly into its waters from behind a thicket of broken, half-submerged trees.

For the first time in days, I felt the river was my companion again, weaving its way playfully through the green tapestry of English countryside. A man with a large beard popped his head above the parapet of his canal boat and warned me cheerfully not to fall into the river. Otherwise, I would get "very wet and very cold". A British Indian woman with a blue denim shoulder-bag asked me the way to Kidlington. When I told her she was miles out of her way and heading for Eynsham instead, she responded genially: "Oh well, it is God's will that he take us to new places."

She was in high spirits. I was in high spirits. The path became paved after King's Lock and took me underneath the Oxford bypass, through a couple of gates and up onto the road beside the Trout Inn. Spurning its spit roast chicken and faux connections with TV detective Inspector Morse, I followed the road into Wolvercote and into the White Hart.

There I found what I'd been looking for. A warm fireplace. I sat down with a bitter lemon in the warmth of its glowing coals and mulled over the past few days.

I had followed Edward Weller's working river, seen its remaining weirs and settlements; but I had seen much more besides. I had seen crack willows and gnarled trees, rookeries and King Alfred, Roundheads and Cavaliers, the bursting of the river's banks and the hovering crest of the Thames Conservancy.

Slowly, in a meandering sort of way, I started to inscribe in my mind what I had seen, and like the traditional draughtsman layering a piece of fine parchment over the base map, began adding the beginnings of my topography to his.

VII
Oxford

"See what I mean?"

I peered into the liquid crystals of Parvesh's mobile phone and saw what he meant. A road that had become a river, a young man struggling through the water on a bicycle, another man in a canoe paddling past him.

"That was November last year," the proprietor of the guest house on the Abingdon Road where I had put up for the night in Oxford continued. "The river came right over the allotments and then over our road. As you can see, people were canoeing up the street.

"And the police had to turn the electricity off at the traffic lights because one person got electrocuted when he touched one of them."

"Incredible," I murmured in empathy. "Incredible."

"Been like this on and off ever since 2007," Parvesh continued. "The thing is the water levels are so high that it only takes a bit of water for this to happen.

"But, anyway, what would you like for breakfast? Bacon, egg, mushrooms, tomatoes, no sausage, no baked beans? Yes, that's fine."

He retired to the kitchen where his wife was cooking, and presently, I heard the reassuring squelch and spit of an egg frying on the hot stove of the couple's chatter – mainly in Hindi, was it, I wasn't sure, but occasionally seasoned with a pinch of laughter and a smidgeon of English.

I rather liked this bed and breakfast, I thought to myself as they busied away. It stood in an area where the comforting honey-coloured stone of the Oxford terraces began to give way to the disconcerting grey of a run-down council estate and the boarded-up windows of pubs and shops that had obviously closed down in the economic depression; yet it was a homely sort of place full of Ercol furniture and wooden banisters.

When Parvesh reappeared five or so minutes later with my breakfast, I wanted to know more about it. "So this house was owned by a toy manufacturer originally? I was reading your guide in my room."

My genial but consistently worried-looking proprietor seemed surprised by my interest. "Yes, the house was built in 1914 by a Eugene Delamare who made toys. This was all countryside around here once, you see, and he wanted a view of the Thames."

He paused for a moment, and looked out the window. "But then in 1921," he added darkly, "they built that housing estate across the road. He didn't like all the riff-raff coming in and spoiling his view, so he moved upriver to Wolvercote."

It was now that his wife, Narinder, appeared. "Shame really," she laughed. "He wouldn't have had to move out now, because the river comes to you!"

We had returned to the weather, the subject never really far away from our thoughts in the wake of 2012, the wettest year on record in England.

"Are people in Oxford worried about more flooding this year?" I joined in. "I think the people of Binsey are. I walked past there yesterday and the houses are surrounded by sandbags."

———m———

I had come from Binsey or thereabouts the day before. After leaving the cosy fireplace at the White Hart, I had walked back to the Trout Inn past an orchard donated in 1934 by a PL Agnew in memory of his son killed in the First World War, and rejoined the Thames Path at Godstow Lock. Passing the ruined remains of Godstow Abbey on the way – the sanctuary in the twelfth century of 'Fair Rosamund', who lived a life of prayer there after being exposed as the mistress of King Henry II – I arrived, half an hour or so later, at a wooden gate and a path that led through wiry bushes and spindly trees into the garden of the Perch Inn at Binsey.

It was after a quick lunch under the low wooden beams of the Perch that I had explored the local village, noticing then the sandbags thrown up tight against the frontages of each cottage I passed.

Binsey is actually located on a meadow cut off by the Thames on one side and a threading of streams and rivulets on the other, which would account for the heightened danger of flooding if the Thames were to burst its banks, and explains why the area is often called the Isle of Binsey.

Yet the area is also known, more interestingly, as 'the isle of prayer'. This was the name given to it by Frideswide, the patron saint of Oxford and founder of an order of nuns very close to where the Perch now stands.

According to legend, Frideswide was the beautiful daughter of a Saxon king of Oxford who was brought up by nuns after her mother had died. She had dedicated herself to God, so when a handsome prince turned up to claim her hand in marriage she fled Oxford under the cover of darkness, hiding among the reeds of the Thames riverbank.

For many weeks, she and her little group of devout supporters travelled upriver, caring for the poor and healing the sick at a sacred well on a meadow cut off by the Thames on one side and streams on the other: this was Binsey, her 'isle of prayer'.

Only when she heard that her father was missing her desperately did she return to Oxford. Once there, she was apprehended by the prince again. This time, however, she prayed to God for help and in an act of heavenly intervention that tends to happen in this kind of tale the prince was blinded on the spot by a bolt of lightning.

It was then – finally, you might say – that Frideswide took pity on the poor prince and prayed again, this time asking God to restore his sight but to diminish his desire for her hand. Water duly burst from a spring, healing the prince, but curing him of any love he'd had for Frideswide. She was now free to set up a priory on the site of what is now Oxford University's Christ Church College, and to perform miracles and that sort of thing as saints are inclined to do, until her death in October 727.

In 1858, the Pre-Raphaelite artist Edward Burne-Jones – soon to become Edward Weller's neighbour in Red Lion Square – created a stained glass window for Christ Church depicting the story of Saint Frideswide. The window was crowned with a beautiful rounded panel showing a ship of souls containing the saint and her acolytes sailing off in the moonlight to heaven.

Crossing the river from Binsey to Port Meadow on the fringes of Oxford on a cold but increasingly bright afternoon many years later, I sensed that I was now entering the realm of Frideswide and the Burne-Jones window, a feeling reinforced when I caught a glimpse of the dreaming spires of the famous university town from Port Meadow.

The meadow itself has played an important part in the city's history, being its traditional recreational ground, a place where people have come to walk and play for more than a thousand years. In the nineteenth century, it was the location of the annual Oxford Races, which invariably generated something of a carnival atmosphere. Travelling by boat, by carriage or on horseback, thousands of visitors would arrive from miles around each year to fill the beer tents lining the course for a day of betting and boozing. Summer thunderstorms dampened the jollities slightly on the first day of the event in 1863, the year when Weller drew up his map of the Thames; but the crowds were out in force again on the second day to watch Mr Crawford's colt take The City Member's Plate after trailing Colonel Crockett's horse for most of the distance.

Leaving the meadow behind, I was soon passing by the 'island' of Osney, enclosed on one side by the Thames and on the others by converging streams. This was once the site of an abbey where, some say, the twelfth century monk, Geoffrey of Monmouth, might have written his *History of the Kings of Britain*. Nowadays it is a citadel of makeshift wooden huts, glasshouses and beanpoles which make up the Osney allotments. Overlooking them, on the Thames side, is a row of anxious terraces furnished with kitchen extensions and loft conversions.

It was not long until I reached Folly Bridge, right in the heart of Oxford.

—⟋⟍—

It was at Folly Bridge one wet July day in 1862 that Charles Lutwidge Dodgson, a mathematics don at Christ Church College, wobbled onto a boat with rowing companion Robin Duckworth and the three young daughters of the college dean, Henry Liddell. The next day, Dodgson started to write a tale that would eventually become *Alice's Adventures in Wonderland.*

I dawdled for a while on the bridge admiring a house with a turreted roof and curious marble statues carved into its red Victorian brickwork. Then, turning up St Aldates, I headed for Christ Church Meadow and the college itself.

The entrance to Christ Church college was through the Meadow Building, built in 1863 by Thomas Newenham Deane, which led onto the college's mellow stone court-yards and cloisters. I climbed up the staircase to the Great Dining Hall and then ambled around the hall itself, study-ing the portraits of the famous alumni on the walls – prime ministers, philosophers and one particular mathematician, Charles Dodgson, aka Lewis Carroll.

Outside again, I found a door that led me into the col-lege cathedral, and after being pointed in that direction by a guide, stood in the chancel looking upwards at its mag-nificent vaulted gothic ceiling, the stone pillars at the side of the aisle spreading out their ribs when they reached the ceiling like tall trees extending their branches. The result-ing patterns were intended to create an image of heaven, the cathedral guide had told me.

She had also divulged that there was a beautiful window in the Latin chapel and moments later I found it: Edward Burne-Jones' stained glass window. Four panels related in vivid greens, reds and blues the story of Saint Frideswide's flight upriver – the arrival of Prince Algar to take her hand in marriage, Frideswide hiding in the bushes and reeds along the Thames with Algar's men in hot pursuit, the saint rowing upriver to Binsey where she established her nunnery and drew water from the holy well, her return to Oxford, the rather violent fate of the young prince, and, finally, Frideswide on her death bed.

Suspended above this story told in glass, there were two flower-shaped windows showing the Tree of Knowledge and the Tree of Life and above these, the stunningly pretty glass image of a Saxon ship, portrayed in lovely shades of red and yellow, sailing away on waters of bright blue and green. The sleeping body of Frideswide lies on deck. A crescent moon hovers overhead in a starry night sky.

For a while, I sat in that dangling moon in that starry sky looking down on the saint in her floating sepulchre, admiring the luminous art of Burne-Jones that had immortalised her. When I finally stumbled out into the wintry light again and onto the Oxford cobbles, it was time to make my way to my guest house on the Abingdon Rd. I hopped on a bus.

—⟋⟍—

The next morning – after the breakfast cooked for me by Parvesh and Narinder at my guest house – I walked down a line of suburbia called Weirs Lane to pick up the Thames Path back into the centre of Oxford. It was a cold but bright morning; and when I got to the waterfront in the neighbourhood of Hinksey it was bustling with people: students from Magdalen and Merton clad in ear muffs and branded sweat-shirts, runners in tight-fitting lycra bottoms with i-Pods strapped to their belts, cyclists wearing helmets and serious expressions as well as families with inclement children in tow. I guess the river in Oxford has always been something of a promenade. On a midsummer's day in 1863, for instance, the waterfront here would have been filled with holiday makers who had turned out for Oxford's annual regatta. It was an exciting day, observed the Oxford Journal, notable for "the defeat of old-established clubs by younger blood", exemplified particularly by the victory of young gun WG Edwards in the Challenge Silver Scull against a veteran called Mr Dolly.

Wrapped up warmly, I strolled for a while upstream until I came across a fork in the river, with an island in the middle. This is where the River Thames and the River Cherwell, which flows down from the north, meet each other. Their confluence creates a natural island fortress that made it conducive for a university to be built here in the Middle Ages. At the southern tip of this island is a pub called the 'Head of the River'.

A few more steps and I was up on Folly Bridge again and making my way up St Aldates, as I had done the day before, towards Christ Church. Instead of going into the college this time, though, I crossed the meadows and slipped up an alleyway beside it which led to the cobble-stones of Merton Street. Here, I reached another alleyway, called Logic Lane, which, I knew from my pocket map of Oxford, would take me up to the High Street.

The lane eases its way around the side of University College, which was "founded by King Alfred for twenty-six students in Divinity" in 1249 according to the eighteenth century antiquary, Thomas Cox. In the centuries that have followed the college has boasted among its alumni the Romantic poet Percy Bysshe Shelley who was expelled for writing a scandalous tract called The Necessity of Atheism; William Jones who founded the Asiatic Society of Bengal in Calcutta in 1784 to encourage Oriental studies; and a High Commissioner of British Malaya called Henry Gurney who was murdered in a guerrilla ambush on a lonely jungle road winding its way up to a hill town near Kuala Lumpur.

I could almost feel their presence. Nowhere on my journey so far had a sense of the past been so palpable as in Oxford. Ancient colleges, stained glass windows, stone bridges – they all seemed to cradle the memory of years gone by: 1167 perhaps, when the university was founded; 1642, when the Cavaliers occupied the city; 1863, when the city welcomed a visit from the Prince and Princess of Wales.

I turned into the High Street. It was here that preparations for the Prince and his new wife, Alexandra of Denmark, reached their height in the summer of 1863; buntings, fancy lights, all hastily erected in anticipation of the Royal cortege making its way up from Magdalen Bridge towards their accommodation in the Deanery at Christ Church. The following day His Royal Highness would receive an Honorary Degree at the Sheldonian Theatre before the Royal party moved on to the gardens of St John's for a bazaar in aid of raising funds for a new wing at the Radcliffe Infirmary.

The royal visit was quite possibly the most exciting thing to happen to Oxford in 1863. That is not to say, however, that the city slept for the rest of the year. On the contrary, it was abuzz with activity; not only with the comings and goings of students, but also with various worthy meetings to tackle the issues facing the municipality: the guardians of the Oxford workhouse on the Cowley Road met to discuss the increasing numbers of tramps on the streets; the street commissioners met to consider an extension to the public lighting hours; and the Institute of Civil Engineers got together to mull over the perennial problem of flooding in the Thames valley.

Others were having more fun. The Ancient Order of Druids toasted the sun over a baron of beef at the Wheatsheaf Inn and hundreds turned up at the Town Hall in November to watch the "Great Polish Wizard, Pann Warschawski" perform his amazing repertoire of magic tricks. Somewhere in the shadows, meanwhile, the criminal classes were also hard at work: in August there was a spate of burglaries on the Iffley Road.

The past is never dead in a place like Oxford; it is not even sleeping. You can see it in the shaft of sunlight thrown through the stained glass window, you can smell it in the wood-smoke filled lounges of the old inns, you can touch it when you push open the wooden door at the entrance to one of the colleges. You don't need history books or commemorative signs to appreciate the past in Oxford because you can sense it at every turn.

But sometimes there is a helpful sign which grabs your attention. Shortly after I had passed All Souls College walking towards Magdalen Bridge, I noticed something above the door of No 48 High Street. It was a metal plaque.

It told me that these premises – now a shoe shop – had once been home to a bicycle repair business run by a young man called William Richard Morris.

—⚏—

The Oxford motor empire began here at the turn of the twentieth century. A genius for all things mechanical, Morris soon gravitated from bicycles to cars, and in 1913 his first car, the Bullnose Morris rolled off the assembly line at a motor factory he had opened at a disused military training college in Cowley, in the city's southern suburbs.

By the middle of the 1920s, the Cowley factory, now Morris Motors, had become one of the global pioneers of automobile mass-production and over the next 30 years or so, it would launch a series of classic brands, including the Morris Oxford, the Morris Eight and the Morris Minor.

By the 1950s, the joint Morris and Austin organisation, under the banner of the British Motor Corporation (BMC), was churning out more than 10,000 cars a week, many of them destined for export. The UK was now the largest car exporter in the world, bigger even than the US.

This is when my father got a walk-on part in the Morris story. In the early 1950s, he became the motoring correspondent on the *Birmingham Evening Dispatch*; and in 1956, he was invited with other journalists to join Morris and other BMC directors on a prestigious British press visit to the company's factories in Australia.

Thirty journalists – including a Norman Dixon of the *Manchester Guardian*, a George Richardson of the newly-founded *Independent Television News* and my father whom everybody just called R, probably because his name was the increasingly unfashionable Ronald – set off on a BOAC Stratocruiser piston-engine plane from Heathrow on Wednesday 22 February, arriving via New York, San Francisco, Honolulu and Fiji for a welcome lunch at the Elanora Country Club near Sydney the following Sunday.

For the following three weeks this broad-shouldered, doubled-breasted, chain-smoking group of men (although the more urbane London types sported a lighter, sharper Italian look) were wined and dined all across Australia, occasionally taking in an assembly plant or a distributor showroom to witness for themselves how truly global the BMC had become. They finally arrived back at the historic Wentworth Hotel in Sydney on a hot Saturday evening in mid-March for their farewell dinner of Poulet de grain roti a l'anglaise followed by Poires belle Helene.

No one assumed at that final soiree, I expect, or indeed, cared very much in between the glasses of Rhinecastle Brut Champagne and the after-dinner liqueurs that this state of affairs could not go on forever. R, who had gushed about the "revolutionary new engineering features" of the "new completely re-styled" Morris Oxford a year or so before, returned home to file stories on BMC's £5 million expansion programme in Australia which, it was hoped, would build on the "remarkable" post-war growth in Austin and Morris sales in that country.

But that same year, almost unnoticed, German car production overtook that of Britain's for the first time, and within a few more years the British motor-manufacturing industry was in terminal decline, brought to its knees by the forces of disintegration that had been gathering in the wings for some time. Although R and other reporters had devoted thousands of column inches to some of these over the years – the angry labour disputes and the emergence of foreign rivals – the final demise, when it came, seemed to have an air of hopeless inevitability about it.

The carve-up began in the 1980s and 1990s. The Morris logo showing an ox crossing the River Isis – as the upper Thames is often called – is now owned by the Shanghai Automotive Industry Corporation. Morris's factory in Cowley, home of the original classic Mini, is now churning out up to 900 new Minis a day under the tutelage of BMW. Flourishing once more, it is true, but under foreign ownership.

—∾—

St Frideswide returning to the city to set up a priory, Lewis Carroll rowing from Folly Bridge upriver to Port Meadow, Morris Minors rolling off the production line at Cowley bound for aspirational car showrooms in far-flung corners of the globe – Oxford was a place of comings and goings. My final afternoon in Oxford was devoted to all those adventurers who had gone overseas in the service of the British Empire – like that luminary of University College, William Jones, who had become a big noise in Calcutta – and come back with their knapsacks filled with booty. I spent it amongst the Victorian glass cases filled with relics from all around the world that make up the vast anthropological collection of the Pitt Rivers Museum.

It was a General Pitt Rivers who had started the museum off in 1884 when he retired from military service overseas and donated all sorts of bric-a-brac – ceremonial masks, musical instruments, amulets and charms containing magical powers and so on – that he had collected on his travels or bought from dealers or at auctions. And then the trickle had become a flood: explorers, anthropologists, archaeologists, colonial administrators, adventurers, all bequeathing the fruits of their plunderous obsessions.

For a couple of hours, I was caught up in it all. Samurai swords and boomerangs on the top floor, wielded by warriors and hunters lost in the hills of Japan or the plains of Australia; the shadow puppets of Java on the middle floor; and on the ground floor a little textile horse belonging once to a secret society in Nigeria who believed that once they mounted it they could gallop invisibly towards their enemies. There were more things too that captured my attention: miniature figurines of Hindu deities here, the neck rings of the Kayan people of Burma there, and a range of bronze objects quite possibly looted in 1897 from the West African kingdom of Benin by imperial British forces.

The evening was drawing in when I finally stepped out into its icy grip. I dived into the streets, making my way through the smell of wood smoke back towards the city centre, half hoping to see my old university friend, Tony, there, walking home from work to the three-room flat he once rented near the Magdalen Bridge before he had gone off to Japan and never returned. Instead, the faces, some old, some young, hurrying past me on the pavements, were ones without a name, soon to be lost anyhow to the gathering darkness.

At one point a college door was thrown open to reveal a group of choristers in red and white and their choir master assembling nervously for the Evensong service, at another point a brilliant white light in a college window revealed shelves and shelves of dusty books in a library; but they were just occasional eddies of light in the swirling currents of the night.

I came up for air briefly at the King's Arms, bathed in light on the corner of Parks Road and Hollywell Street, where I sank a pint of Bombardier beer in front of the log fire in the oak-panelled bar somewhere at the back of its labyrinth of rooms. Then I fell into the streets again, winding my way down Broad Street and up to the disembodied busts of 13 Roman emperors on the gate posts of the Christopher Wren-designed Sheldonian Theatre. With their laurel leaved hair and stately togas draped over stately shoulders, they were ghostly reminders of an imperial city that believed it was eternal, until, like all empires before and since, it had finally succumbed to the barbarians and heretics knocking at its gates.

Oxford was full of echoes of empire, both living ones such as its famous university sitting at the centre of a vast web of international connections feeding it with information and ideas, people and money, and dead ones such as Pax Britannica, the mementos of which were now displayed forlornly in glass cases at the Pitt Rivers Museum.

I hung around for a while, peering into the mad, bulging eyes of one particular Caesar – those of Nero probably – but soon the bitter cold of the dark night began to bite once again. I needed light and warmth, and after casting my eyes in vain around Broad Street, suddenly remembered where I could find both. I had visited this establishment a couple of years before, and hoped it was still around, and hadn't succumbed to the economic downturn. I hurried on in the cold down Broad Street and turned left into Turl Street. Then, when I got to a Saxon church called St Michael at Northgate, I turned right.

I need not have worried. Makan-La, a Malaysian noodle bar, was still there, a little window of sombre light next to an independent bookshop now closed up for the day.

I sat down on a hard wooden chair at a small table, and after pondering the menu for a while, ordered char kuay teow – fried noodles with squid and chicken – which was a particular favourite of mine from a few years before when I had worked in Southeast Asia.

A couple of students held hands over a table opposite; and in the corner an irate academic related to a female colleague an epic and vainglorious tale of how, inexplicably, he hadn't been copied into a very important email.

And me? Well, it was just me and the river and Edward Weller now, and the noodles of course. In the kitchen below, a clanging of pots and the furious scraping of chillies and garlic at the bottom of a spitting wok heralded their arrival. Picking up my chopsticks, I plunged in.

VIII

Onto Abingdon

Turn right out of the guest house I was staying at on the Abingdon Rd and, as the name of the road suggests you will fairly promptly, if you are in a car, arrive in the town of Abingdon. But my route along the River Thames was rather more mercurial, picking my way through kissing gates, fields and locks firstly in a south easterly direction across the Oxfordshire flood plain before turning right again towards the town.

At the outset, the path was busy with other walkers, heading to and fro along the stretch that leads to the pretty church and lock at Iffley; while the river was full of sculling boats, the oarsmen and women thrusting through the water to the animated instructions of a coach riding a bicycle on the path alongside them.

Once at Sandford Lock, however, where cottages long ago replaced the mill that is displayed here on Weller's map, I was on my own again. Empty meadow after empty meadow interrupted by occasional belts of muddy wood-land took me the five miles or so to the weir and the lock at Abingdon. Crossing these, I turned onto the final approach to the market town; the spire of its church, St Helen's, edging gradually closer until I was right underneath it.

Opposite the church was the old county hall, an elegant building of Corinthian pilasters and arched windows built in the seventeenth century by a protégé of Sir Christopher Wren. It was now the county museum and it closed at 4pm. I had half an hour, so I stepped in.

I was glad I did because I learnt a lot about Abingdon in that half hour. It was the oldest continuously occupied town in Britain, being the location of a settlement ever since the Iron Age; it was the home of the MG sports car; its old gaol had been built in 1811 by Napoleonic prisoners-of-war; and its well-known school, Abingdon School, had produced such luminaries as the members of the band, Radiohead, and a travel writer called Eric Whelpton who was apparently the inspiration for Dorothy L Sayers' fictional detective, Lord Peter Wimsey.

I also learnt that it was a handsome town. An excitable museum curator with a pleasant puppy-fat face led me and several other tourists – accompanying us for health and safety reasons I presumed – up a ladder inside the building's crowning dome onto the rooftop to see the panoramic views of the town and the surrounding countryside.

"That's Bridge Street to the south and that's the market place to the north, the abbey to the east and the old Morlands brewery to the west," the museum employee informed us all in a brisk 360 degree spin. "Lovely, isn't it?"

We all concurred. Looking over the edge, trying to fight the feelings of vertigo that often fill me with the urge to throw myself off whenever I find myself on some breezy precipice at the top of a tall building, I giddily drank in the panorama of red terracotta roofs and graceful Georgian townhouses. "So, what brings you here?" the curator suddenly asked, looking at my muddy walking boots and rucksack.

"I'm walking the Thames."

"Oh, I would love to do that, walk the entire river," the young man gushed. "I often walk it into Oxford from Abingdon," he added, gazing northwards towards the university town and the low limestone hills of the north Berkshire ridge. "I love the Thames around here."

My feet aching after hours of walking and my rucksack sagging on my back, I couldn't find an appropriate response. I mustered a smile and gazed over his shoulder towards the chalk downs that lay to the south.

To the east of this chalk ridge were two hills, one of them looking like a sugar-loaf – completely bare except for a clump of trees clinging Mohican-style to its peak. These, I knew, were the famous Wittenham Clumps, which mark the spot where the River Thames is joined by a much lesser stream from the northeast – the River Thame.

It is here that Edward Weller, together with contemporary mapmakers, renames the great river. Before Dorchester where the two waters meet – as I think I may have mentioned before – the Thames is often called 'Isis', the river flowing metaphorically from the provenance of the fertility goddess of ancient Egypt. Afterwards, it is just the muddy old Thames, feeding the hundreds of littoral communities that line its banks with fertile soil but no longer doing so in the name of an Egyptian goddess.

Edward Weller finished the first section of his map of the Thames here, at the end of the river's upper reaches. There, at the Wittenham Clumps, I would be finishing the first stage of my own journey.

—ᴍ—

"A visitor to our church? Welcome, come in," an elderly man said to me in Abingdon's main church the next morning. "Don't trip over the medieval vacuum cleaner."

Jim had seen me hovering in the foyer of St Nicholas Church, which stands at the gateway of the Abingdon's Abbey of St Mary, and was keen to usher me in. "I'm Jim the verger," he said, extending a hand. "And this is Ellie." Ellie, a petite woman knitting behind a stall stacked with church guides and mementoes looked over and grinned.

"And no, it's not my perfume. It's all the flowers left over from a wedding at the weekend," Jim continued. And now I could smell the fragrance of them, permeating the musty but sanctified air all around us – roses, freesias, gerberas and the noxious inflorescence of gypsophila.

"Can I take a look around?" I asked.

"Yes, of course. It's 840 years old. Seen a few changes over the years, of course."

St Nicholas's hadn't seen that many changes over the years, as far as I could tell. With its wide arches and a wooden pulpit with ornately carved griffins perched around its corners, the church was still dressed largely in the regalia of its original medieval design. I took my time wandering around, reading the memorial plaques of people long gone, like the unfortunate Abingdon man who had died from wounds sustained at Gallipoli, and admiring some of the stained glass windows.

The truth was I was in no hurry to leave the sociable glow of the town for the bleakness of the Thames Path on another bitterly cold day. I had checked into my hotel the previous afternoon after my visit to the county museum and then spent an enjoyable evening at the Parasol Chinese restaurant in the middle of the town, listening to a crowded table of well-lubricated locals break out into their version of *Love me for a reason* as the Boyzone track oozed out of the restaurant speakers above them.

"Let me be the one, girl. Love me for a reason," they sang volubly. After their concluding salvoes, one of them, a jolly man with ruddy cheeks, wanted to know where the increasingly quiet family on the next table were from.

"Germany," they murmured.

"Ah, Germany! Nena. 99 Red Balloons! Loved that song," he cried, and warmly embraced them one by one – the mother, the father and then the two children.

Ellie and Jim also wanted to know more. "Walking the Thames," I said in reply.

"Bit cold for that, isn't it?" Jim was concerned. "Are you camping out at night?"

"No," I laughed. "I'm doing it the luxurious way. Staying in guesthouses and hotels."

"I went camping once," Ellie piped in. "Never again."

"Yes, I'm not really into camping either," I said. "Far too cold and wet. Too much like hard work."

"I went on a church camp to Yorkshire once," Jim recalled. "The river nearby broke its banks and flooded our campsite.

"I folded up my tent there and then and sold it the following week. Never camped again."

"Oh dear. Well, that's why I'm staying in warm guest houses," I said, not quite sure how we had ended up dwelling on Ellie and Jim's tenting tragedies.

"Oh well, I must be off," I added. "Got to be in Dorchester by this afternoon."

IX

Dorchester

By lunchtime I had got as far as Clifton Hampden, about five miles downriver, via the Culham lock cut, from Abingdon. In time for lunch at the Barley Mow, in fact – a pub immortalised by Jerome K. Jerome in his 1889 book about a journey up the Thames, Three Men in a Boat.

In the story, Jerome, his bumbling friends George Wingrave and Carl Hentschel, and a fictional dog called Montmorency, approach the village from the opposite direction, having sailed upriver from London in search of "rest and a complete change" from the capital and an "old-world spot far from the... surging waves of the nineteenth century world".

Due to their general ineptitude, however, the three mock-musketeers from the city manage to turn their holiday into a series of comic mishaps. They bring with them all the wrong provisions, leaving behind all the essential items; and triumph in turning the simplest of tasks such as putting up the awning over the boat at night into an epic disaster.

The critics hated it – the Eton boys on the books desk at Punch magazine particularly sniffy about the "vulgar" English of a solicitor's clerk who had not even been to university. Vulgar perhaps because they didn't like any sort or irreverence that wasn't theirs.

But the public loved it, buying up Jerome K. Jerome's whimsical, self-deprecatory adventure story in their droves, quickly turning it into a smash-hit. The book has never been out of print since.

"A wonderfully pretty village, old-fashioned, peaceful and dainty with flowers" is how the Three Men in a Boat author described Clifton Hampden, and, approaching the village from the northwest, I could see he was right. It was a beautiful hamlet of thatched cottages spilling down to the river on its left bank.

In Edward Weller's day, I would have been forced to catch a ferry across to the right bank to reach the 650-year old Barley Mow. The Clifton ferry was centuries old, the earliest records showing that Exeter College, Oxford, acquired it in 1493 from a local draper called Roger Roper.

The college owned it right up to 1861 when preparations were begun for the building of a bridge. That bridge, designed by Gothic revival architect George Gilbert Scott, opened in 1867.

It was a typical Gilbert Scott affair. The man responsible for the Albert Memorial and the Midland Grand Hotel at St Pancras Station built a magnificent crossing of red-brick with a span of six Gothic arches. While he was at it, he also renovated St Michael and All Angels Church, which sits like some Transylvanian castle on a rocky promontory above the river.

I crossed the water, taking refuge in the bridge's triangular pedestrian turrets as cars passed by; and arrived in the beer garden of the pub that Jerome K. Jerome described as "the quaintest, most old-world inn up the river".

"Its low-pitched gables and thatched roof and latticed windows give it quite a story-book appearance, while inside it is even still more once-upon-a-timeyfied."

He was right again, although I suspect the writer who condemned Maidenhead on his way upriver as a "town of showy hotels" would not have appreciated the Barley Mow's modern pub chain atmosphere, which urges customers to step back in time into the pub of Jerome K. Jerome while digging into their 'honey glazed belly pork'. Still, after a lunch amid the wood-panelled walls and low beams of this very old inn, I felt set up for the last few miles of my walk onto Dorchester. Warmed by 'hand-battered' cod and chips, I followed the signpost for Days Lock that took me back down to the river from the pub and onto the wide meadows again of the Oxfordshire floodplain.

It was a lovely stretch of the Thames. The river was wide and full, flanked on the opposite shoreline by large houses, elegant lawns and boathouses, as it orbited around a sugar loaf hill crowned with a coppice of trees on the horizon. It was the Wittenham Clumps again, and they would be with me now for the rest of my journey on the upper reaches of the Thames; a lonely wood on a lonely hill edging closer and closer, until at Day's Lock, you could not avert your gaze.

At the lock, however, I turned left. The clumps were tomorrow's expedition. For now, I was tired. I wanted to rest. I wanted to check into my hotel for the night. A scramble over fields, past a series of grassy dikes which once made up an Iron Age fort, took me into the village of Dorchester.

—✕✕—

The confluence of the Thame and the Isis rivers at this point once made Dorchester an important place, and after a cup of tea in my room at the White Hart, I ambled down the village's charming high street, which has been used as a film set for numerous Agatha Christie films and television murder mysteries, to Dorchester Abbey, one of 33 minsters that the Saxons built along the River Thames. The abbey, I had read, contained a beautiful Tree of Jesse erected in the fourteenth century, depicting the ancestors of Christ in stained glass and sculpture.

The abbey I stepped into from its south porch seemed to be a Spartan, simple affair – lofty arches and plain stone walls – but as I walked through into the nave the building became more ornate – beautifully carved pews and pulpits leading the eye to the north wall of the chancel and the Tree of Jesse, a resplendent interlacing of stone and stained glass.

I stood and admired it for a while, and then explored the abbey a little more, wandering past a couple of effigies of medieval knights before chancing upon a small secluded chapel hiding behind the eastern wall of the chancel.

It, too, had a beautiful stained glass window. It was not the window that caught my eye on this occasion, however, but a disintegrating Union Jack suspended high up in an archway to the side of it. On one of the pillars of the arch there was a plaque which read:

"This flag was used at the funerals of all the members of Her Majesty's forces who died as prisoners of war at Kuching in Borneo during the world war of 1939-45 and was the first flag to be hoisted after the Japanese capitulation."

There was another plaque below which provided more information. The flag, it transpired, had been brought home from Borneo by a young officer called Leslie Bickerton after the liberation of the camp in September 1945. Bickerton had it raised in Oxford City Church in memory of his fallen comrades of the 35th Light Anti-Aircraft Regiment of the Royal Artillery, a local regiment drawn from servicemen in Oxfordshire and Berkshire who were among the prisoners of war who had died at Kuching. The flag went missing, however, when the church was converted into a college library. It turned up many years later, in the 1990s, languishing in a dusty store room at the church of St Michael at Oxford's Northgate, which I had walked past a few nights before on my way to the Malaysian restaurant, Makan-La. From there, it was taken to its last resting place in Dorchester Abbey.

—〰—

It was a few years ago – in May 2011, to be precise – when I found myself on the parapets of a nineteenth century fort peering over the edge at the city of Kuching which lay spread out before me.

The city had been firmly on my itinerary on a trip to Southeast Asia that year, seeing old friends in Singapore where I had worked as a journalist for a few years at the turn of the century, and visiting some of the places I hadn't managed to get to while I lived in the city-state. Top of my list was Kuching because I had always wanted to go to the jungles of Borneo and I had always wanted to visit a place that had the audacity to be simply called 'Cat'.

The origins of the name go back to the days of James Brooke, a British adventurer who had breezed into Borneo in 1841 to help the local sultan put down a rebellion of Dayak tribes and Malay villages and ended up being crowned as the Rajah of Sarawak, setting up a dynasty that would last over a hundred years. Some say that Brooke called the village which would eventually grow into the capital of Sarawak after Sungei Mata Kuching (Cat's Eye), a small stream that fed the main Sarawak river; others say that the first rajah pointed to the village and asked its name, and the locals, thinking he was pointing at a cat, gave him the Malay word for the feline animal – Kuching.

Whatever the truth of the matter, the Brooke rule was firmly entrenched by the time Edward Weller was drawing up a map of the island of Borneo for the 1863 *Dispatch Atlas*, a reality that the mapmaker reflected in his division of the island into separate realms. The area to the north of the central spine of mountains that crosses the land from the northeast to the southwest was called Borneo Proper, full of English names like the Woody Hills or Dead Tree Mountain etched out in Weller's fragile typography because this was the area over which James Brooke and the British Empire held sway. South of the spine, in the region I can only assume the Victorians regarded as Borneo Improper, the land seemed to be split into smaller principalities – in the east there was the Territory of the Sultan of Sooloo, and in the south there was the valley of the River Coti and a plateau of probable danger for the Victorian adventurer simply known as Nomadic Tribes.

Sitting in his studio in another town on another river thousands of miles away, Weller, the draughtsman, could probably only dream of such places. Born in Marylebone on 1 July 1819, he is likely to have never left London, learning his trade and applying it in the city that was his life, except for holidays he later spent with his wife and children in St Leonards on Sea on the Sussex coast.

At the age of 11 or 12, the young Edward was left £50 by his uncle, Sidney Hall, a London mapmaker, to pay for an apprenticeship in the mapmaking business. And that charted the course of his life. In 1851 he turns up in the census as a 'map engraver' living at 15 Cadogan Terrace in Chelsea with his wife Mary Anne from Stepney, who he had married four years before, and their three children

– Edward, Francis and Mary – as well as two servants and a 56-year old lodger, a spinster called Louisa Laforestier. The same year, he was elected as a fellow of the Royal Geographical Society.

And in 1853, he finally inherited the Hall map-engraving business in Bury Street, Bloomsbury, which had been run by his aunt Selina Hall ever since the death of her husband, astutely breaking through the Victorian discrimination against women by signing all her maps 'S. Hall'. With the business now his, the nearest Edward Weller ever got to 'Mount Kini Baloo', on the northern tip of Borneo Proper, or 'The Chinese Widow' as the British called it for some reason, was in that intimacy forged between his pen and his paper.

The next decade or so, however, would see him make his name from maps of places he had never visited. The British Library, the Royal Geographical Society and antique shops across London hold hundreds of charts he produced in those years: among them, maps of the Americas, maps of British counties, historical atlases for schoolchildren, and for those scripturally inclined, illustrations of the Holy Land. A copy of the Royal Geographical Society magazine from 1863 carries a number of maps – for instance, one of Manchuria as well as one of the coastline between Karachi and the Arabian Sea port of Gwadar – that Weller drew up for the society in his capacity as its official cartographer.

It was at meetings of the society that he probably met the explorers and naval men who laid the groundwork for his charts – explorers like Nye Elias, who charted the Yellow

River, and Richard Burton, seeker of the source of the Nile, whose mission in life was to set up camp on the banks of an inhospitable river or hack through a steamy jungle to make the first rough drawings of the terrain on behalf of the Admiralty or the Foreign Office.

Perhaps the stories of their adventures lingered with Weller. Perhaps that chance meeting with Nye Elias in the corridors of the RGS after the explorer had returned from China in the late 1860s got him thinking about the twists and turns of the Yellow River.

Or perhaps, after listening to a paper given in the RGS lecture theatre in 1863 by the naturalist, Alfred Russel Wallace, on his famous journey through Borneo and the Malay archipelago, he had walked down to Charing Cross Bridge, and dreamt, just for a moment, that he was drifting out on the open sea, with no compass or lights to guide him, drifting among the nutmeg rocks and emerald isles of the Orient.

—⁓—

My own visit to Borneo many years later had taken me to the ruins of the wooden bungalow overlooking the estuary of the River Sarawak where Alfred Russel Wallace had stayed on his arrival in Borneo and where, under the brooding Mount Santubong and the humid, grey skies of the 1854 rainy season, he had fumbled towards a theory of evolution, echoing the efforts of Charles Darwin sitting in a cold study thousands of miles away in Kent. I had stayed in a Malay-style lodge nestling in the reeds of that same estuary for a few days before moving upriver to Kuching itself, where I had checked into a small hotel housed in one of the old trading warehouses (godowns) on the river front and gone out to dinner at the deftly named James Brooke Cafe & Bistro.

It was there that I learnt about Fort Margherita. It had been built in 1880 by the second rajah, Charles Brooke, in honour of his wife who bore that name. It had said as much in the menu notes to my Margherita Fish Curry. The next morning, I decided to go and see it for myself, and by the time the sweltering equatorial sun was ascending to its high noon, I was climbing the wooden stairs of the neo-Gothic tower and peering over the parapets.

It was a wonderful view. To the left, was the concrete and glass of Kuching's modern hotel quarter. Straight ahead were the line of the waterfront godowns, built in the nineteenth century when steamships would arrive at the jetties from Singapore and beyond. In the middle of them, elegant, severe, was a square surrounding the courthouse, built in 1883.

And to my right, the silver line of the Sarawak river coiling its way towards the sea, towards the precipitous Mount Santubong and the estuary below it.

It was into this estuary that the ships of colonialists and refugees had entered Sarawak over the centuries. First, it was the low galleys of Hindu adventurers from the

Majahapit empire in Java. Then, the flimsy sails of Chinese junks fleeing from repression and starvation in Guangzhou and Funan, floating into the harbour on the winds of hearsay that there was gold in the hills of Borneo.

By the 1840s, it was the ships of the British Admiralty, come to defend James Brooke and his newly-acquired fiefdom. Alfred Russel Wallace would have watched them from his verandah on the other side of the bay, preparing to sail away to subdue the Dayak pirates hiding in their mangrove strongholds further up the coastline.

Then, early in the morning of 23 December 1941, it was the steel hulls of Japanese troop ships slipping stealthily into the bay.

In the ensuing chaos, it's difficult to say what happened to many of the residents of this British colony. In the last desperate hours of freedom, government officials managed to destroy much of their wireless equipment before they were rounded up with other Europeans to surrender to the Japanese occupying force in the Main Bazaar area. Some were then herded into the grand Astana building on the north bank of the river, built by Rajah Charles Brooke in 1869, while others were thrown into a dark room below the police station.

In the following months, the European prisoners of war were relocated to the infamous Batu Lintang camp, three miles to the south of Kuching.

Others, however, managed to escape from Kuching in the final hours before the occupation. Some of the locals, if they had not been killed in the bombing raids or rounded up afterwards, hid with relatives in the outlying kampongs. A small collection of Europeans, meanwhile, succeeded in getting out onto the road leading to the border; their cars, packed with hastily assembled families and belongings, heading to Pontianak in the Dutch East Indies, where they would board evacuation ships bound for Australia. Many, though, never made it. They were caught out on the road by in their Morris Eight Tourers and shot dead on the spot.

As for the Allied troops, some withdrew over the border to the Dutch East Indies to fight another day; but one regiment stayed on to fight it out with the enemy in the jungles surrounding the city. The second battalion of the 15th Punjab Regiment, a British-Indian army, made a last stand under the thick jungle canopy of Mount Santubong. There, amid the twisted and tangled aerial roots of giant forest trees that soared towards the sky like the columns of a Gothic cathedral, they held out for three months without food until the Japanese troops finally flushed them out.

They were marched to the Batu Lintang POW camp, where they joined civilians from Kuching and allied soldiers who had surrendered to Japanese forces elsewhere – in Malaya, Singapore and the Dutch East Indies – among them the men from Oxfordshire and Berkshire who made up the 35th Light Anti-Aircraft regiment of the Royal Artillery.

Many of the prisoners of war died there, from disease or malnutrition in the camp's brutal conditions, their coffins covered with the Union flag that I would find many years later hanging in a chapel in Dorchester Abbey.

—⚹—

I would need to add the flag to my map of the Thames, I thought as I turned to make my way out of the abbey. The transparency that I had mounted onto Edward Weller's original and on which I had started to add my own observations and notations. A Saxon door, the clashing of Roundheads and Cavaliers on a bridge, the ghostly pillboxes. Some shading here, a line there.

The dreams of William Morris. A certain ratio, almost imperceptible, a certain texture.

The Oxford motor empire, the Barlow Mow pub, the floods of 1894, 1947 and 2007. Sketches, tones, contours of history as high as the fathoms of the Thames estuary are deep.

Never erasing what Edward Weller had laid down on his base map. But continuously adding to it.

And now I would add a little smudge of watercolour in the shape of a horse-shoe and in the colour of yellow, the national colour of Borneo, in memory of the local men who had fallen in Borneo and who were part of the memory of the Thames. This would be the ox-bow lake of international remembrance that the Thames had created when it had cut away at the curves in its banks, and the currents of British history had broken through.

Yes, that was it. A smudge of watercolour. A smudge of watercolour would mark the spot. That would almost complete my representation of the upper reaches of the River Thames.

X

Wittenham Clumps

I had a few more steps to make before I reached the end of the first stage of my pilgrimage along the Thames. They had been a beacon ever since Abingdon, and the morning after my arrival in Dorchester I couldn't wait to get my walking shoes on and head out to them – the lonely trees on a barren hill, the Wittenham Clumps.

"Be careful when you climb up to the trees," said the woman behind the hotel reception desk as I went out after breakfast. "It's very steep, and it can be quite slippy."

Only a handful of people were out braving the cold as I made my way over the fields that morning, past the ancient Iron Age fort again, and towards the river. Yet the two rounded mounds – named the Sinodun hills by antiquarian writer John Leland in 1542 – rising out of the flat lands of the Oxfordshire plain which I could see now on the horizon seemed curiously inviting. One of them largely barren, except for its little crown of trees. A sinister crown of trees, in the way they seemed to appear like airy spires out of a cold nowhere; but, at the same time, alluring.

I accepted their invitation and walked to the bridge that spanned the Thames at Day's Lock. Next to the bridge was a house with the trademark Thames Conservancy plaque informing passers-by that it had been built in 1924. I took the path that ran alongside it and found myself in Long Wittenham, the hamlet at the foot of the climb.

I lingered for a while in Long Wittenham's pretty church, admiring the alabaster effigies of Sir William Dunch, who died in 1612, and his wife Mary, the aunt of Oliver Cromwell – one of a number of memorials to the Dunch family, the local notables who owned the village for more than 200 years following Henry VIII's dissolution of the monasteries.

Venturing outside into the churchyard afterwards, I found another interesting memorial – a tombstone to a Marion Frances Wood who had died as old as the century in 1999 after "devoting much of her life to nursing in St Luke's Hospital, Chabua, Assam". She had journeyed to the Himalayan foothills where scores of different races – Bengalis, Sikhs, Afghans, Chinese, Burmese, southern Indians, Assam hill tribes – had worked in the tea gardens set up by British planters, and where nursing outreach work had meant cycling through thick jungle and sleeping at night in remote villages with a lantern hung outside your hut to scare away the elephants. And then many decades later, I presume, she had journeyed back to a quiet retirement in the mellow English fields of her birth. These must have been two very big expeditions to make, I thought as I gazed at her gravestone; ones which put my forthcoming ascent to the clumps into a certain perspective.

Nevertheless, I was out of breath when I finally reached the coppice of ancient beech trees at the summit and surveyed the view. There was a map of the panorama etched out on a bronze tablet a few yards to my left, and after catching my breath again, I went over to examine it.

At the bottom of the hill, according to the map, slightly to my right, there was Day's Lock, which I had passed through about twenty minutes before, and not far behind it, Dorchester Abbey.

Orbiting around these landmarks were an abandoned Second World War airfield called Chalgrove, a hamlet called Christmas Common, possibly named after a Christmas day truce in 1643 during the English Civil War, and RAF Benson, the frontline support helicopter base still sending out crews to fields of conflict such as Afghanistan. Due north was the pretty village of Clifton Hampton, and nudging up to this Sylvan cluster of cottages, in this cosy bronze firmament of English Arcadia, a place called Paradise Wood where a charity called the Earth Trust was busy planting oak, ash and walnut trees in one of our last stands against climate change. Not far away, the Culham Laboratories were also doing their bit, smashing atoms together in an effort to find a carbon-free energy future through the harnessing of nuclear fusion, the delicately uncertain process that powers the sun.

Spanning outwards to the northwest, there was the Victorian Gothic spire of Appleford Church and, in addition, a strange brick folly peeping out from among a clump of Scotch pines, which was built in 1935 by an eccentric aristocrat called Lord Berners. Finally, to the west, were the six cooling towers of Didcot Power Station, for almost 43 years puffing long plumes of coal-fired steam out into the Oxfordshire skies but now lying dormant, having been switched off for the eco-friendly good just days before I arrived.

All morning it had been grey, but as I stood beside the clumps a sort of radiance began to emerge from behind the clouds, holding the landscape together in a soft vellum of light. Running through it all, a silver river emerging from a silver sky horizon as if it was flowing down from the heaven itself. From here, it would glide gracefully into its middle reaches, the next stage of my journey.

A young painter called Paul Nash – later to become a famous war artist – would have stood here beside the Wittenham Clumps on the crest of the Sinodun Hills a hundred years ago, delighting in a place that would become his lifelong obsession. "I felt their importance long before I knew their history," he wrote later, referring to the remnants of an Iron Age fort near the Clumps. "It was the look of them that told most, whether on sight or in memory. They were the Pyramids of my small world."

He had first seen the trees in 1907 at the age of 18 or 19 on a visit to his uncle's house at Sinodun House near Wallingford, a few miles upstream. He was attending art classes at Chelsea Polytechnic at the time, having left school at 17, and may well have been inspired by their artistic potential. Or perhaps they offered some sort of sanctuary from a life at home that was probably being made increasingly difficult by his mother's spiralling bouts of depression.

His mother died in 1910 – "a release from the strain of constant anxiety" – and in 1911 Nash moved out of the family home to take rooms at 19 Paulton Square in Chelsea, close to the Thames. The same year he wrote enthusiastically about another visit to the Wittenham Clumps in a letter to a friend describing the "grey hallowed hills crowned by old old trees, Pan-nish places down by the river wonderful to think on, full of strange enchantment ... a beautiful legendary country haunted by old Gods long forgotten". A year later, he joined his father and his sister and brother on another holiday to the area, and produced his first drawing of the Clumps.

The Wood on the Hill depicts the coppice from the bottom of the hill near the river. A gate and an open field draw the eye upwards until we reach the crown of trees at the top. A flock of birds is circling above it.

It was a peaceful scene that perhaps encapsulated the relative serenity of the time to which Nash belonged, the Edwardian era, before it was obliterated within a few years in the artillery fire of the First World War. Nash himself was dispatched to the European killing fields in 1917, first as a soldier to Ypres, then as the war artist who produced arguably the most iconic painting of the war, the *Menin Road*. The painting shows two soldiers picking their way through a battle-scarred landscape of flooded trenches and shattered tree stumps, illuminated by apocalyptic beams of light emanating from an angry sky.

Although Nash went on to become a very successful artist, he was never quite the same again according to his family and friends. The horrors of the Western Front had left him prone to dark moods and depression.

But there was one place in the world which would always bring him a sense of peace – those "grey hallowed hills crowned by old old trees" he had written about in a letter before the war. He would return again and again to paint the Wittenham Clumps during his life.

Gazing over the soft green folds of the Thames valley from my vantage point at the clumps many years later, I could see why.

The Middle Reaches

LONDON, 1863

"If those are Oriental Pearls, Sir, then they are most definitely from Ceylon."

"Are you entirely sure?" asks Edward Weller in a quizzical fashion. He is well used to his old friend, Theo, making grand unsubstantiated claims.

"I am absolutely certain, my dear Edward. That's the main source for them," says Theo, equally well accustomed by now to his friend's persistent habit of scrutinising every self-evident fact. "The oyster beds in the straits of Manaar between Ceylon and India. Isn't that right, Mr Scott?"

Henry Scott, just about to sink a fork into his own favoured object of desire, a steaming lamb cutlet, lends his support. "He's right, Edward. Small consignments of them come off the steamers and the clippers from Madras and Bombay, along with all the spices and dyes and precious woods."

"I'll take your word for it then," Edward Weller says, his soft green eyes smiling at his two old school pals from

Marylebone. Henry is in the shipping business, after all. "Well, Ceylon or no Ceylon, I hope my wife likes it," he adds, and holds up the seed pearl pendant he has bought Mary Anne as a symbol of his devotion, one that he hopes she will wear at a big dinner party he is throwing for fellow members of the Royal Geographical Society and friends in a few days' time.

"I'm sure she will. Let's drink to that, and to your good wife, of course," Theo pronounces, and raises his tankard of beer. Another toast. The three companions have been raising their glasses to something or other in this same wooden booth in the same chop house in Change Alley for around a quarter of a century now. They can't put their finger on why, exactly, but it's their favourite dining room in London. Something about their preferred spot by one of the grubby windows, about the gravy stains on the table-cloths, and about peering through the smoky yellow gas lighting at all the exotic maps of the world hanging on the walls which lifts this place, in their opinion, above all the other dining establishments in town.

"Of course, you know how they find the pearls, don't you?" says Theo, warming to his theme now that Weller's inevitable examination of the facts has been satisfactorily squashed. "They dive for them."

His friends let him continue. "Once a year, when the British authorities announce another pearl fishery season, hundreds of boats turn up at a little place called Aripo on the west coast of Ceylon, each boat with ten divers on board. And they dive down to the bottom of the sea to find oysters with pearls in them. No equipment, of course. Just a peg on their nose!"

"How on earth do they stay underwater long enough to pick the oysters?" Henry asks.

"They're native Tamil divers and they've been doing it for years. They descend with two ropes from the boat, one which has a string bag attached to it ... and the other which ..." Theo pauses for dramatic effect, "... the other which has a loop in it with a stone attached. The diver puts his foot in the loop and the stone pulls him down to the bottom of the sea and all the dangers of the deep."

"The dangers of the deep?" Edward Weller and Henry Scott ask in unison. Weller's interest, in particular, is growing. As it happens, he is about to begin an illustration of Ceylon for the Weekly Dispatch.

"Yes, the dangers," Theo says triumphantly, wiping some gravy off his waistcoat with his napkin, pleased that he now has the full attention and credulity of his long-term compatriots. Spinning a good yarn is his stock-in-trade. As up-and-coming Bayswater's foremost property agent, he is proud of his abilities in this respect. "Stingrays, scorpion fish, and sharks even. A man can make a tasty breakfast if it is the shark's desire."

"But the main problem, of course, is running out of air. The divers have about a minute to fill their bags with oysters before they begin to swallow water. At that point, they give the rope with the bag a tug and the puller up on the boat above – the munduck as they call him – will haul them up as quickly as possible."

"How do you know all this?" Scratching his head through his curly mop of brown hair, Weller is suddenly vigilant again. During his time as the Royal Geographical Society's official cartographer he has been spellbound by the fantastic stories that travellers have brought back from the Orient – stories of lofty pagodas clinging to the edges of river gorges; picturesque villages fringed with bamboo trees stumbled upon in the recesses of secluded valleys, a Buddhist stupa found in the jungle – but in the end he knows that if these great journeys are to be turned into accurate maps he has to be attentive. He has to be particular about the cut of that coastline, fastidious about the exact meander of that river, mindful as to the accuracy of the explorer's intelligence. Alert to any possible breaching of deadlines for the society's journal too. Sometimes these travellers can be a bit vague about passing drafts of his maps in time for the copy deadline. Too much time in the jungle, he has always supposed.

"A London jeweller interested in buying a house in Craven Hill Gardens told me," Theo says. "He was in contact with the Arab pearl merchants based in Ceylon – the ones who wait all morning on the shoreline for the divers' boats to come in so they can inspect their catch.

"It's a long wait in the tropical heat, but it's worth it for these beautiful Oriental pearls."

Beautiful Oriental pearls. Weller looks proudly again at the pendant he has bought his wife – made of the cheaper seed pearls to be sure but beautiful all the same, set as they are in an intricate filigree web of ten-carat gold. There is a brief silence before Henry suddenly quips: "Well, it's rather like waiting while Mrs Tyburn tries to retrieve our steam puddings from the bottom of Baker's Chop House, isn't it?"

The long-time friends laugh. Well, yes, it has been rather a long time since their mutton joints and cutlets and their gravy and their French beans and potatoes. But even as they speak there is a muffled shout from the kitchens below, then the squeaking of the dumbwaiter's rope pulleys clearly discernible through the chitter-chatter of the busy restaurant, and the puddings arrive on a tray ay the top of the food shaft.

Moments later, the scowling proprietress, with the tray in her hand, is upon them. At the same time, as if to herald her arrival, a gust of wind outside sends a splatter of rain onto the adjacent window pane. Edward, Theo and Henry peer out through the glass.

It has been raining most of the day, and now that the early winter darkness has enveloped the capital, the wind has picked up, sending billowing sheets of precipitation dancing up the Thames, dappling the umbrellas of commuters waiting to board a ferry at Hungerford Stairs, rapping against the masts of the oyster boats anchored up at Billingsgate fish market, slapping the passengers travelling on the top deck of the No19 Omnibus on Oxford St.

They are playful things, these rainy phantoms of the skies. They pose at one moment as nothing more than an ethereal dampness clinging to the sides of tomorrow's steamer to Marseilles; but in the next moment they are spinning around to nearly blow the ship workers off the quayside. One minute tickling the faces of the last few shoppers of the day on Regent Street with a light spray, the next drenching them from head to toe in a sudden downpour. Tapping wispily on the front doors of the gentlemen's supper clubs on the Strand, they give the emerging groups of brandy-sodden revellers a soaking.

The answer is to stay indoors. All across town, soft pools of yellowish light shine out in the watery imbroglio, fortresses of comfort and conviviality in the storm. There is the tinkling of glasses inside the gas-lit gin palaces, singing in an East End pub, the racing results in a Fleet Street tavern.

And then there is always home. Edward Weller is asking the head waiter at Baker's to arrange a hackney cab to take him back to Red Lion Square. Mary Anne will be waiting for him in the drawing room.

The gas lights will be on in thousands of homes across London. Journalist George Augustus Sala is placing an umbrella in the willow-patterned umbrella stand in his hallway after returning from a long day at the *Telegraph*; and in the grand drawing room of a house near Regents Park, the naturalist Alfred Russel Wallace – who Weller will soon meet in the corridors of the Royal Geographical Society – is attending a dinner party which will end in a séance. The famous scientist has turned his thoughts to spiritualism after a similar evening a few years back when the inexplicable jingle of a glass chandelier and the rustle of a lady's dress got him thinking. What if the laws of nature didn't explain everything?

Just around the corner at 2a New Cavendish Street, meanwhile, novelist Wilkie Collins is resting on the Ottoman in his smoking room, watching the spatters of rain on the window in a desperate effort to forget the crippling pain of his gout. But in the end he knows there is only one answer. A small bottle of the laudanum sits in his spirits cabinet.

He pours the liquid opium into his glass.

XI

The Elephant at Pangbourne

I couldn't make them out at first through the spatters of light rain on the glass, but gradually a line of ruddy terracotta chimney stacks poking out of a red-tiled citadel of Edwardian rooftops took on form and substance as the view through my window. I was waking up from a good night's sleep in a room in the Miller of Mansfield Hotel in Goring, a pleasant riverside village about ten miles south of Dorchester.

Together with its twin village, Streatley, on the opposite bank, Goring had become an important settlement historically because of the meeting of two ancient paths at this spot, the Ridgeway, arriving from the west, and the Icknield Way, from the east. These bridleways, which between them followed the chalk ridge running across England from the Wash on the Norfolk coast to Seaton in Devon where it plunges into the sea, were used for thousands of years by cattle drovers, traders and invaders who needed to make quick progress over high ground. Bronze Age and Iron Age communities built forts and burial barrows along the ridge, which was also used by the Saxon and Viking invaders in their marches towards Wessex, the land of King Arthur and King Alfred. The parish church standing adjacent to my hotel was a fine stone edifice built in grand eleventh-century Norman style, from the days when this was a by-way for drovers from the West Country moving their livestock to markets in the Home Counties.

But for me, after a walk from Dorchester the previous day that had oozed old world charms in the form of the primeval-looking Little Wittenham Wood and the fossilised buildings of historic Shillingford, the verdant holloway of foliage on the approach to Benson and the ancestral cedar trees on the way to Wallingford's pretty market square, this place felt less like an ancient meeting point than a gateway of some sort, the beginning of something new. It is here that the Thames enters a gentle gorge called the Goring Gap, which was cut out of hills by a glacier in the last Ice Age, breaking through the chalk range that traverses England.

Edward Weller divided his 1863 map of the Thames into three parts – the upper reaches, the middle reaches and the final descent through London towards the sea; and Goring and Streatley are placed near the beginning of his second segment, the middle reaches, like a couple of rather homely Pillars of Hercules heralding the entrance to a confident new realm. Beyond this point, I knew, was Berkshire, a land of rolling hills and riverside houses with lawns running down to the water's edge and tea under the loggia, a landscape differing in tone and tempo to the starker, flatter Oxfordshire plain upstream.

My assumptions buoyed by a good breakfast of salmon and scrambled egg, I stepped out into the beating heart of Middle England.

—✺—

I found the river behind the parish church, curving silently towards the Berkshire Downs to my right – a set of mellow hills furnished with beech and pine. The water would now carve a course between the downs and the Chiltern Hills receding gently away from me on the left bank.

All was very peaceful at first. A melancholia of willow trees lined the river's right bank and a cluster of small pleasure boats lazed in the shallows beside them. A little further along, I passed a fisherman who grunted reluctantly in reply to my morning greeting, and then further along still I found a silent mouldering ruin of a house, its insides laid bare to the elements, a white door suspended forlornly in the rubble of an upper room only hinting at all the comings and goings once carried out under the dwelling's roof.

But this was a river transformed from a couple of months before when I had completed the first stage of my journey at the bare and ghostly Wittenham Clumps. It was now green and lush and bursting with life; and, gradually, the silence of my wanderings began to give way to the rising timbres of a late spring. After half a mile or so, I had reached a place where a slither of an island had emerged in the middle of the water, and, here, the annual liturgy of renewal began to unfold. The discordant trumpeting of Canadian geese, the liquid honey notes of the blackbird and a welter of croaking phrases and creaky cadences that I did not recognise signalled that I had entered the meadows and woodlands that characterised the countryside between Goring and Whitchurch.

The chorus ushered me into a wide pasture that flanked a Thames now turning eastwards again towards the sea. Ahead of me was the Gatehampton Viaduct, built by Isambard Kingdom Brunel in 1838, carrying the Great Western Railway to and from London. The railway was a prominent feature on Edward Weller's 1863 map of the Thames, its striped grey livery slicing its way through a landscape otherwise only criss-crossed by narrow country lanes. It was also a prominent feature in the real landscape; and a beautiful one too, its amber, semi-elliptical arches suspended picturesquely above the green valley floor.

The sight would not have been so beautiful, however, for the hundreds of bargemen who depended on the Thames commodities trade in the 1800s. In the same way as it had ruined Lechlade's cheese trade upstream, the Great Western Railway decimated commerce up and down the middle reaches of the river overnight. Before the opening of Brunel's transport masterpiece in 1841, barge-masters at the river ports of Oxford, Abingdon, Wallingford, Reading and Henley shipped thousands of tons of iron, copper, tin and metal goods downriver to London, building on an already well-established traffic in malt, timber and grain. In the other direction, came luxury groceries and foreign imports from London as well as ashes and rags used as manure on farms upstream.

Within ten years of the arrival of the GWR freight trains, however, toll income from the water-borne cargo traffic had fallen by half. It was never to recover.

Now a First Great Western train, the modern incarnation of the GWR, rattled overhead as I passed underneath within yards of another one of those Second World War pill-boxes standing deserted in the shadow of one of the railway arches.

After a while I reached a low-roofed Edwardian bungalow at the water's edge, its mullioned windows thrown open to the warmish air. Here, the Thames Path turned inland, crossing a field before joining a public bridleway at a point where the Chiltern Hills begin to rise from the valley floor. A couple of horses ridden by a middle-aged woman and a young girl were approaching as I turned onto the bridleway. "How far is it to Whitchurch?" I asked the woman, my tiring feet half hoping that the short but strangely wearing three-and-a-half mile trek from Goring to the next village downstream was nearing its conclusion.

"Oh, you've got quite a long way to go yet," the woman laughed. "About two miles, in fact, and it's all uphill from now on. A big hill to climb at the end."

I thanked her as cheerfully as I could, and pressed on up the flinty path, which ascended gradually into a thicket of trees, a mixture of juniper, ash and pine as well as the gaunt trunks of silver birch spilling down the hill to the water's edge.

The climb became harder and the wood grew thicker until soon the river only came into my view intermittently – far down below in the valley, a little smudge of silver spied from time to time in between the trees.

Finally, I reached a sort of plateau lined with farms and about ten minutes later I joined the B471, which drops back down into the valley and into Whitchurch-on-Thames. From the top of the hill there, I could see a great cedar tree and underneath it I could see the lofty gables of the village's houses projecting high above its high street, rising from a patchwork of warm red brick and flint, braided with bay windows framed in creamy coloured wood. An embroidery of Edwardian England stitched into the fabric of an ancient landscape.

In an era of mapmaking before contour lines or contour layering were introduced, Edward Weller depicted the promontory on which I now stood as a ridge of grey shading with a small road falling out from the bottom of it. I now followed his chart and made my way down the steep high street past all the grand houses I had seen from the top, most of which had been built during the 'river boom' in the years preceding the First World War when it became fashionable for wealthy people to acquire a home in this part of the Thames valley. After the war, the houses became empty white elephants, tenant-less except for caretakers, and were later converted into flats as they fell into the hands of building speculators. Now, the wheel has turned full circle once again with houses on the high street regularly going for in excess of £1 million.

At the bottom of the hill, I took a detour into the graveyard of the Church of St Mary Virgin, and then into the church itself. A curious hot-potch of Anglo-Saxon, Norman and Medieval features, this hallowed building contains some interesting wall plaques, including one commemorating Philip Lybbe-Powys of Hardwick House and his wife Caroline Lybbe-Powys who kept a famous diary of her hectic social whirl of winter balls and country house gatherings in the area in the middle of the eighteenth century; and another remembering Sir John Forbes, physician to Queen Victoria's household, who wrote a number of travel books with earnestly lengthy Victorian titles like *A Physician's Holiday: or a month in Switzerland in the summer of 1848*. The nave of the church, meanwhile, is paved with the family shields of the Whistlers, distant relatives of James McNeill Whistler, the American artist who in the 1870s painted a series of broodingly mysterious night scenes of the River Thames in London called the Nocturnes.

I emerged from the church into a cluster of red-brick cottages sitting on the margins of the Thames and onto a pathway that took me up onto the iron toll bridge that crosses the Thames here to take foot and road passengers into the streets of Whitchurch's more bustling neighbour, Pangbourne. I paused momentarily on the bridge to admire the lovely view of a silent, reflective Thames, flanked on the one side by the Chiltern Hills and on the other by a wide meadow; and then I plunged back into the traffic.

Pangbourne, sitting at the point where the tiny River Pang joins the Thames, is a pretty place, filled with quaint buildings of Edwardian, Victorian and Georgian provenance as well as timbered cottages surviving from the seventeenth century. There is also a handsome church with a 130 foot spire dedicated to one of the more obscure apostles, St James the Less, and next to it a cottage where

Kenneth Grahame, the author of The Wind in the Willows, lived from 1924 until his death in 1932.

In the middle of it all was my accommodation for the night, The Elephant Hotel.

On the outside, The Elephant was a building firmly rooted in the Old English vernacular, its facade an amalgam of discreet nods to centuries of architectural style, from the Victorian sash windows enclosed in a latticework of white Tudor timber to the redbrick tiles of its Edwardian roof and the grand classicism of its portico entranceway.

On the inside, however, it was an emporium of all things Indian. A large wooden elephant painted in grand Mughal style greeted me as I entered the hallway while an oriental rug underfoot cushioned my aching soles. By way of explanation, a little brochure at the reception desk told me that the hotel offered "a return to the opulence of the Empire".

Moments later, I was turning the key to a room called 'Orient', which had a magazine picture of Yul Brynner as the King of Siam in the blockbuster film, The King and I, plastered on the door. Pausing momentarily to appreciate the imperial opulence, I fell onto the bed and fell asleep.

—◁◁—

I awoke an hour later with a question that had obviously begun to vex me in my dreams. Why was this hotel called

The Elephant? There couldn't be, I reasoned, too many elephants in Berkshire. That evening, I put the question to a young, clean-cut man behind the hotel bar.

"There was a pub here called The Elephant, but it was renamed The Copper Inn in the 1960s," he replied. "It carried on being the Copper Inn until a few years ago. But then the present owners decided to change it back to its original name."

"Not sure why the place was called The Elephant originally," he added. "But the pub was built in the time of the British Raj in India, the empire and all that. Must have been owned by one of those colonial types."

Sitting down at a corner table, I was happy with this answer for a while; happy, at least until I had finished the steak and chips and the pint of bitter I had ordered.

But when I thought about it again, I began to doubt the ease of this breezy calculation. After all, if it all had been simply to do with the Raj, then every Fox & Goose and Rose & Crown in the land would have been called The Elephant or The Banyan Tree & Turban at one time.

What appeared at first glance as a bit of glib hotel branding, precipitated possibly by the cold air of global tourism clashing somewhere over Pangbourne with a warm front of Raj nostalgia, seemed to me, all of a sudden, something of a mystery.

I opened up my Ordnance Survey map of the area as if it might contain some revelation.

Rather surprisingly, it did, at least in that sudden wave of optimism that a pint of beer always manages to give me.

At first, all I found were the comforting names of middle England – places like Woodcote, Coombe End Farm, Bottom Wood, and further downstream larger, but no less cosy, places like Sonning, Shiplake and Henley.

But then unexpectedly I saw it, inscribed in blue, nestling in an area full of green forest about four miles to the north of Pangbourne. A spot on the map declared simply as Maharajah's Well, a little bit of India in a foreign field.

It was late May. The evening was still light. I ordered a taxi straight away.

Half an hour or so later, I arrived in a cab at a crumbling village hall on the fringes of a village called Stoke Row.

A sign opposite it pointed the way to an iron structure that looked liked one of those bandstands you find in Hyde Park, except for the fact that it was crowned by a magnificent dome that looked like it would be more at home in the deserts of Rajasthan than among the rolling hills of the Home Counties.

I walked up to it and peered inside. Sure enough, there, underneath the dome, on top of the iron winding machinery, was a golden statue of an elephant.

—ɷ—

A couple of yards to the side of the well there was a wooden post that contained booklets explaining the history of the Maharajah's Well. I picked one up and, prompted by a sign on a metal post topped by a little blue dome, made a donation to the upkeep of the monument.

The well, it transpired, was the brainchild of the Maharajah of Varanasi in the 1860s, who, after a casual conversation with an Oxfordshire-born civil servant in India called Edward Anderson Reade about the lack of access to clean water in Stoke Row, decided to become a benefactor to this impoverished rural community.

Work started in 1863 – when Weller was drafting his maps for the *Dispatch Atlas* – and on 24 May the following year a well, descending 368 feet (deeper than the height of St Paul's Cathedral) was officially opened. All the work, which involved men digging a four foot wide tunnel entirely by hand, had been carried out by the Wallingford firm of RJ&H Wilder; and the whole project, which included a system for lifting the water using two nine gallon buckets being wound up and down by hand, was lauded as something of a feat of engineering. The local villagers now had access to up to 700 gallons of water a day; and the Maharajah also

provided them with a four-acre cherry orchard that would
help to finance the well and a warden whose job it was to
keep the machinery in good order and to "guard against
mischief or abuse".

But the benefaction of the Maharajah did not stop
there. He later added a footpath that would make access
to the well easier and in 1882 donated food and drink for
local festivities prompted by what some now might see as
a rather odd reason for a street party – Queen Victoria's
survival of an assassination attempt.

Contacts between the locality and Benares were lost,
however, in the years following the death in 1886 of
Anderson Reade, the middleman in the whole business;
and they were not resurrected again until 1958 when a
new Maharajah happened to ask a visitor to Benares from
Oxford whether the well still existed, sparking a renewed
interest in a utility which had fallen out of use after a public
water supply arrived in Stoke Row in 1927. A fund-raising
campaign subsequently raised enough money for the
Maharajah's Well to be restored as a public monument.

It was a nice story, but did this really have anything to do
with The Elephant Hotel at Pangbourne, I wondered more
soberly the next morning on my journey down the Thames.
It was possible, just possible, that the answer might lie at my
next destination, Reading, which was the location, according

to my smart phone, of the Berkshire Record Office containing all the parish registers and archives of the local area. If I could just find out who owned the pub in the 1860s.

The views over the river on the path to Reading from Pangbourne were lovely, despite the continuing cloudiness of the skies. To my right, there were broad meadows of long grass and buttercups and purple clover; to my left; on the opposite side of the river there was a row of launches moored up, in some instances, next to black and white-timbered boathouses, and in others, just anchored to a couple of wooden posts in the shallows. In the distance, the soft green line of the heavily-wooded Chiltern Hills rolled down towards the water's edge.

There was a break in the trees at one point, making way for Hardwick House, the neat red-brick mansion of Tudor style which once played host to the winter balls of Caroline Lybbe-Powys, and is said to be the inspiration for EH Shepard's illustrations of Toad Hall in The Wind in the Willows, though this prize is also claimed by Mapledurham, an Elizabethan manor house located further downstream. Mapledurham also boasts the Thames' last working water mill, which churns out stoneground flour, and, in addition, has been equipped with a new turbine to produce green energy, a very modern take on the Thames mill which was traditionally employed not only to produce flour, but also to pump water, make paper, hammer sheet metal and treat cloth, all long before the halting of climate change was ever a consideration.

It was at Mapledurham's lock that I decided to catch my first passenger boat along the river. This was partly provoked by a sign on the lockkeeper's cottage that London was 78 ½ miles away – still so far! – and partly driven by my lifelong love affair with ferries.

My passion had started with a ferry crossing on Lake Windermere during a family holiday as a child, but what really did for me was the Star Ferry in Hong Kong where I spent some time working in the early 1990s. There was something about standing in the gangway at Kowloon, waiting with hordes of other commuters for the sound of the bell and the green light to board the diesel-fume spluttering steamer creaking and straining against the pier; there was something about the bad-tempered crewmen gathering in the ropes ready for departure and the sight of the skyscrapers of Hong Kong Island gradually drawing closer which got me hooked forever.

Thereafter, I caught a ferry on my travels whenever I could. I took a ferry from the Greek island of Samos to Patmos in order to see the glistening port of Skala draped around a curving bay. I boarded a ferry in Singapore so that I could see the spectacular peaks of Batu Sirau and Nenek Si-muka wrapped in their carpets of emerald jungle green on Tioman Island in the South China Sea. I wobbled onto a tiny launch in the centre of Phnom Penh, which, after chugging through the flat, dusty basin of Cambodia, finally reached the Vietnamese border town of Chau Doc just as night was falling.

The Salters steamer that arrived at 12:15 at Mapeldurham Lock wasn't quite in the same league as these. Still, it was a happy moment when I boarded the 'Reading', a sleek low-lying vessel with a front lower deck covered with a blue awning and two decks at the stern: the upper one open to the elements.

Salter's Steamers is a family firm which was established in Edward Weller's day – at Folly Bridge in Oxford in 1858, to be precise – to build and let boats largely for the university market. Its boats quickly gained a reputation for good craftsmanship and soon the fledgling firm was exporting to all corners of the empire.

It was a prescient moment to launch a boat company on the Thames too. As the commercial barge traffic declined in the wake of the Great Western Railway's arrival on the scene, the river was becoming a place of pastime, recognised as such by the Thames Preservation Act of 1855 which called for provision for it to be "preserved as a place of regulated public recreation". The skiffs and punts, skulls and launches of amateur boaters which were beginning to fill up the river then, particularly during the Regatta season, were joined in time by passenger steamers offering a quick spin on the water for day-trippers arriving on the railway from London. This was, by the way, much to the chagrin of Jerome K Jerome, who, as a rowing man, hated steam launches. By the time *Three Men in a Boat* was published during the 1880s heyday of the river as a place for pleasure craft, Salters was running its own service from

Oxford to Kingston-on-Thames. It has been running passenger services ever since and continues to build boats.

My service to Reading in May 2013 entered Mapeldurham Lock on time. The captain and his assistant held the boat steady with ropes on the posts at the side as the water drained out, and within minutes we were crawling slowly out of the gates and into the Kentwood Deeps beyond.

There were just three of us on the boat – the captain, his young assistant on a summer job and me. Quietly, we slipped along with the lush greenery closing in on either side of the river, its brown surface now as still as a mill-pond. Later on in my travels, I would read at the River and Rowing Museum in Henley that the Thames above Teddington Lock was really a series of "managed lakes" between each lock and weir system; and certainly it was true that the character of the water had changed since my early days on the waterway. In its infancy, particularly before it reached that first lock at Lechlade, the Thames seemed to trickle and gush in a determined fashion towards its ultimate goal, the sea; but once past Oxford, the pace of the river had appeared to slow down, sauntering now, the directions of its currents more difficult to determine.

Either way, the steamer chugged on – Salters coal steamers had actually been diesel-powered since the 1950s – towards the county town of Berkshire, passing by a grey brick escarpment carrying the Great Western Railway line and a couple of factory buildings before the waterway opened out again into vistas of pleasure again, flanked with boathouses, large Victorian houses and smart riverside apartments.

There had been hints, though, of something quite different again, a series of tower blocks on the horizon as we approached the town; and after disembarking at Caversham Bridge and walking along the towpath to Reading Bridge I turned towards the town centre and a landscape wholly new to the river – glass towers, ring roads and busy people in suits talking importantly into their mobile phones. Oxford had been busy but this was different somehow.

I swapped my walking boots for my loafers on the steps of Clearwater Court – the corporate headquarters of Thames Water – and stepped onto the edges of a roundabout. If I took the turning straight ahead, I would find myself on the M4 heading east (after quite a while I should think). Alternatively, I would find myself in Bracknell.

Thankfully, there was a tiny sign lurking below the urgency of this traffic directive. It pointed the way to the town centre.

XII

Reading

Some of the world's greatest metropolises have sprung up at the meeting point of two rivers: Khartoum bubbles up where the Blue and White Niles become one; St Louis emerges at the marriage of the Mississippi and the Missouri; Allahabad pops up at the great swirling together of the Ganges and the Yamuna.

Reading, sitting on the confluence of the River Thames and River Kennet, cannot really be said to be one of them. It possesses no great Mughal forts, no Ragtime heritage, and no souks to speak of. It is not even a city like its close neighbour, Oxford, which lies on the convergence of the Cherwell and the Thames 30 miles away. Despite Reading's greater size, it remains a town.

Yet I rather liked it. A jumble of Victorian civic buildings and modern office blocks and shopping malls, it didn't look much at first. But, after picking up a map called 'Global Reading' at a Fair Trade shop on London Street and finding out more about it, I began to appreciate this slightly unloved place that has consistently failed in its long-running campaign to be recognised officially as a city.

The premise of the map published by the Reading international Solidarity Centre, a charity dedicated to raising awareness of world issues in the local community, was that Reading was a global town long before the likes of Microsoft, Kyocera and other multinational technology giants set up home in its wealth of business parks, putting it at the heart of the UK's 'silicon valley'. Their map, illustrating various places of historical interest, showed that Reading has been influenced by the movement of people, goods and ideas from every continent for nearly two thousand years. Like Oxford upstream, it is a place consistently caught in the cross-currents of international history.

The map references started with a Saxon cemetery found near the Dreadnought Inn at the junction of the Kennet and the Thames, and moved on to a Viking warrior's grave unearthed in the 1830s during excavations for the Great Western Railway – evidence of the Viking army camp set up in the area in 870. Down the road, there were the ruins of a Norman abbey established in 1121 by Benedictine monks from the great monastery at Cluny in Burgundy. Saxons, Vikings, Normans; wave after wave of foreign conquest – Reading was already proving to be an early history of the River Thames in miniature.

But it was not only the world that came to Reading. By the eighteenth and nineteenth centuries, Reading was venturing out into the world. A derelict malthouse on Fobney St and a demolished biscuit factory on King's Road recall a thriving industrial town which threw up Simonds brewery and Huntley & Palmers, making India Pale Ale and hundreds of varieties of biscuits, respectively, for export all around the world. There was also Cock's Reading Sauce, also produced on King's Road, which was a heady concoction of soy sauce from China, anchovies from the Black Sea, chilli, ginger and cloves which sold as far afield as China, Argentina and West Africa. The gardens of the Taj Mahal, meanwhile, glowed with petunias grown by Reading corn and seed merchant, John Sutton.

Where trade went, people followed. After spending 14 years in Bengal, Major Charles Marsac returned to England in 1779 and bought Caversham Park in Reading, spending lavishly on the house and gardens. He was one of many 'nabobs' who settled back in Berkshire in the late eighteenth century after making money with the English East India Company out in India, earning the county the nickname of 'the English Hindoostan'. Another was Thomas Pitt, who in 1702 bought a diamond from a gem dealer in Madras for £24,000, selling it a few years later to French royalty for £135,000 and retiring on the proceeds to the country estate of Swallowfields, a few miles south of Reading. Wild rumours continue to circulate as to the provenance of the Pitt Diamond, as it is known. Some say it was snatched from the eye socket of a Hindu deity; others say it was stolen from the Golkonda mines in Andhra Pradesh by a slave who hid it in a self-inflicted wound in his thigh.

Reading-born painter William Havell, meanwhile, joined a British trade mission to Beijing in 1816 as its official artist, his sketches and paintings recording the journey to China via Madeira, Rio de Janeiro and the Cape of Good Hope. The ship was wrecked in the Java Sea on its return journey, though Havell and many of his fellow shipmates lived to tell the tale.

Memorials all across town attest to Britain's military, political and trading power in the nineteenth and twentieth centuries. There is a statue in Eldon Square of Rufus Isaacs, the Liberal MP for Reading before the First World War who became Viceroy of India in the 1920s; there is a huge statue of a lion which commemorates the men of a Reading regiment who died in a battle in Kandahar in 1880 in the Second Anglo-Afghan War; and there is a plaque to a Danish prisoner-of-war in St Mary's Church who was held in Reading prison during the Napoleonic Wars.

It was during and after the two world wars that the world began to come back to Reading. More than 600 Belgian refugees ended up in Reading during the First World War. During and after the Second World War, refugees from Europe – Poles, Hungarians and Ukrainians especially – stayed in camps in the area, many eventually settling in and around Reading.

They were joined In the 1950s and 1960s by migrants from the Commonwealth – mainly from the Caribbean and the Indian sub-continent – seeking a better life in Britain. Encountering racial prejudice in the early days, housing and jobs were first difficult to come by, but slowly these communities etched out a living and a presence in the town. The first mosque in the town opened its doors in 1965, a Sikh temple later sprung up on Cumberland Road and more recently a Hindu temple established itself on Silver Street.

There are also a number of Caribbean churches in what has become a very multicultural sort of place. Afro-Caribbeans make up nearly seven per cent of the population, South Asians nearly ten per cent and there is also a large Polish community. There are refugees from war zones and troubled countries overseas – Somalians, Algerians and others – and, in addition, a growing Nepalese presence.

Thousands of Gurkha veterans and their relatives have chosen to settle in the UK after they successfully acquired British settlement rights in 2009 following a famous campaign led by actor Joanna Lumley. The community in Reading is now 5,000 strong and includes a mix of ex-Gurkhas and their dependants, skilled migrants and students.

—ᗡᗡᗡ—

After walking around the town all afternoon, I made my way up Castle Hill past a beautiful Cedar of Lebanon which was planted during the French Revolution by French priests who had settled in Reading after escaping Robespierre's reign of terror. I was heading towards the Berkshire Record Office on Coley Avenue. I wanted to see if I could find out something more about The Elephant Hotel at Pangbourne.

"We've got the deeds for that property from 1756," said the archivist at the information desk. "And a map of the area from the 1870s.

"While we source those, you could look at the censuses on the computer here."

I scrolled through the censuses of 1861, 1871, 1881 and 1891 but came up with nothing. I hadn't much to go on, just the vague address of Church Road, Pangbourne; and the online responses were just as vague, a red line of script to the effect that there was nothing matching my enquiry.

The archivist came back with the deeds and the map. The spidery writing of the eighteenth century deeds announced that the original building had been owned by the Breedons, the family who owned the local manor and over a couple of centuries produced a number of MPs, a number of high sheriffs of the county and a few doctors and rectors of the parish, as well as being the benefactors of a school which opened in Pangbourne in 1863.

But a 1756 document didn't prove anything about the 1860s. I turned to the map from the 1870s, and, to my delight, found what I was looking for. There it was, The Elephant Hotel on Church Road in bold writing on an old parchment showing Pangbourne and the surrounding fields.

But my delight quickly gave way to despair. So what if there was an Elephant Hotel in the 1870s? How long had it been there? Who owned it? Did they have any connections with the Maharajah of Benares or, indeed with Edward Anderson Reade who I later discovered in a couple of old documents in the British Library was wrapped up in a rather exotic story himself. He had apparently found a moonstone in India, which he had brought back to his family seat in Ipsden in Oxfordshire. It turns out that Edward's brother happened to be the novelist Charles Reade, who, as I think I mentioned earlier, was part of a set of word-smith friends who used to meet in a pub near the Strand. A set of friends which coincidentally included Wilkie Collins, who was later to write a detective novel about a certain moonstone.

Elephants? Connections with India? Moonstones even. History can hold some strange secrets. But it was all a far cry from the light, airy rooms of the Berkshire Record Office on a bright spring day. Sitting on my functional office chair, with no particular answers to any of my questions, I knew I wouldn't be able to establish a link between the hotel in Pangbourne and the golden elephant of Stoke Row.

The final letdown came when I turned back to the computer database and looked up the Berkshire newspaper archives. The pub had actually been called The Elephant and Castle in 1863 (though, by 1870, it was indeed being referred to as simply The Elephant) and was being run by a rather shady character called William Ford. In April 1863, Ford was declared bankrupt and the fixtures and fittings of his pub put up for auction by his creditors. By 1865, he seems to have been back in charge of the pub, but still unable to keep out of trouble: in February that year, he was summoned before the Reading County Bench for alleg-edly assaulting a former employee and later on, just before Christmas, he was before the local magistrates, accused of running an illegal gambling den in his hostelry.

In fact, Pangbourne in Weller's time seems to have been a scurrilous sort of place, local young men regularly appearing in court, charged with running amok through the streets of Pangbourne at midnight after a night of boozing in the local pubs. Not even the establishment of public gas lamps in the town in November 1863 seems to have thrown any improving Victorian light onto the situation.

My visions of maharajahs and elephants quickly fading, I headed back into Reading town centre.

On a pedestrianised street near the railway station I found a modern cafe catering to the latest settlers in the town – the Nepalese. I had tasted Nepalese food a few times – most memorably in a restaurant near Paddington station in London when I first moved down to the capital to find work in the mid-1980s – and had loved its earthy tastes and textures. It was time, I thought after the disappointment of the record office, to savour it again.

A young Nepali waitress came over as I wedged myself into a seat at a table near the window and handed me a menu. "You eaten Nepali food before?" she smiled. "Do you need help with the menu?"

"A long time ago," I replied, looking at the bewildering array of dishes available. Dal bhat – lentils and rice. Tarkari – vegetables in a curried broth. Momo – dumplings. There was a lot of buffalo meat on the menu, but there also chicken and lamb.

"The dumplings?" I enquired.

"Yes, the dumplings. Different," she grinned.

I played it safe in the end, and opted for the lamb thali. That way I could sample a bit of everything – a meat curry, some dhal, some rice, some vegetables in a curry broth. And at £7 for the whole lot, I could hardly go wrong.

"So what does 'sapana' mean?" I asked after placing my order, referring to the name of the cafe, Sapana Home.

"It means 'dream'," the waitress replied. "Actually, it's the name of our proprietor who's in London at the moment."

It might also have referred to the painting on the wall that had caught my eye. A pretty picture of a thatched village sitting on a hill with a dramatic snow-capped Mount Everest watching over it. A nostalgia for the homeland? Dreams of home? If that was part of the meaning behind the name of the cafe, it didn't seem to be of particular concern to my waitress. Otherwise, it seemed to me, she would have mentioned it.

Nor was it for the lively group of Nepalese on the table next to me. They were discussing work at one of Reading's large software firms.

"I tell you, I was sitting on that beach in the Seychelles on Christmas Day with the sand between my toes," said a small round man wearing a smart pair of slacks with an orange T-shirt tucked smartly into them. "And I took that call from the office. I needn't have done. But I did."

"Yes, I can see why you did it," his friend concurred. "You have to show leadership towards your team, don't you."

"Yes, yes, you do," the small man said excitedly. "My Singapore manager said he would have done exactly the same thing. Leading by example, you know."

Singapore? Tropical beaches? Leadership? Reading was obviously a globalised go-ahead sort of place. I sank into a lamb thali as good as I had ever tasted.

—w—

Go-ahead places need their landmark projects, and in Reading this is currently the Oracle shopping centre, which hugs the sides of the Kennet not long before this little river from Wiltshire converges with the regal Thames. The following morning, I found myself lost somewhere between Debenhams and House of Fraser on its upper mall, looking for a bag shop which might provide something portable and light to carry my walking shoes when I wasn't wearing them.

In its way, it was a striking place. The glass frontages of the myriad designer shops housed on three floors under a great glass dome, the hustle and bustle of shoppers from

Reading's diverse communities, the smooth escalators that took you places you never quite wanted to go – it was a development that the mall's builders and the local council probably believed, probably quite rightly, had helped to put Reading on the retail map.

A website dedicated to the mall that I found on my smart phone told the story. More than £250 million had been invested in the development when it opened in the late 1990s. There were "72,000 sq metres of shopping and leisure" spread over three levels and over 22 acres if you included the 'al fresco' dining area and the car park, which could accommodate 2,300 vehicles. A wide variety of public art had also been employed "to enhance the overall appearance of the scheme", particularly on the riverside.

But if the Oracle caused a stir around Reading when it was built, that was nothing compared to the retail sensation caused by the opening of Whiteley's department store in London in the year of my map – 1863. Perhaps, the Victorian gentlemen reading the latest editions of the London papers in the Reading public news rooms noticed the breaking business story amid all the column inches that year dedicated to the American Civil War and the Polish uprising against Russian rule.

The residents of Bayswater in central London may have seen the Yorkshire draper, William Whiteley, with the mutton-chop side whiskers perusing an empty shophouse on the corner of Westbourne Grove in the winter of 1863 – not long, in fact, after the opening the Metropolitan Underground Railway at nearby Paddington. On 11 March, the day after the wedding of the Prince of Wales to Princess Alexandria of Denmark, he opened for business, and was an instant success.

Whether it was the opening of the railway which made transport out to Bayswater easier or the perfect timing of the royal wedding, or whether it was because Whiteley was bringing the new concept of the department store to London's growing middle classes, or as is most likely, a combination of all these things, his shop was packed to the gills within hours with fashionable young ladies rifling through his stock of hosiery and ribbons, gloves and lace. By the time the year was out, this customer base had become a seething mass, and Whiteley had extended the number of his departments to include, among other things, haberdashery, dresses and hats.

Perhaps, who knows, Edward Weller's wife Mary Ann was one of those first customers feeling the texture of a piece of silk between her thumb and forefinger under the attentive eyes of one of the Yorkshire businessman's shop girls, while her husband sat in Red Lion Square etching out in minute detail, on one of his maps of London, the elegant town houses and handsome squares which were beginning to emerge in Bayswater at the time.

Whiteley, who had arrived in London in the mid-1850s with less than £10 in his pocket but determined to set up his own drapery business, steadily added to this map over the next few years, and by 1871 he ran a row of ten shops in Westbourne Grove, containing more than

17 departments and a refreshment room. By 1890, the department store was a huge and prosperous concern, employing more than 6,000 staff. Nothing, it seemed, could stop this inexorable rise of William Whiteley, not even the John Lewis store which had opened up on Oxford Street in 1864.

Nothing, except for one thing perhaps. His taste for Whiteley shop girls, and young women in general. He married his first shop assistant, Harriet Sarah Hill, who was with him at the very beginning in 1863. But over the following decades he went through quite a few more – extra-marital affairs which eventually contributed to his divorce from Hill in the early 1880s.

A few years before that a Louie Ellen had joined the store as an assistant and become Whiteley's mistress, having a child by him.

More significantly, though, for my tale, she had a sister called Emily Mary who was married to a stockbroker named George Rayner. The two couples struck up a friendship and started to take weekend trips together.

William Whiteley was moving in important circles by this time – the tea magnate Thomas Lipton, for example, was a close friend – but in April 1879 a little boy was born in the Rayner household in Teddington, who was ultimately to prove his undoing.

George and Emily Rayner split up in 1888 and their son, Horace, was sent to boarding school in Brighton, and then spent some time in Russia as a clerk for an English company. A good-looking young man with cultivated manners, Horace was soon, nonetheless, drifting from one job to another and from one desperate loan to another. His mother died a lonely alcoholic in 1898, and his father George Rayner, for some reason, didn't want much to do with him. His simmering resentment began to grow.

William Whiteley's nemesis, when it came, came – coincidentally for my story – out of Edward Weller's neighbourhood. Although he was married by now, Horace had spent most of 1906 in cheap London boarding houses, drifting from one attempt at self-employment to another, his family finances drifting dangerously into penury. On the 4th of January 1907, he checked into a small lodging house called the Gerhard Hotel at 23 Red Lion Street in Holborn, just round the corner from Red Lion Square.

Three weeks later, just after his breakfast at the Gerhard, he started making his way over to Bayswater. Around the same time, William Whiteley, now an elderly man of failing health, was leaving his home at Porchester Terrace in Bayswater for the world famous emporium he had started back in 1863, arriving as he had always done for the last 40 years just after 10am.

At 12.30pm a young man arrived at Whiteleys, asking to see the 'Universal Provider' as the grand old man of department stores was known, and as William Whiteley always kept an open office he was let in.

At 1pm, the door of the office swung open and the stocky figure of William Whiteley emerged, looking pale and agitated. He asked a store assistant to fetch a policeman at once. Then his visitor emerged.

"Are you going to give in?" Horace Rayner demanded.

"No," said Whiteley.

"Then you are a dead man," and with that, the young man pulled out a revolver and fired two shots at point blank range into the head of the Universal Provider. Then he turned the gun on himself.

Testifying later at the trial of Horace Rayner, who had proved better at taking Whiteley's life than his own, Jacob Gerhard told the court that during his three week stay at the hotel he owned in Red Lion St, Horace had told him that he was the son of a London businessman worth over £2 million, who was originally from Yorkshire.

Horace Rayner had no claim to the family fortune, but he was, he believed, the son of William Whiteley.

XIII

The Golden Gleam

You cannot see it from the Thames, but once you have finished your cup of Darjeeling or something similar at the Sonning Lock tea garden, and turned right up the lane into the churchyard of St Andrew's, you find yourself in a village that Jerome K Jerome described as "the most fairy-like little nook on the whole river". Half-timbered cottages, wisteria climbing around their dainty windows, an Edwardian village hall with a big round clock – Sonning slowly reveals itself as an English rural idyll.

But I was slightly disappointed that an architectural treasure called The Deanery was not open to the public after I had developed a misguided idea in my mind that it would be. "You mean the big house?" said the handsome blond woman serving behind the bar at The Bull. "No, you can't visit it. It's owned by Jimmy Page, you know, the guitarist with Led Zeppelin."

"Oh well, I'll go and take a look, all the same," I said. "Could I leave my bags here for a while?"

"Yes, of course. Your room won't be ready until three, so you might as well." The young woman shrugged her shoulders.

The Deanery was a house designed at the beginning of the twentieth century by the famous British architect, Edwin Lutyens, the creator of so many beautiful country homes dotted around the British Isles. His house at Sonning apparently bore all the hallmarks of his particular oeuvre – the use of traditional craftsmanship, the subtle combination of brick, tile and timber forms, the combination of formal geometry and romantic English earthiness. Architectural historian Christopher Hussey once described it as "a perfect architectural sonnet".

What I found on Thames Street was merely the opening refrain of a sonnet; just the mellow, high red-brick walls that surround the Deanery's allegedly beautiful garden, one of Lutyens' trademark turrets and a cluster of amazingly lofty chimneys, again bearing his stamp. The rest of the estate – the vaulted buttresses, the giant timber oriel, all the flowers and all the herbs – were bricked off, literally. Jimmy Page had bought his stairway to heaven. Understandably, I suppose, he was keeping it to himself and a few friends.

Sonning was a bit like that. I strolled down to the eighteenth century flour mill which was converted around 30 years ago into a famous dinner theatre, and nearly fell through the floor when I found out that a ticket for that night's performance was £45.50 with or without dinner. Meanwhile, the Edwardian village hall rather predictably housed a social club which was strictly members-only.

It did not matter too much though. I knew I was going to be an honorary member of this exclusive club for one day. I had booked a room at the Bull, "a veritable picture of an old country inn," according to Jerome K Jerome, "with low, quaint rooms and latticed windows, and awkward stairs and winding passages". I was going to enjoy it.

I did, as it turned out. Rather too much. The sun had come out properly for the first time on my journey along the middle reaches, and sitting in the pub courtyard in the green-gold light of a glade of trees, I drank a pint of beer. And then another.

I woke up a couple of hours later in a low, quaint room with latticed windows called Harris in homage to *Three Men in a Boat*, listening to the babble of beer drinkers still drinking in the courtyard below and lazily inhaling the drowsy afternoon scent of the wisteria spilling in through my window.

—⚬—

It was as if the character of the river changed for a while after that sunny afternoon in Sonning, or was it that the river was beginning truly for the first time to catch me in its spell? I don't know, but for the next couple of days I began to fully appreciate the words of Lewis Carroll when he wrote of his journeys down the Thames at Oxford:

Ever drifting down the stream

Lingering in the golden gleam

Life, what is it but a dream?

Wandering down the Thames between Sonning and Marlow that first weekend of June felt like a dream. For the first time really on my journey, I let go of my everyday cares and worries, and surrendered myself to the river. I forgot my sore feet from walking for miles and miles along an uneven towpath and my aching shoulders from carrying a heavy rucksack, and savoured each twist and turn of the historic waterway.

The weekend started with the 11.45 ferry from Sonning to Lower Shiplake – a low enclosed launch piloted by a short burly captain with a mop of black wavy hair and an ear-ring who, in answer to my curiosity about the responsibilities involved in being in charge of a passenger boat, showed me his Maritime and Coastguard Agency licence, and warned me with a friendly grin about the dangers of the river.

"Oh, I've had some hairy moments, I can tell you," he said. "It's the motor cruisers driven by novices or by people who've had a bit much to drink you've got to steer clear of. I've had to take quick action a few times."

And then the day continued with a tramp through the village of Lower Shiplake, where the path leaves the water for a while, winding in between some very expensive houses with 'Beware of the dog' signs on their front gates before returning gently to one of the prettiest stretches of the river – the approach into Henley.

The view of the river here was as delicious as the birdsong carried on the summer breezes blowing softly all around me. To my left was a sea of wild meadow; to my right, across the river, emerald green hills unfurling themselves onto the river bank, the occasional turret or tower of a half-hidden house peeping out from behind a cluster of trees. One of them, incidentally, was Park Place (noted by Weller on his 1863 map), which has recently been sold to an unknown Russian oligarch for £140 million.

A break in the trees as I approached Henley was identified on my modern map as 'Happy Valley', but the real happy valley waited for me on the other side of the Marsh Lock broadwalk, which takes the rambler halfway across the river on a wooden footbridge to avoid the lock weir and then returns him or her to the bankside.

On the other side lay Mill Meadows and the promenade into Henley town centre, and here, everybody was out on the water enjoying the summer sunshine: earnest Steve Redgrave types in sleek sculls, laughing families with excitable dogs in small motor launches, rich Russian oligarchs in gin-soaked cabin cruisers, a riverboat crammed full of blazered blue-bloods, drinking themselves into a merry afternoon oblivion.

On the bankside, meanwhile, a musical event had assembled. Hundreds of people thronged the meadow, eating food from catering tents, chatting, shouting at their children and sometimes watching the local bands thrash out their dreams on the iron bandstand in the middle of the park. There was a girl who played heavy metal guitar, there was a boy who bashed his drums to a heavy rock backing track, and a ukulele orchestra, who looked half-startled when the crowd applauded them. I applauded them too, and then, feeling hungry after my walk, took myself to a food stall where a grumpy man hovered over a giant paella dish.

It was just a few weeks away from the annual Henley Regatta and you could already feel the festival spirit building up in the town as it would have done every June since 1839 when the famous rowing gala was first held. Thunderstorms threatened the first day of the event in 1863 – the year of my map – but the crowds still turned out in their thousands, who knows, perhaps Edward Weller and his family were among them – and by the afternoon the rain had passed over, ushering in the heats for the Grand Challenge Cup. One of these, won by Oxford Brasenose College by a whisker, was "one of the finest and fastest races ever seen at Henley" according to one observer quoted by the Reading Mercury.

A brilliant sun came out to meet the Henley spectators on the second day of the 1863 Regatta, as it did for me the following day in June 2013 when I left the town, caressing my meander across fields and meadows towards Marlow, past more revellers in pleasure boats. This time it was a flotilla of about 20 tugs with fancy funnels and union jack bunting, each filled with plump rosy-cheeked men wearing slow-boater hats and striped blazers and women squeezed into cocktail dresses. They were celebrating the golden anniversary of the Queen's coronation apparently.

And then there other vessels of a more racing nature, one of them a dragon boat thrashing through the water at great speed.

I passed Temple Island, which is the starting point for the Henley regatta, and followed the path in a wide arc towards Hambledon Lock before it cut inland towards the village of Aston.

After that, I remember only a collection of scenes as I drifted downstream in the golden gleam of a summer's day. I remember the heron standing like an old man hunched in a grey overcoat in a field. I remember the stuffed fish in glass cases in the bar at the Flowerpot Hotel in Aston. I remember the green slopes around Culham Court and the red kite hovering high overhead.

I can recall the white Gothic arches of Medmenham Abbey, home in the eighteenth century to the bawdy rituals of Sir Francis Dashwood and other high society members of the notorious Hellfire Club.

I can recall all the mobile homes clinging to the banks of the river on the approach to Hurley surrounded by low picket fences as if they were moats protecting private kingdoms.

I can recapture as if it was yesterday all the Asian families camped out in Hurley Riverside Park, the vivid colours

of their saris and topis mingling around kebab sticks sizzling on makeshift barbecues.

I can summon up, if anyone cared to ask, the mellow
stones of Bisham Abbey.

Finally, at around 4 o'clock, as if in some strange
sort of reverie, the delicate steel lines of Marlow
Suspension Bridge appeared on the horizon. Gently
ushered towards it by the sun, I strode the last few hundred metres, turned left up a grassy slope and onto the
High Street.

—〜〜—

"It always seems to be summer when I look back," wrote
George Orwell of his childhood in two of the places I had
just walked through, Lower Shiplake and Henley. "I can
feel the grass round me as tall as myself, and the heat coming out of the earth."

Born in Bengal, India in 1903 – where his father worked
for the Opium Department, a morally dubious arm of the
British Indian Civil Service responsible for the export of
4,000 tons of narcotic to China each year – Orwell, aka
Eric Arthur Blair, moved back to England in 1907 with his
mother and sister, settling in Henley. After five years there,
the family moved to a Victorian house called Roselawn on
Station Road in Shiplake. I must have walked straight past
the place, which has recently been on the market for £1

million apparently, when the Thames Path took me past Shiplake station.

Orwell was very happy in Henley and loved Shiplake, according to his biographers, never really forgetting the lost, golden world of his childhood beside the Thames before the First World War. The writer best-known for his vision of a future dystopia in *1984* recalled these days extensively in a novel called *Coming up for Air* where the protagonist, walking amongst the crowds along the Strand in London just before the Second World War, suddenly finds himself reminiscing about his life as a boy in Lower Binfield, a thinly disguised Lower Shiplake.

By the same token, Orwell never quite warmed to the world he encountered once he had left that dreamy riverine world of "great green juicy meadows" and "blue hills". In an essay for *Time and Tide* magazine in 1936, he railed against "the machine civilisation which makes one part of the world indistinguishable from another". In his most famous essay about the state of the nation a few years later, *The Lion and the Unicorn*, he hit out at England's "vast new wildernesses of glass and brick" in which the inhabitants lived "a rather restless, cultureless life, centring round tinned food, Picture Post, the radio and the internal combustion engine".

Some of these words don't sit very well seventy years on, making Orwell sound like an old-school Tory, which he certainly wasn't. Even if you substitute 'ready meals' for 'tinned food', and then finish the line off with '*Hello* magazine, the internet and cheap flights to Spain', the quote still has a hollow patrician ring to it.

But in the view expressed in *Time and Tide*, he probably hit the proverbial nail on the head, his words echoing down the decades to our own age. 'One part of the world indistinguishable from another' – doesn't that sound very familiar? In spite of all the pomp and bluster in the modern media about our freedom of choice, don't we all live in identikit towns, shopping and eating at all the same John Lewis's and Costa Coffees? Sometimes, it seems to me, that we do.

Perhaps we all need a river to escape to. Like the one George Orwell lived besides as a child, the one where it was always summer. Like the one I drifted down a hundred or so years later, in the golden gleam of a sunny weekend.

XIV
Marlow

Another writer with one or two things to say about modernity was Mary Shelley. In March 1817, the nineteen year old daughter of feminist thinker Mary Wollstonecraft and political philosopher William Godwin, arrived in Marlow with her new husband, Percy Bysshe Shelley, and the mistress of Lord Byron, Claire Clairmont; and completed a book which ever since has caught our imagination.

She had started it in the summer of 1816 in the company of Clairmont, Shelley and fellow poet Byron at a villa on the shores of Lake Geneva, where waking from a nightmare one stormy night she conceived the idea of a scientist, who, like the Greek god Prometheus who stole the secret of fire from the heavens to bring to life the species of mankind that he had moulded out of clay, decided to create his own creature out of lifeless matter.

The book she started there and then and finally finished in the elegant white house with its long Georgian sash windows in West St, Marlow, was called *Frankenstein, or The Modern Prometheus.*

The Shelleys lived in a Promethean Age. The persistent rattle of the looms in the swelling industrial towns all across Britain said it all. By the time the couple were living in Marlow, Britain was well into the first phase of the most fundamental transformation in human history, a transformation powered by scientific innovation and steam – the Industrial Revolution.

It did not go unchallenged. You may remember the journalist William Cobbett writing about the hardships of the farm labourers in Cricklade in the 1820s, caught up in the imperatives of this emerging industrial system, a system he called 'the thing'. And he was not the only one. There was growing anger at the harshness of the new factory conditions, and the political crackdowns on free speech introduced by nervous governments that seemed to accompany them.

From the coffee houses and the non-conformist churches around Piccadilly to the waterside workers of Wapping, from the silk weavers of Spitalfields to the old dissenting stronghold of Southwark – up and down the Thames and all across the nation, amongst intellectuals and workers alike – the cry went out for liberty from this oppression; and liberty, in general, which after all had been the birthright of every Englishman since King Alfred assembled his parliaments at Shifford and other Saxon settlements, and King John was forced to sign the Magna Carta in 1215.

To this general clamour, the poet Shelley added his voice, composing *Laon and Cythna* in Marlow about two characters who spark a revolution against the despotic ruler of the fictional state of Argolis, a thinly veiled attack, many say, on the British government of the time.

More directly, he produced a political pamphlet which called for a meeting at The Crown and Anchor Tavern in London (the address was undisclosed lest government spies got hold it) to consider the motion that "the House of Commons does not represent the will of the People of the British Nation". He signed it 'The Hermit of Marlow'.

Meanwhile, in the form of Frankenstein's monster, a scientific experiment which had spun out of control, Mary Shelley added her comment.

—ᴍ—

Over the year that the Shelleys lived in Marlow, Percy Shelley became a familiar figure in the town – a slender figure covered in briars and flowers wandering home from a day by the river, spent writing amongst the ruins of Medmenham Abbey or on his boat lazing under a willow near Temple Lock. A brilliant poet, but also probably a troubled one. The body of his estranged wife Harriet had been dragged up from the bottom of the Serpentine in Hyde Park only a few months before, a suicide that had freed him to marry his lover, Mary Godwin.

Whether he was thinking of Harriet, or his perennial debt problems, or of his pregnant wife back in the house on West Street, or his latest poem, he would almost certainly have ended his day on the river at Marlow Bridge on his route back up the High Street and onto West Street.

It is here that I stood for a while one June evening nearly 200 years later, admiring the view downriver towards Marlow weir. I'd had a lovely evening in historic Marlow, chancing upon an irreverent revue at a local theatre called *Two Bald Blokes Do Shakespeare*. Now, before I turned in for the night, I had decided to walk up to the bridge.

I was on a different structure to the small timber affair Shelley would have ambled across. I was on the famous suspension designed by civil engineer William Tierney Clark in the 1820s, which would turn out to be his prototype for the beautiful crossing he later built over the Danube to link Buda and Pest.

Otherwise, though, the view would have been one that Shelley more or less recognised: the formidable line of water gliding inexorably onwards towards the sea, the exuberance of foliage fringing the bankside and, in the distance, the bright greens of a low hill draped with beech trees, which is said to be the Wild Wood of Kenneth Grahame's imaginings in *The Wind in the Willows*. The author lived much of his childhood over the brow of the hill in the pretty village of Cookham.

The Shelleys did not stay long in Marlow. Within the year, haunted by personal tragedies such as the suicide of Harriet Shelley, and probably pursued by the heavily-indebted poet's creditors, they were packing their bags for Italy.

I watched the advancing dusk gather over Marlow Bridge, thinking about Mary Shelley and her husband gathering their belongings in the house with the Georgian sash windows on West St. By the time the evening light had finally drained away, they were gone.

Percy Bysshe Shelley did not return. An itinerant life spent living out of suitcases in Florence, Venice and Naples ended in a sudden storm off the northern coast of Italy on 8 July 1822. The poet had been sailing out in the bay with his friend Edward Williams. Their bodies were washed up on the beach at Livorno.

Mary, who had been waiting for his arrival further up the coast, returned to England the following year with their only surviving child, a boy who had been born in Florence in 1819.

She returned to the River Thames, moving in with her father and stepmother in the Strand first of all and then taking up lodgings in Kentish Town.

XV

The Garibaldi

"It was that Italian bloke, you know, the one who united Italy. He was a guest at the big house – do you know it? – the one up on the hill over there," grinned the young man on a crutch at The Garibaldi, gesturing with his one free hand vaguely. "He must have come down here for a pint or something. That was in 1864. The pub took on his name after that. It was definitely under his name in the 1871 census."

I had taken a detour into the village of Bourne End looking for a spot of lunch after a beautiful trek through velvety green meadows from Marlow when I'd stumbled on the pub in a small lane full of snug redbrick terraces. Now I was standing under its low roof surrounded by paint pots and wooden planks and the warm, sweet scent of drilling, chatting about the pub's intriguing name and the work obviously being carried out.

"We're refurbishing the pub because we've just bought it from the Punch Taverns brewery," my informant continued, seeing the question formulating on my lips. "By 'we' I mean the local community."

"Oh, that's brave," I said.

"Yes. Punch spent next to nothing on it for 20 years, and then put it up for sale last summer. And we all know what that means."

I looked blank.

"It means that it'll be converted into flats or something worse. So, all the residents of this street, we decided to buy them out. There are 35 of us, all of us shareholders."

"How much did it cost you?"

"More than £300,000. But it's worth it. The Gari, as we call it, has always been a bit like the extension of all our living rooms. We want to keep it that way."

A small wiry man put a lime soda on the bar for me. The young man nodded at him. "This is our new landlord," he explained. "And we hope to have all the work finished in a few weeks, so we can open up for business properly."

"Well, good luck with it all," I said, raising my glass and looking at him with admiration. Whether the crutch was the result of balancing precariously on too many wooden planks during the renovations, I wasn't sure; but one thing was certain I thought: Garibaldi would have appreciated the efforts of these local residents to take destiny into their own hands. On a small scale, it showed a bit of Garibaldi pluck.

—m—

But how did Garibaldi end up at having a pint in Bourne End? Well, he did indeed come to stay in 1864 at the 'house up on the hill' – the stately home of Cliveden House perched on a grassy outcrop above the Thames – as the young man at The Garibaldi had told me. It was during a triumphant visit to England a few years after he had played a pivotal part in the making of modern Italy.

Giuseppe Garibaldi's tale starts in 1825 when the young Italian is growing up quietly in Nice, the son of a sailor and small trader from Genoa. Genoa was then part of the kingdom of Piedmont, one of the many petty states on the Italian peninsula, all of whom spoke some sort of Italian dialect, but had been ruled directly or indirectly by foreign powers – the Austrian Empire, the French, the Spanish Bourbons and so on – ever since the final fall of the Western Roman Empire in the sixth century.

But that year, Giuseppe joined his father on a business trip to Rome and a dream was born. "The Rome that I beheld with the eyes of my youthful imagination," wrote the freedom fighter much later, "was the Rome of the future – the Rome that I never despaired of even when I was shipwrecked, dying, banished to the farthest depths of the American forests – the dominant thought and inspiration of my whole life." Not long afterwards, he joined the Young Italy movement led by the exile Mazzini agitating for that long, lost ideal – a united Italy.

Many adventures followed, as is, I suppose, par for the course for a revolutionary hero: Garibaldi took part in a failed insurrection in Piedmont, was sentenced to death in absentia and fled to Brazil. After making his name as a guerrilla freedom fighter in South America, he arrived back in Europe in 1848 to take part in another revolution in Italy, which again was brutally suppressed.

It all went quiet for a while after that. The savage disappointments of the unsuccessful 1848 revolution together with the tragic death of his wife Anita during a bloody retreat from Rome sent Garibaldi back into merchant seamanship where he had made his living before becoming a revolutionary, finally settling into a house he had built for himself on the little island of Caprera, just off the north coast of Sardinia, ready to spend the rest of his life reading, writing and fishing.

But then his moment arrived. Uprisings in Sicily against Bourbon rule at the beginning of 1860 suddenly offered an opportunity; and, on 11 May that year, Garibaldi arrived in two ships at Marsala on the island's west coast with his Red Shirts, a ramshackle military force of 1,089 volunteers.

Many battles and heroics followed – not least Garibaldi's lone stand against a cavalry charge at the Battle of Milazzo – but within months the Red Shirts were marching up the Italian peninsula, and on 7 September, 1860, they arrived in Naples amid cheering crowds. They had come to liberate southern Italy from the yoke of the corrupt Bourbon monarchy. When Garibaldi finally got to the waterfront, he stood up in his carriage, removed his cap and gazed at the city filled with waving hats and flags all around him. His life's mission had become a reality. Italy would be one again. He had come home.

Not only that, but it had been one of the most famous military victories in history thanks to the signals that had been furiously pulsating through the copper telegraph wires between Europe and London all that summer, surfacing as inky dots and dashes in newsrooms across Fleet St. The words of an embedded reporter from the Illustrated London News, Charles Arrivabene, and the ever improving electric telegraph service had transformed the march of the 'Thousand' into one of the great media events of the century.

Fleet St had been following Garibaldi's story for quite some time, partly because of the Victorian reading public's growing taste for romantic heroes and partly because his story had been kept in the public eye by London's growing Italian immigrant community, most notably by political refugee Giuseppe Mazzini. By the time Garibaldi 'liberated' Naples, his story would have been known not only in the little Italian cafes springing up all over Holborn, Soho and Clerkenwell but also amongst London's middling sort of people, the office clerks, the shopkeepers, the skilled workers, the new professionals, for whom the daily newspaper had become an important part of their daily ritual. It is very likely that the mapmaker Edward Weller had opened his *London Daily News* or *Illustrated London News* one morning that September and enjoyed the apotheosis of Garibaldi's tale.

So, when the freedom fighter arrived in London in 1864 on a triumphant visit, about half a million turned out to welcome him. They lined the streets, hung out of windows and from railway arches, sang the Garibaldi hymn, waved red scarves and cheered the man with the deeply set brown eyes and friendly charming smile wherever he went. Little girls ran up to with him with bunches of flowers, Prime Minister Lord Palmerston and the Gladstones dined with him, while the poet, Tennyson, was wooed by his "divine simplicity". There was also a run on Garibaldi biscuits. Who knows? Perhaps, Edward Weller, the draughtsman who had recently mapped the coastline between Naples and Sicily for the *Dispatch Atlas*, bought a tin box of them for his excitable household in Red Lion Square.

For a few weeks, Garibaldi, the romantic adventurer whose sole mission, according to a reporter on the Manchester 'Examiner and Times', was to "give liberty to the down-trodden" and "freedom to the oppressed" was lauded and celebrated. Garibaldi fever had gripped the nation. No-one, it seemed, was immune.

Least of all, the women of the Duke and Duchess of Sutherland's household at Cliveden, who, according to the government minister, Lord Granville, went "temporarily a little out of their minds" during the Italian freedom fighter's stay in the household. Both the Duchess and her daughter-in-law, Anne, the wife of the third Duke, sent swooning letters to the Italian after his departure, while Mrs Seeley at the Prince's Gate wrote of her "anguish" when she looked at the small bed where the Italian's "noble head" had once rested.

Garibaldi left Cliveden in a hurry and sailed out of Fowey harbour in Cornwall a few days later, returning to the comparative safety of his newly-united homeland. The Italianate mansion of Cliveden, meanwhile, went on to cement its reputation for warm hospitality. The owners in the first half of the twentieth century, the Astors, entertained the likes of Winston Churchill and Amy Johnson here in the 1920s and 30s. Later on, the third Viscount Astor, William, installed a swimming pool where one weekend in July 1961, his house guest, the Secretary of State for War, John Profumo, met a society call-girl named Christine Keeler. The rest, as they say, is history.

—⁓—

Although I could not see the house up on the hill from the river valley below, I could almost feel its historical presence as I tramped onto the handsome village of Cookham from Bourne End. And the next morning, after a night in a bed and breakfast resting a large blister now emerging on my left toe, it popped up in my thoughts again.

It was after I had negotiated a narrow path that winds between the hedges of the large properties on the outskirts of Cookham, when I suddenly arrived at the river again, and was met with the heavenly vision of the hanging beech-woods of the Cliveden Estate spilling down to the water on the opposite bank, cottages peeping out seductively from behind them. The vision got me thinking about Garibaldi's visit to Britain again. And all those years dreaming of his homeland across the sea: in Nice as a teenager, holed up as a freedom fighter in the jungles of Brazil, on a little island off the north coast of Sardinia when he was living in exile.

Imagine too, all the yearnings, all the melancholy, of the émigré Italians in their shops and restaurants in Victorian London; and also of all the other exiles seeking shelter in the Thames valley over the centuries: of Brutus and his fellow refugees from the windy plains of Troy; or of the children fleeing from the Spanish Civil War who ended up at Buscot Park.

Imagine their nostalgia for their far-off homelands. Revived again only in the pictures they hung on their walls: a painting, perhaps, of an ephemeral Capri suspended in the electric blue waters of the Bay of Naples; or a photograph of a family home that had been destroyed by the firebombs of Franco's allies. Or perhaps that picture of a village in the Himalayan foothills which I glimpsed in the Gurkha restaurant in Reading – the popular haunt of Nepalese expatriates.

My thoughts were still wandering from Garibaldi to the Himalayas and back again when I finally arrived – around midday – at the clanking, mechanical clutches of Boulter's Lock in Maidenhead.

XVI

Visions of the River

In 1947, my father toyed with the idea of moving to Maidenhead. He had seen a notice among the classifieds from the Maidenhead Advertiser which was offering a salary of £8 a week for a general reporter.

But, in the end, he decided, according to one of the musty diaries that I had found in that attic room in the old stone house in his home village many years later, that he didn't want to go back to a "small weekly paper".

When the Second World War broke out in 1939 he had been an apprentice reporter on the small weekly *Banbury Advertiser*. Fifteen years old at the time, he had been too young to join the war effort; but in 1943 he finally got his call up, and on Thursday 8 July that year his ship slipped out of the Firth of Clyde bound for West Africa.

I would like to say "slipped out unnoticed" – after all, when things 'slip out' in stories, it is usually unnoticed. Unfortunately, however, the German U-boats had probably already clocked the three-vessel convoy, and a couple of days later the young Ronald William Wilcox found himself on a rope scrambling down the side of a fast-sinking ship into a flimsy life-raft below. Luckily for him the raft was picked up after a few hours drifting on a burning sea by another ship in the convoy. It was not until the following Wednesday that those raft survivors finally made it to Casablanca.

Things got easier after that for my father, arguably for the entire remainder of the war. From Casablanca, he was transported by boat and train to Freetown in Sierra Leone and then onto a port town called Takoradi in what is now Ghana, but was then the British Gold Coast. There, he was shown the jungle wireless hut where he would spend the next two years, furiously tapping out Morse code messages between British High Command in London and the Takoradi Air Base. The base was a staging post for RAF planes flying onto the North Africa campaign or protecting ship convoys in the Atlantic.

It was a routine life, dominated by shift work; but on his days off, R – as many of his fellow servicemen called him just as work colleagues would do later – would slip his Kodak Brownie into a small rucksack and make his way in his pith helmet and baggy shorts into town or into the local fishing villages to take photographs. One day he took a picture of an Ashanti tribeswoman with her three children, on another day the snap of his lens caught a solitary canoe skimming across a lake, on another he captured a beautiful grove of palm trees on a local beach.

Now, though, in 1947, my father was back at home in the village near Banbury after being demobbed. From his diary, it is obvious he was kicking his heels a bit. He spent a lot of time going to football matches like the fixture between Reading and QPR he went to watch at the old Elm Park stadium in Reading; visiting a young woman called Joan in Bedford who always seemed to be out shopping when he turned up; and applying for newspaper jobs again, toying with several different prospects, including the idea of ending up in Maidenhead.

If he had applied for that job and got it, he probably would have spent a lot of his time early on filing stories on the famous flooding of the Thames which devastated the Berkshire town that year. More than 1,400 local homes were underwater after heavy rains in late March, making the town one of the worst affected areas along a river that had burst its banks at numerous points along its 184-mile course. Soldiers from local British and American army bases were hurriedly drafted in to help with the local rescue and relief efforts. They were caught on camera by the Pathe newsreels, pulling boats full of families and possessions along the water-logged streets of the town, and carrying infants to safety in their arms.

The Thames was out of its banks for two weeks.

The waters were safely contained as I walked along the riverside promenade between Boulter's Lock and Maidenhead Bridge sixty or so years later, admiring the large elegant houses alongside it. The dredging of a seven-mile flood relief channel between Maidenhead and Windsor carried out about ten years ago ten seems to have had the desired effect: when places like Oxford and Kelmscott succumbed to the torrential rains of 2007, Maidenhead held out.

After about 15 minutes, I reached the famous bridge, a double-arched red-brick viaduct designed by Isambard Kingdom Brunel in 1838 to carry the trains of the newly-opened Great Western Railway. It was (and remains) an iconic structure, its low bearing and wide arches soon becoming the subject of one of Turner's most famous paintings – Rain, Steam and Speed – which depicts an ephemeral Great Western locomotive steaming across it in a sooty haze of coal dust and golden twilight.

Joseph Mallord William Turner is possibly the most renowned artist of the Thames, depicting the river time and time again during a life spent living beside it. He was born in Maiden Lane, just off the Strand in London in 1775, and died on Cheyne Walk in Chelsea in 1851; and in-between times lived in Brentford, Isleworth and Chiswick. Close our eyes for a moment and we can all picture a Turner painting of the river even if we are not sure it is a Turner – sailing ships out in the stormy estuary, a wherry approaching Millbank at moonlight, and, perhaps the most famous of all, *The Fighting Temeraire*, that image of a ghostly but golden three-mast galleon being pulled to her last berth – the breaker's yard at Rotherhithe – by a dark, squat steam-powered tug. Voted the nation's favourite painting in a poll conducted by Radio 4's Today programme in 2005, it encapsulates the essence that paintings by this inspired son of a London barber were all about: light. The light breaking through the London fog, breaking up into brush strokes of gold, ruddy brown, yellow; the light emanating from a dirty, dark but strangely luminous old river.

James McNeill Whistler saw light too. The American artist whose English ancestors were all buried, if you recall, within the Church of St Mary Virgin in

Whitchurch-on-Thames, painted several moonlit scenes in the 1860s and 1870s of industrial London as seen from a boat out on the river after dark. But in contrast to Turner's vivid romanticism, the light in Whistler's Nocturnes is moodier and more troubled.

A couple of artists in the following century saw the Thames in a different way. Where Turner and Whistler had seen a mysterious luminescence, Paul Nash and Stanley Spencer saw something sacred. I had seen the vision of Nash back at the Wittenham Clumps near Dorchester; and, at Cookham, just the day before, I had seen Spencer's.

There is a gallery dedicated to Spencer in this charming riverside village, the community in which he lived and worked most of his life; and, in this gallery you will see how the artist – who like Nash attended the Slade School of Art just before the First World War and later served in that war – carved out a very original path for himself.

For the Cookham boy, the Thames was like one of the rivers which had originally flowed out of the Garden of Eden, a place where the religious and the secular meet and are united in some sort of holy tryst. In a 1933 painting, a real-life character in the village Granny Tubb is comforted by angels after being frightened half-to-death by a strange sunset caused by the passing of the tail of Halley's Comet. Two years later, there is a painting of St Francis preaching to the birds in the passageway beside Spencer's childhood house, Fernlea; and then there is the unfinished work spreading right across one wall on the middle floor of the gallery, the one of Jesus Christ preaching at the Cookham Regatta in its golden age, the regatta which the artist recalled from his boyhood. For Stanley Spencer, the Thames was the river of heavenly visitations. A sort of church.

—〰—

I enjoyed my hour in the house of Stanley Spencer's imaginings, a former Wesleyan chapel on Cookham High St, the chapel where the artist had worshipped with his mother as a child. I liked his paintings.

But for me, the Thames is most strikingly portrayed in all those railway station posters designed to entice day trippers from grimy London to the river in the 1920s and the 1930s. You know the ones, the ones with voluptuously lime green trees, aquamarine skies and big bold bulbous white clouds.

They were created apparently by a new generation of advertising designers employed by the four big railway companies of the time, who were waking up to new ways of targeting the droves of British people who were now going to the movies at least once a week. Designers like Edward McKnight Kauffer and Charles Mayo working for Great Western in the 1930s added a touch of Hollywood glamour to the familiar, grey landscapes of England. Kauffer's portray of Windsor, for example, had an impossibly blue Thames surrounded by ebullient forest with a bright orange castle peeping out above the canopy, silhouetted against a yellow sky.

There was a growing number of travel publishers too in the 1930s who were selling their guides on the back of their colourful book covers. Sitting in a tiny attic room at the top of an eighteenth century building in Holborn, looking out through one small window onto the sooty chimney pots of Red Lion Square where Edward Weller had produced his maps in the previous century, Brian Cook and his production team did the business for Batsford. One of his most famous covers is a depiction of Ye Old Bell at Hurley, the Thameside village near Marlow, for Batsford's guide to *The Old Inns of England*. This traditional timber-framed coaching inn is transformed into a building of yellow and orange stripes, with purple window lattices and a purple pub sign. The church opposite is bright yellow and the trees surrounding it are a dizzy kaleidoscope of colours.

The map of the Thames, from its source to the sea, engraved by Edward Weller in 1863, was the vision that had brought me to the river; but a little bit of me, I must admit, had wanted to find Brian Cook's or Edward Kauffer's river when I got there. That aspirational, art-deco fantasy of the good life.

Under their guidance, my view of Maidenhead Bridge at this point of my journey would not be of a weather-worn, red-brick structure nailed down in the sediment of a brown river, but a ribbon of bright saffron hovering over azure waters, flowing like blue martini towards Windsor.

Those sturdy black and white mock-Tudor houses on the right bank, meanwhile, would be marshmallow pink and white; and the balding man in a flabby blue T-shirt and baseball cap puffing past me in his sculling boat would be an angular sliver of quartz powering through a river of curling waves.

There were many memorable scenes that afternoon as I walked through the chameleon countryside of my imaginings towards Windsor: the patchwork of emerald green fields to my left, divided up between florid lines of broccoli-shaped bushes; and the neatly trimmed horse chestnut tree at Bray Lock which looked liked one of those exotic palm trees you get in Torquay; and the cabin cruiser which floated past me containing, not as I thought at first glance, a dumpy group of middle-aged friends in beige shorts, but instead a row of Hellenic faces with long thin eyebrows, almond eyes and rosebud lips dressed in light summer dresses and Oriental shawls, accompanied by the long slim silhouettes of men in debonair evening suits.

My journey also took me through avenues of lavender blue trees looking like parasol umbrellas perched on cocktail sticks; gardens of pink roses and olive green topiary; and two bridges, one a baby blue motorway crossing erected in a latter-day brave new world of 1961 and the other, the Summersleaze footbridge, which hovered over the Thames like a watery brushstroke on a scroll of Chinese silk.

I passed an island, I think it was Monkey Island, which was fringed with yellow iris, and I stumbled upon a tree covered in jungle green creepers. I saw the black chrome Gothic towers of the Oakley Court Hotel peeping up behind ultramarine cedars and amber willows, and I saw a golden fleet of motor boats anchored up in the Windsor Marina.

Overhead, in the brilliant blue skies punctuated with delicate streamers of white cloud, planes with a glint of the Caribbean and the Far East in their holds were lowering their landing gear for their final descent into Heathrow.

From the vicinity of the marina, I trekked around the bottom of the Dorney Rowing Lake, which had accompanied me unseen all the way from Summersleaze bridge and past the redundant church of St Mary Magdalene at Boveney with its low flint nave and high timber tower, which was built in Norman times for the bargemen working on the Thames. There is a mystery attached to this church. According to the record books, it had a graveyard in 1859, but since then there has been no hint of consecrated ground. No one can explain how or why.

I was nearing Windsor now. The town's racecourse had now appeared on the far bank and occasionally I would catch a glimpse of St George's Chapel at Windsor Castle on the horizon. Then, accompanied by a flurry of blue dragonflies I turned a corner, and there it was: the magnificent turrets and towers of a bright orange castle sitting on a canopy of ebullient green forest just over the blue Thames from Brocas Meadow.

I collapsed in a heap on the meadow in the sunshine, sipping at my water bottle and gazing exhaustedly over the water.

After a while, though, when I had recovered a little, I got out my notebook and started to record what I had seen on my six-mile walk from Maidenhead. The mysterious church, the jungle-green creepers, Summersleaze Bridge.

The colourful patchwork of fields, the Gothic towers of Oakley Court, the baby blue motorway bridge ... A tall young man was walking past me when I looked up momentarily from my notes.

"What are you doing? Drawing a picture of the castle?" The man, ordinary-looking, really, with a hint of black stubble on his chin, was suddenly beside me. "Oh, writing in your diary, is it? Well, it's a lovely day for it, isn't it? A perfect day for a picnic. Looking over the castle and everything."

"I tell you what," he continued in his wide southern vowels as I struggled for an answer, a little taken aback. "I tell you what. We could get Jesus down and we could have a bash. You, me, Jesus, Peter, and all the other disciples. Right here on the meadow. A nice picnic. A right old bash. What do you think?"

"Er .... yes, sounds like quite a good idea," I stuttered, not knowing quite what to say.

He looked a little disappointed by my hesitation. "We all know each other, you see," he said, in way of explanation. "You, me, Jesus, the disciples."

"Yes, I see," I said.

"Well, anyway," my bringer of strange tidings suddenly decided, perhaps clocking for the first time the baffled look in my eyes. "Well, anyway. I'll tell Jesus that you were here."

With that, he bounced off down the path on which I had just arrived.

Perhaps, I wrote in my travel journal there and then. Perhaps Stanley Spencer was right all along.

Perhaps this was the river of heavenly visitations.

XVII

Runnymede

I'm sure the Queen's apartments at Windsor Castle are very luxurious, but my suite in the Victorian attic rooms of the Clarence Hotel on the outskirts of the town – the last room they had available – was also rather sumptuous, in its own peculiar way.

It was something, I think, to do with the ostentatious sash curtains hung over the window and the mirrored wardrobe in which I hung up my clothes. Or was it the thick green carpet that started in the bedroom and carried on into the bathroom and up the side of the bath?

Or was it the scantily clad beauties dipping into a Roman bath depicted on the bathroom tiles? Or the bath tub itself, fitted out as it was with strange Jacuzzi protrusions looking like something out of communal washroom in a Soviet gulag?

I wasn't sure, but it did make me feel like a Roman emperor who had somehow been transported forward in time to the 1970s. Suitably pampered after a night there, I was set up for another day on the Thames Path.

The path took me first around the perimeter of Windsor Home Park, following the loop of the river here as it circles the promontory on which the royal castle stands. Then it took me across Victoria Bridge onto the left bank and through some thick woodland into the elegant village of Datchet. Here, I stopped for a bite to eat near the village's handsome war memorial which commemorates the 54 local men who died in the First World War and the 30 who died in the Second. Nine months after I passed through, the village green on which the urn-crested memorial proudly stands would be temporarily underwater as a result of the 2014 winter storms and the subsequent Thames flooding.

There used to be a bridge across the river at Datchet, a flimsy wooden affair which collapsed a couple of times before it was finally demolished in the mid-Victorian era when the local road to Windsor was re-routed to make way for the expansion of the castle grounds. After the second collapse in 1834, the councils of Berkshire and Buckinghamshire – the two counties that the river divides at this point – came up with the bright idea of each building their own half, which they did: Berkshire building its half in iron; Buckinghamshire, erecting its bit in wood. Needless to say, the crossings did not meet in the middle, and the final span of Berkshire structure had to be cantilevered so that it would not need support from the Buckinghamshire side.

It quickly became unsafe, so I suppose it was lucky for everyone that Queen Victoria's consort, Prince Albert, forever tinkering with the grounds at the castle, oversaw the building of two replacement bridges in the 1850s, one called Victoria, the one I had just crossed; and the other, naturally enough, called Albert. Albert was a bit like that, forever the one for grand gestures. He master-minded the Great Exhibition of 1851, personally engi-neered the museums quarter in South Kensington and, on a more personal note, bought his wife a beautiful brooch crowned with four Scottish freshwater pearls on their third wedding anniversary. Unfortunately, he died suddenly of typhoid at Windsor Castle at the relatively tender age of 42 in December 1861, and was temporarily entombed at St George's Chapel in the castle before being finally laid to rest a year later in the Frogmore Mausoleum in Home Park. Edward Weller carefully recorded the Victoria and Albert bridges on his map of the Thames in 1863, together with the soon to be non-existent Datchet Bridge. Queen Victoria, meanwhile, commissioned the first of her many mourning jewels featuring black pearls, which she would wear for the rest of her life.

It was on Albert Bridge, downstream from Datchet, that I met a rather jolly middle-aged couple who were cycling around the country lanes between Staines and Windsor. They were very impressed by my mission to walk the length of the river.

"Remember to stop when you get to the end. Don't want you ending up in France," the woman beamed.

"Oh, no. You wouldn't want to do that," agreed her partner, wincing at the prospect.

"At the rate I'm walking at the moment, I'll be lucky if I get to Old Windsor," I laughed.

But I did get to Old Windsor, a couple of kilometres downstream. And not long after that, I got to a wide green meadow called Runnymede.

—∿∿—

The energetic proprietor of the Magna Carta Tea Room at Runnymede recognised my type immediately. "Walking the Thames, are you?" he asked, eyeing me up and down, as he served me up a very welcome pot of tea.

"Er, yes. Do you get many of us?" I asked. I was curious actually because so far I had only seen two other walkers who were obviously doing the whole journey – two men wearing red charity T-shirts near Marlow. Everybody else, as far as I could tell, had just been walking the dog, or was out on a weekend ramble.

"Only thousands of you every year," he said, smiling. "But you're the lucky one. Most of the other walkers stumble in, usually. Drenched from the rain lashing down outside. You've got fantastic weather for it."

I did have fantastic weather. The sunny skies, which had first appeared on that dreamy day in Sonning, had continued to follow me to this point; and after my cup of tea I was quickly out again to enjoy it a bit more, crossing the meadow and climbing half-way up a hill to a Doric-style temple sheltering in a glade of oak-trees, from where I looked out in the bright sunlight over the plain of Runnymede.

It was hereabouts, or perhaps on the wooded island in the middle of the river which I could just glimpse from my vantage point, that King John on 15 June 1215 was forced to sign the Magna Carta limiting his absolute and arbitrary powers and proclaiming the equality of all men before the law. Although the historic document contains much that is rather specific to thirteenth century England – promises to abolish evil goings on in forests and so on – clause 39, which states that "no free man shall be taken, imprisoned, outlawed, banished or in any way destroyed, nor will we proceed against or prosecute him, except by lawful judgement of his equals and by the law of the land", is the clause that underpins the founding charter of every modern democratic society and would-be democratic society around the world.

The whole area – from the island in the middle of the river to the JF Kennedy and Commonwealth Airforces memorials hidden in the trees around me and the Greek-style columns I stood between – is dedicated to the lofty ideals of freedom and democracy. And as if to nail home the point, at either end of the meadow rose those amazingly lofty chimneys again, the trademark stamp of Edwin Lutyens that I had first seen back at the Deanery in Sonning, perched on top of the Fairhaven Memorial Lodges that he designed as gateways for the area in the early 1930s.

With their steeply angled roofs and long chimneys, they bore all the hallmarks of the country house he designed for Sonning, combining a sense of the traditional English vernacular with a grand neo-classicism.

But by the early 1930s, Lutyens was no longer the architect of English country homes. He had become the architect of empire, who had only recently returned from the opening of the new city he had designed in British India. In January 1913, he and the architect Herbert Baker had been commissioned to build a new capital in Delhi, and since then Lutyens had spent half his working life in India.

It was the hope of the Foreign Office civil servants who had employed him that Lutyens would incorporate Indian styles in his architecture in the same way as Victorian architects had done in their great civic works in India in the previous century – buildings such as the Gilbert Scott-designed university in Bombay. On his first two visits to India, however, the Bloomsbury-based architect was decidedly sniffy about all the Oriental domes and Mughal pinnacles that adorned the Victorian buildings of Bombay. "All pattern" and "veneered joinery", he sneered.

But on his third passage to the sub-continent at the end of 1913, he and his collaborator, Herbert Baker, went on a Christmas tour of the holy city of Varanasi, Lucknow, and the Buddhist centres of Sarnath and Bodhgaya; and for the first time the two architects were captivated. Lutyens admired the Buddhist stupa at Sarnath; it later became the inspiration for his dome at Delhi. The next day in Bodhgaya, where the Buddha attained his enlightenment, Lutyens saw the stone railings built for Ashoka, the Buddhist king of the once mighty Maurya Empire; he later threw up something similar around the perimeter of the Great Place in New Delhi.

It did not stop there. The leaf pattern of the pipal tree – the tree under which the Buddha sat – reappeared in the new Indian capital as did the geometrical patterns of the Hindu temples of Varanasi.

The city that Lutyens and Baker built was finally opened in January 1931, a monumental synthesis of modern western classicism and traditional eastern design.

Monumental, but also subtle. Not long after he attended the official opening, Lutyens was still distancing himself from the grand designs of his Victorian predecessors. "There are two ways of building in India," he said, "one to parade your buildings in fancy dress at a Fancy Ball, mixing dates and styles .... or to build as an Englishman dressed for the climate, conscious only that your tailor is of Agra or Benares, and not of Savile Row or Petticoat Lane."

—m—

Englishmen had been dressing for the climate in India ever since an administrator with the East India Company called Job Charnock founded Calcutta as a British trading post in 1690, and a captain in the Company army Robert Clive won the Battle of Plassey in 1757 which delivered large swathes of Bengal into the hands of the bankers and merchants sitting thousands of miles away in Leadenhall Street in the City of London.

By the time Edward Weller was drafting out his maps of the subcontinent, British power – despite the little local difficulty of the Indian Mutiny in 1857 – was well-established across the length and breadth of its sun-parched plains, criss-crossing them with its railways and firmly anchoring the port cities of Bombay, Calcutta and Madras to its international network of commerce and trade. Even as the Red Lion Square cartographer drafted out a map of southern India in 1863 for the Dispatch Atlas, work was beginning on a telegraph connection between London and Calcutta.

The map – a copy of which I picked up in the antiques shop off St Martin's Lane for £9 not long after I had discovered Weller's Thames chart – was, like his illustration of the English river, full of Victorian bustle. There was the railway line running all the way from Bombay on the west coast to Madras on the east, which had been achieved in 1862 by the linking up of the Great Indian Peninsula Railway and the Madras Railway. There was a large area called Nizam's Dominions, which was one of the princely puppet states that the British Raj had set up in India. In addition, there was a very useful inset sketch which helpfully illustrated the three administrative units by which the British ruled India – the Madras, Bombay and Bengal presidencies.

Beneath the veneer of British India, however, there was also a much older country peeping out from underneath the mapmaker's tidy Victorian grid. You could see it. There was a place etched out in tiny writing called Trichnopoly, which was originally a rock fort temple built by the ancient Hindu kingdom of Pallava. There was the age-old Portuguese community in Panjim, hugging the banks of the Mandovi River in Goa. There was Cochin, which for many centuries was the key port for spices being traded between the Spice Islands of the Indonesian archipelago in the east and Arabian and Greek merchants in the west. There was also, on Weller's inset sketch of India in its entirety, the great Ganga herself, oozing somnambulant down from the Himalayas, the bedrock of so many ancient civilisations, and the sustenance of the Mughal Empire before the arrival of the British.

And like all those ancient civilisations and the Mughal Empire before it, the British Raj would soon be gone. As Edward Weller drafted out his chart of India, it was entering the zenith of its power – the port cities, particularly Bombay, were flourishing; the railway network was expanding at a rapid rate; and trade was booming as the British took advantage of the great riches of the country: its timber, its famed textiles and its Golkonda gem mines, as well as the pearl fisheries between the Coromandel Coast and Ceylon. Yet, within a few years a million people had died in the devastating famine of 1866-7 in Orissa, and many more would die in a series of famines which would plague the country for the remainder of the century, caused not only by the failure of the monsoons, so crucial to Indian agriculture, but also by an economic system – the same system that William Cobbett had described in Cricklade back in the 1820s – which demanded that rural grain stores be continually emptied to satisfy the forward contracts of merchants and exporters sitting in far-off Calcutta or Bombay.

And then there was the sticky issue of that document called the Magna Carta. The liberal vision underpinning British rule in India – and also Lutyens' new city containing the Indian Parliament buildings – was that Britain's long march to liberty which had started with the Magna Carta and proceeded through a series of electoral reform acts and a tangle of laws covering education, justice and so on would be reproduced in Asia.

It is well-documented that this vision was never quite delivered, the economic exploitation of Britain's foremost colony always being the priority. Within 20 years of the unveiling of New Delhi, the British Raj had packed up its bags and left.

XVIII

Approaching London

"I hear this ferry service is very old," I said, passing the time of day with the white-haired man with a sharp nose who was at the wheel of tiny motor launch shuttling me across the river from Shepperton to Weybridge.

"Yes, it's even older than me," the man joked, alluding to a boat crossing that has been running almost continuously for 500 years.

Then, before he could say any more, we were on the other bank.

It was a very short trip, but as I soon realised, it carried a significant change in the character of the river. From Staines, where I had woken up that morning in a room in the riverside Swan Hotel which sloped at a slightly alarming angle towards the water, the Thames curls through the last vestiges of rural England – the fertile loop of Penton Hook, the bramble of Dumsey Meadow – before finally shrugging off the shackles of provincialism at the bottom of Ferry Lane where I had asked about the venerable boat crossing.

Once on the other bank – in Weybridge – the character of the river changed dramatically. The pleasant riverside bungalows and houses which had accompanied me through Windsor and Staines gave way to grey buildings and construction sites; the perfumed aromas of the water meadows gave way to the asphalt smells of suburbia; and the great metropolis of London, the traffic, the dirt, I could feel, was beginning to close in around me. In Edward

Weller's day, Shepperton and Walton, towards which I was heading, were just tiny hamlets in a tapestry of green fields; but, today, 150 years later, my final approach into London was palpable.

I surrendered to it, allowing myself to be washed downriver, constantly being deposited, resettled, moved on. One moment, I found myself amid the clanging and thudding of the new bridge being built at Walton; the next, I was walking under a line of trees filled with squawking parakeets, which apparently have become a feature of the London suburbs in recent years though nobody knows quite how.

I stopped for a drink at a pub called The Weir whose landlord was fighting a campaign to stop a football stadium being built by the local council on the green land behind his hostelry and I stopped again at Sunbury Lock with its view of the distinctive eighteenth century tower of St Mary's Church in Sunbury on the north bank.

From there, I moved on in the shadow of a long grey wall – old reservoirs and gravel pits lurking behind it – towards Molesey, the path eventually opening out into a pleasant grassy strip which was once part of Hurst Park Racecourse; here, in Weller's time, were held the very popular Hampton Races, a sort of poor man's Ascot where the silks and satins worn by the ladies were imitation and where, instead of champagne in the hospitality tent, amusements were those laid on by travelling gypsies – drinking booths, horse circuses and carnival masks.

Over on the other side of the water, I could see the out-lines of a domed temple built in 1756 by the famous actor-manager David Garrick to celebrate the work of William Shakespeare; and not long afterwards, I was walking alongside the colourful houseboats moored up on Taggs Island, originally developed in the 1850s and 1860s by a boatbuilder called Thomas Tagg and now jointly owned by the houseboat residents.

It would not be long now, I knew, before I would catch my first glimpse of Hampton Court. I passed East Molesey Cricket Club, which played its first game in 1735, and then it was there, in the distance – the familiar Tudor chimney pots of the royal palace, and, in front of it, Hampton Bridge, arching over the water in the mizzle of a grey, damp day. It was busy with traffic. It was busy with red London buses.

—⁂—

The royal palace of Hampton Court, which in the Victorian era was thrown open to London day-trippers arriving on the South Western Railway, is, of course, associated with one particular English monarch more than any other: Henry VIII. This Tudor king of legendary excess engineered a huge expansion of the palace that he appropriated from his chief minister, Cardinal Wolsey, in 1528, adding the Great Hall, hundreds of rooms and pleasure gardens. Over the next 20 years, he would entertain a succession of for-eign ambassadors here as well as a procession of unfortu-nate wives.

So it was of no great surprise that after tramping the streets trying to find a place to stay in Hampton, I eventually wound up in a hotel room named after his third wife, Jayne Seymour. It was in a 300-year old establishment next to the Lions Gate called the Kings Arms, which helpfully told me all about her in a booklet they provided on a table in the room. The 19-year old Seymour, it said, died of post-natal complications at Hampton Court in October 1537, less than two weeks after giving birth to a baby boy. Her labour had been difficult, lasting two days and three nights, and it is rumoured that she died after King Henry, in his desperation for a male heir, had ordered the baby to be cut from her to prevent a stillbirth.

The final irony is that the boy went on to become the sickly Edward VI, while the daughter of Anne Boleyn who Henry had had executed the year before became the very able Queen Elizabeth I, who presided over an English golden age of literature and exploration.

Still, I went down to the bar that evening determined to honour the infamous King Hal in some way, and after looking through the menu, chanced on the idea that I might do it through some kind of empathetic gluttony. Confit of pork belly with crispy crackling, Ox cheek stew – the menu was full of promise.

In the end, however, I opted for fish and chips. Hearty and filling as this was, I would not, I knew, begin to rival the roasted swan or peacock that Harry would have opted to order for his bar snack, or even hold a candle to the copious amounts of ale and red wine with which he would have washed it all down.

Then, perhaps, the king would have been taken by royal barge in the twilight to one of his other palaces on the royal river – downstream perhaps to Richmond Palace or upstream to Windsor – serenaded as he went by the lutes of his court musicians.

I made do with a Phil Collins ballad wobbling through the bar sound systems. I'd had two pints of beer, though, and by the third stanza my eyes had begun to moisten with the beauty of everything.

XIX

The View from the Hill

If in Tudor times, the Thames was the river of royal palaces – Hampton, Richmond, St James, the Tower and so on – by the eighteenth century it was also the playground of aristocrats. Great houses sprang up all along the river's approach into London – grand affairs with turrets and stone doorways as well as picturesque gardens which tried to reproduce the imagined pastoral paradise of Arcadia in Ancient Greece.

These were still the major feature in 1863 when Edward Weller faithfully recorded them. You get a glimpse on his map of the Stuart-era Ham House in Richmond, the neo-Gothic Strawberry Hill House in Twickenham, the neo-Palladian Chiswick House built by the third Earl of Burlington in 1729, and Syon House in Brentford. Syon House was where Henry VIII's coffin was brought in 1547 on its final journey to Windsor only to be licked clean by wild dogs after it burst open during the night.

After all, there wasn't much else to record in terms of human settlement on this stretch of the river in 1863. Although Surbiton, Kingston, Teddington, Twickenham, Richmond and Kew all appear on Weller's map, they are represented as small clusters of buildings surrounded by fields and country lanes.

Change came very quickly, however, after the 1860s, driven inevitably by the railway tracks steaming out of London on Weller's map – the Windsor Line, the London & South Western Railway and the North & South Western Junction Railway – as well as by the momentous opening of the Metropolitan Underground line in 1863. In the last quarter of the nineteenth century, Weller's fields and hamlets were swept away by a relentless tide of suburbia. Once Wandsworth, Putney and Barnes downriver had fallen to the developer, it was only a matter of time for Kingston, Kew and Richmond.

Inevitable as it all seemed, though, the pastoral character of much of this stretch of the metropolitan Thames has held out to a large extent, due in part to a famous campaign led by local people to save 'the view from Richmond Hill' from the developers at the turn of the twentieth century, which led to the Richmond, Ham and Petersham Open Spaces Act of 1902. This piece of legislation is seen as one of the earliest and one of the most successful environmental campaigns in British history.

It was a campaign I had to thank when I boarded a ferry at Hampton on a sunny June Saturday a century later, and was accompanied by bright greenery for most of my journey until I reached the vicinity of Kingston upon Thames.

Kingston itself was full of new development – smart riverside apartments, shopping malls and multi-storey car parks – but it wasn't long after I got off the New Orleans-styled 'Yarmouth Belle' at the town's pier that I was in parkland again, in the form of Canbury Gardens, and rambling on through a swathe of emerald green riverbank running alongside a deep blue river dotted with the white sails of weekend pleasure dinghies.

Half a mile north of Kingston – exactly – I stumbled across an elm tree named as 'the half mile tree' on a plaque in front of it because it was exactly equidistant between Kingston and Teddington Lock. Apparently the original elm tree on this spot, which had been recorded in 1863 by an ordnance survey map, had been 500 years old. The elm in front of me though, was a younger version, planted in 1952 to replace the original which had fallen into a dangerous condition.

Half a mile later – exactly – I was at Teddington Lock.

—◠◠—

Teddington was the largest, most complex lock that I had come across on my entire walk down the River Thames, and the reason for it was summed up by a makeshift clock stuck on the wall of the lockkeeper's cottage. Its hands were set at a quarter to four – the time of the next high water.

This is where the soft rippling waterway of the shires finishes, and the tidal river begins. From now on, the water levels would rise and fall twice a day in sympathy with the highs and lows of the North Sea surging into the Thames Estuary. As a result, the builders of the modern complex in 1857 planned three locks: a conventional launch lock, a narrow skiff lock and a very large sea-going barge lock which is 198 metres long and holds eight million litres of water. Its weir, meanwhile, is the largest on the river with 20 electrically operated sluice gates capable of letting 55 billion litres of water through a day at peak flow.

The lock has a bit of heroic history attached to it too, being the assembly point for a flotilla of a hundred small private boats bound for Dunkirk in 1940. They were organised by the Tough Brothers boatyard at Teddington Wharf, joining the thousands of motor boats, lighters and barges which chugged across the channels to rescue the thousands of French and British troops stuck on the beaches of northern France.

Once past the lock, the river leaves the jurisdiction of the Environment Agency and falls under the authority of the Port of London; but the scenery did not change much as I tramped on towards my bed for the night in Richmond. The towpath was still draped with the vivid finery of alder, ash and willow, and the riverbanks still carpeted with cow parsley, nettles and dock leaves. The brick and concrete of the gathering metropolis were pushed away to fringes, and, if anything, were in even further retreat as I entered the prospect from Richmond Hill.

I was by the foot ferry crossing to Twickenham at this point, listening to loud rock music pumping out from somewhere on the opposite shoreline. A festival or something like that? I decided that once I had checked into my hotel in Richmond I would head out again to try to find out what was going on.

The elegant Stuart mansion of Ham House was now on my right hand side, and a few steps further on I was skirting Petersham Meadows, behind which, somewhere in the trees, was the Star & Garter, a former care home which has recently been sold to a London property developer, but in Edward Weller's time, one of the most fashionable hotels for miles around, attracting royalty and aristocracy from all over Europe. It was a particular favourite of Charles Dickens who held several celebration dinners there, including one to mark the publication of David Copperfield in 1850. Weller duly marked it on his map.

I could not see the building but perhaps people standing on Richmond Hill could, thanks to the efforts of the local campaigners in 1902 to save the Petersham meadows and therefore the view from the hill.

They would not have been able to see me, or if they could, I would have appeared as just a tiny speck on the horizon, but I certainly could see Richmond now. Neat rows of Victorian and Georgian town houses spread softly over the sides of a green limestone ridge.

—␣␣␣—

As soon as I had checked into my hotel, I headed out again, as I had promised myself, in search of the music I had heard over the water that afternoon. More in hope than expectation, I took a bus to Twickenham town centre and from there walked down to the waterfront, which faces one of the Thames' many islands or 'aits' as they are sometimes called.

My fears were confirmed as I turned the corner of Wharf Lane and onto the Twickenham embankment. The festival, the show – whatever it had been – was packing up.

"Have I missed all the fun?" I asked a grumpy-looking man loading a drum kit onto a truck.

"Twickenham Festival. Finished," he grunted sharply. And I could see he was right – food stalls, arts and crafts stalls, the music stage, all being taken down by their owners, and by the band roadies, now eager to get home after a long day of revelry. Disappointed, my eyes wandered over to the island in the middle of the river.

A few yards up, there was an arching footbridge over to it. I took it, and moments later was on a shadowy pathway twisting and turning between the tin shacks and low bungalows of the legendary Eel Pie Island.

In Weller's day, the island was a popular resort for boating parties brought by pleasure steamer from central London to enjoy a day out eating – you guessed it – eel pies, under the shade of the willow trees or perhaps enjoying the music that was laid on at the Eel Pie Hotel, which had been put up in 1830. Charles Dickens described the hotel as a "place to dance to the music of the locomotive band". Presumably, he meant the brass bands that often played at the opening of a new railway station in the nineteenth century, which would be followed by pompous Victorian speeches and celebratory dinners.

But it wasn't brass that made Eel Pie Island famous. It was jazz and blues. In 1956, trumpeter Brian Rutland, who ran a local band called The Grove Jazz Band, started up free jazz sessions at the island's old hotel, building on the tea dances held there in the 1920s and 1930s; and soon afterwards impresario Arthur Chisnall took over the running of the club, booking in some of the big names of the time such as George Melly, Acker Bilk and Cy Laurie. Melly described the ramshackle hotel with its ornate columns and arches as being like something out of a moody Deep South Tennessee Williams play.

In the decade that followed, jazz gave way to R&B and rock and roll, and the headline acts became many of our household names. The Who and The Rolling Stones played on the island. So did David Bowie and Eric Clapton.

In 1967, however, the venue was forced to close down because the owner could not meet £200,000 worth of repairs required by the police, and the old hotel was occupied by squatters. There was a brief revival two years later when the club reopened as Colonel Barefoot's Rock Garden, but in 1971, faced with a demolition order, the Eel Pie Island Hotel burnt down in mysterious circumstances.

To this day, though, the island retains its off-beat character. It is an eclectic mix of modest bungalows and rundown shacks with tin roofs, which sustains a number of artists' studios and a couple of boatyards.

—ᵚᵚ—

Eel Pie is the sort of place that the two volunteers I met the next morning on a tug boat moored up in Richmond were fighting to preserve. They were Honor, a rather distinguished looking woman possibly in her 70s, and Helen, I think that was her name, a 30-something with lively eyes and a pinched nose, who were members of a local environmental group called The River Thames Visitor Centre.

"It's happening all the way up and down the river," Helen explained as I wandered around the small exhibition the group had set up in the cabin of the boat they had renovated. "Luxury flats and private moorings pushing out the old communities, the traditional boatbuilders, the houseboat owners."

"There's a boatbuilder up the river from here," she added, waving her hand animatedly. "He's been here for generations, and the developer of some luxury flats next door comes along and wants to reduce his working hours because he's disturbing their residents. I mean, he was there first."

Her comrade in arms, Honor, smiled sweetly. "Do you like our boat?" she said, changing the subject. "It's a lighter, one of the vessels that would have shipped all sorts of things to and from the docks up in London. Taking things like Welsh coal up to the docks, and coming back with rubbish to be disposed of from central London."

I said I did.

"Would you like to support us? Just a pound, and we can put you on our email list, keep you informed of our activities. We rely on voluntary contributions, you see."

"Don't you get any support from the local council or other bodies?" I asked.

Helen interrupted. "Support from the council? You must be joking," she laughed. "They're more interested in flogging off expensive riverside real estate than protecting the river!"

"Well, they have invited us onto a consultation committee," Honor added quickly.

"Oh, yes, they have, I suppose." Helen calmed a little, taking the cue from Honor's soothing tones.

"Well, I think you're doing great work here," I said, taking note of all the diagrams and pictures of the Thames environment that formed part of their interesting exhibition.

And I did think they were doing good work.

The Thames needed people like Honor and Helen to continue the fight to protect its environment and preserve its traditional ways of life, I thought. Just as it needed the residents of Hedsor Road in Bourne End to save their community pub, and needed the people of Richmond at the turn of the twentieth century to fight for the view from the hill.

They were important struggles. Because you never know what you've lost, until you've lost it.

XX

Kew

Soon after leaving Honor and Helen in their lighter, I passed under Twickenham Bridge and was walking along the fringes of Richmond Deer Park. A cormorant was holding its large black wings out to dry on a tree as I tramped past Richmond Lock. A heron stood totally motionless by a swampy ditch to the side of the towpath, his eyes fixed on the water. It was focused on the business of the day.

In contrast, the memorial engravings on the line of wooden benches that now accompanied me on the footpath were preoccupied with another day, with people who were once fathers, mothers, brothers, sisters, best friends, but had now passed away. As so often during my marathon walk, I found the Thames to be a river of remembrance as much as a river of the present. There is something about this line of water, it seems, that makes people erect memorials to lost ones along its shores. Churchyards often overlook its banks, a flag hangs at its confluence with the River Thame remembering the fallen in Borneo in the Second World War, and there are numerous statues all along its course, not only remembering the famous and the eminent, but also remembering relatively ordinary people such as the very moving statue to four schoolboys who died in a skiing accident that I stumbled across on Ray Mill Island by Boulter's Lock in Maidenhead. I suppose it's because a river often contains the recollections of our happiest days, playing on its banks maybe, walking hand-in-hand with a lover along its shoreline, wobbling in that day-hire punt, laughing because you have just managed to avoid the slipstream that was heading for the weir. The river just keeps rolling on, but we stop and stare into its reflections, finding in them the days we once held in rapture.

So, now I was walking past a line of benches which remembered those treasured days with loved ones. There was Bill Cashman, who was born in 1944 and died in 2008. His epitaph was 'Two of a Kind'. I had no idea what it meant until I reached the next bench along where there was an inscription to someone who was possibly his son. It read 'Matt Cashman 1976-2005' and his tribute was 'Unforgettable' and then 'Bodhisattva', which I presume was some reference to Buddhism.

A Greg Hutt was remembered a few benches along. But for some reason he was better known to his friends as Jabba the Pizza. He had died in 2009 at the tender age of 38 or 39, but leaving, it seemed, some invaluable advice for his friends. "Live your dream, travel the world, I'll be watching you", read the words carved into the wood.

The next bench was an appreciation of a Bruce Boa who was born in 1930 and passed away in 2004. His eulogy was a simple one. "Go with the flow," it said.

I followed the advice, and was soon passing Old Isleworth on the opposite shoreline, its Georgian houses and medieval church tower peeping out coyly from behind another Thames island. Then there were three tower blocks in Brentford on the horizon, and a little after that the entrance to Kew Gardens.

—m—

The Royal Botanic Gardens at Kew came into being in the mid-eighteenth century at a time of growing fascination with China and the Islamic world, two regions just opening up to western trade. It was an enthusiasm that an ambitious young architect called William Chambers reflected in the buildings he designed for the gardens, throwing up next to classical buildings such as Kew's famous Orangery a model of the Alhambra and his own version of a Chinese pagoda. The pagoda was ten storeys high and originally sported gilded wooden dragons hanging from the roof of each tier until they vanished one day, some say to pay off the debts of the spendthrift George IV.

Kew really came into its own, though, in the Victorian era with the construction of the two iconic glasshouses – the Temperate House and the Palm House – and the river steamers, which brought hundreds of thousands of visitors to the gardens every year.

I took time out from the Thames Path for a couple of hours to amble around them too. I've never been an expert on plants and trees, but I do love tropical palms – particularly after my time working in Singapore – so I decided that at least the Palm House would justify the rather steep entry fee.

As it turned out, I enjoyed all of it. I circled William Chambers' pagoda and also walked up to his classical temple, the Temple of Aeolus, which is named after the

Greek god of the winds. I wandered 59 feet up in the air around the highest branches of Kew's tallest trees, courtesy of its treetop walkway; and then safely on terra firma again chanced upon a pagoda tree – a gnarled, sinister looking thing propped up on metal struts, which probably reflects its ghoulish reputation. In Chinese folklore, demons are drawn to it. The last Ming emperor, Chongzhen, hanged himself from a pagoda tree after peasants stormed the Forbidden City in 1644.

Eventually, I got to the Palm House. I stepped into its warm, moist embrace, which reminded me immediately of roaming around the last untamed pockets of jungle remaining on the island of Singapore, and lost myself in the palms – coconut palms, queen palms, triangle palms from Madagascar, their deep verdant fronds gleaming in the white light spilling in through the grand atrium. There were other plants with them. Bamboo and rattan springing out of the greenery. Prickly jackfruit and bulbous papaya and mango hanging from trees, all fighting for space in the indoor rainforest.

There was also a pipal or Bo tree, the shade of which sheltered the Buddha around two and a half thousand years ago when he reached nirvana, and whose pinkish young leaves much later inspired the colour scheme of Edwin Lutyen's new city at Delhi. These leaves begin their life growing on the branches of another tree, slowly intertwining with it until they eventually smother it.

Before leaving, I stopped beside the distinctively slender stalk of a rubber tree. There is an interesting story attached to this plant, sprouting from the development of Kew Gardens into the main seed laboratory for the British Empire and the growing demand for rubber in the late Victorian era. In 1876, Kew raised 70,000 seeds which had been swiped, at the instigation of the India Office in London, by explorer Henry Wickham from a cluster of Hevea brasiliensis trees in Brazil. Only 2,800 germinated, but this was enough to ship on to the Peradeniya Botanic Gardens in the British colony of Ceylon (now Sri Lanka) as well as British Malaya, where they flourished in the tropical heat and formed the foundation of a highly successful rubber plantation industry. To this day Asia produces 90 per cent of the world's supply of rubber despite the fact that this sticky, elastic material isn't native to it. Also to this day Brazil regards Wickham as a 'bio-pirate'.

The semi-clandestine consignment of rubber seedlings arrived in Ceylon on a British ship in September 1876. A few months later, the botanical painter Marianne North, whose artwork is now exhibited at Kew, arrived in the colony on her way back from Japan, coincidentally spending some time staying at the house of an English judge near the Peradeniya gardens.

Born in Hastings in 1830, North had spent a good deal of her life putting together sketchbooks of her extensive travels in Europe and the Middle East with her father, the Liberal MP Frederick North; but upon his death in 1869 she decided to turn her hobby into a mission, devoting the rest of her life to travelling around the globe in search of rare flowers and plants to paint. Painting, she said, was "a drug like dram drinking, almost impossible to leave off once it gets possession".

The result of this obsession was an extraordinary set of paintings drawn from an astonishing series of trips, which took her over the next decade to, among other places, Jamaica, Brazil, Borneo, Java, Malaysia, Sri Lanka, India, Australia and South Africa. She was a driven woman by all accounts, charming but also autocratic and unconventional; a woman who spurned the official residences overseas which were open to someone of her social standing in favour of boarding houses, the homes of friends and acquaintances, even a remote jungle hut. In an age when women rarely travelled alone, it is said that she revelled in the adventure of it all.

In 1879 she offered her collection to Kew Gardens; and, in the same year, work started on an art gallery to house it.

The Marianne North Gallery, a villa containing 837 paintings depicting 900 species of plant, was my final port of call at Kew Gardens, and in a way the most interesting. Open the wide wooden door, and you find yourself in a cabinet of curiosities containing tier-upon-tier of brightly-coloured paintings stretching up to large clerestory windows just under the ceiling. Walk around and you will come across the most vivid and most diverse selection of exotic plant and tree pictures that you are ever likely to encounter. There are close-ups of a red water lily in southern India and one of the red flowers of a Madagascar tree; there are oils of cacti and white rhododendrons; there is a pretty rendition of an aloe flower in Tenerife, also a sketch of the fearful Seychelles pitcher plant, lid open in readiness to seduce its victim to climb inside and be dissolved in its horrible digestive fluids.

And if birds and trees are more your thing, there are those too – humming birds hovering around a Brazilian climbing shrub in one picture, an African baobab tree in the garden of an Indian princess in another.

Sometimes, though, Marianne North pulled back from her close-ups to give a wide-panning shot of a landscape. There were florid interpretations of the Taj Mahal and Jaipur, and also one of the Sarawak River in Kuching, which looked as beautiful and as sultry as I remembered it from my visit to Borneo a couple of years before.

There was another scene that I recognised. It caught my eye as I was glancing through the Ceylon section. Picture 229. A moon-crescent sweep of beach, a wide grove of coconut palms leaning towards the sea, a rocky outcrop at one end of the bay. It was billed as 'a coconut grove on the south coast near Galle' or something like that. I knew it immediately. It was Unawatuna.

—⟋⟍⟍—

There are many levels of reality – the sacred and the profane, the metaphysical and the everyday. So much so that it is difficult to accept one in favour of another: instead we have to accept the utter strangeness of things.

This is the world-shattering conclusion that a travelling companion called Tom and I reached one evening in the coastal village of Unawatuna in 1991 over our second large bottle of beer, our reasoning aided by the strange quality of the evening and the three weeks we had spent drifting without a care in the world around the beautiful tropical island of Sri Lanka. We were eating rice and curry by candlelight (the local electricity generator had broken down) in an eighteenth century Dutch-built bungalow, while the monsoon gales blew outside and torrential rains thundered down on the terracotta roof above our heads.

The night was to turn stranger still. Finishing our meal, and with the rain abating, we left the guest house to take the path to the hotel on the seafront where we would meet with people whose acquaintance we had made on the beach that afternoon. It was a 15 minute walk through the coconut palms, passing makeshift wooden shacks and shops, catching a glimpse now and then of the crescent beach through the trees. Halfway along, there was a long stone wall which enclosed a house set back from the path shrouded in darkness. Beyond the house there were more colonial Dutch bungalows, one of which had a picture of a young man in an army uniform on its gatepost; he was a government recruit who had been killed in an enemy ambush in the island's long-running civil war with the Tamil Tigers. We stopped for a while to look at his picture, before slipping through the final stretch of houses and onto the beach front.

At the hotel we met four Londoners and a German guy. I forget all their names now, but two of the Londoners had been working in Australia and New Zealand and were now slowly making their way back to Britain via Asia. The other two were a gay couple who both worked for a housing association in the British capital and were on four week holiday in Sri Lanka.

We spent the evening eating and drinking well, watching the stormy waves break against the reef out to sea and swapping stories. The young German, who had relatives in high places in Sri Lanka, talked about the political problems in the country; the London couples spoke of their regrets of returning to the grey skies of London; and Tom and I told the others of our travels: how we had caught the train up to the city of Kandy on the edges of the Sri Lankan tea country, where we had joined in with its Buddhist Poya Day celebrations beside its pretty lake, and then caught another train rattling through the lime green plantations up to the former hill station of Nuwara Eliya, founded by the British as a cool sanctuary away from the rest of their colony sweating down on the plains. All these places were incorporated on the map which Edward Weller drew up in 1863 for the *Dispatch Atlas* of Ceylon, as Sri Lanka was known then, except for the incredible railway lines that British engineers threaded through the island's hill country, looping across gorges and around waterfalls and through the middle of pine forests and tea estates. The first line was built in 1864.

We all talked late into the night, the candles on our table flickering and the wooden hotel verandah, which would be destroyed later on in the 2004 tsunami, creaking under the pressure of the monsoon winds. The village's electricity generator was still out of action, so every time a candle was blown out by the wind, a waiter rushed over to relight it.

Finally, around two in the morning, the waiters started packing up the chairs, setting them up on the tables. Our friends retired to their rooms in the beach resort, and Tom and I set off alone again for our walk back to our guest house.

Although there was a full moon it was very dark. We tried to scramble on the beach where the moonlight was flicking off the water but the waves kept sweeping us off our feet so we cut in again beside the shacks and onto the path. Everywhere was deserted – people had long gone to bed. The wind continued to blow strongly.

Suddenly we both saw a figure on the path some thirty metres ahead. It looked like an ageing Sri Lankan man wearing a sarong, but there must have been something unusual about him because I remember asking Tom: "What's that?"

"I don't know," he answered. This was definitely something strange – an old man wandering alone through beach palms in the monsoon season at two in the morning. We both hesitated, and thought about turning back to the beach again.

The figure, meanwhile, seemed to notice us, and he got off the path, now standing to the side of it.

There really was no way we could return to the beach with the tide coming in, so we carried on until we were a few steps away from him.

And then we realised. It seems amazing to relate now, but the figure was grey from head to foot, and I was sure that I could see straight through him to the trees behind. He said nothing, and on a second feverish glance, he seemed to be hovering, not standing on the ground. Just a sarong floating above a sandy footpath. I turned to Tom. "It's a f.....g ghost," I said.

"Yes," he said.

And then we were running as fast as we could. Running past the Dutch bungalows, past the shacks, past the photograph of the soldier who had been killed by the Tamil Tigers.

We were still running when we saw our guest house ahead of us and we continued running until we had reached the gate to the front garden.

We shut the door of our shared room firmly behind us. What had we seen? We weren't really sure, but one thing was certain: neither of us slept that night.

—m—

I could barely walk, let alone run 22 years later on the Thames Path between Kew and Putney. My ramble around Kew Gardens must have added another couple of miles to a ten-mile journey from Richmond to my cheap hotel off Putney High Street, and I was feeling it. At first, it was only my feet that ached, but by Mortlake it was my ankles, my hips and my back too. By the time I reached Hammersmith Bridge, every step I took was like wading through a particularly thick porridge. I think I may have mentioned that I am more of an ambler than a serious walker, and from Hammersmith onwards all I could dream of was a bed waiting for me at the end. Given those sentiments, it was of course inevitable that my progress seemed achingly slow, every step forward somehow metamorphosing into two steps back. Barnes Bridge, Hammersmith Bridge, Putney Bridge all slipped further into the distance as I struggled towards them while the Sunday joggers skipping past me had reached them and were on their way back before I could offer them a grimace. With my antique map in mind, I tried to imagine the ghosts of the 1863 University Boat Race spectators lining the banks between Mortlake and Putney – which, won by Oxford, was rowed downstream that year – offering me some sort encouragement, cheering me on; but it didn't really work and the vision of resting my aching feet on a lovely, soft bed prevailed.

If my dreams were of a bed, though, William Morris's hopes for this stretch of the river was of a future utopia. The famous interior designer who, you may remember, started his professional life in offices opposite those of Edward Weller on Red Lion Square, spent much of his later life in his mansion at Kelmscott upstream dreaming of a new socialist dawn. That dawn, he supposed in his classic book *News from Nowhere*, would appear in Hammersmith in the form of a classless, moneyless society based on the common ownership of the means of production.

The protagonist in the book, a William Guest, falls asleep in the nineteenth century after returning home from a meeting of the Socialist League and wakes up to find himself being transported downriver by a Hammersmith sculler in the twenty-first century. The Thames is unusually clear, he notes, and all the "smoke-vomiting chimneys" of the Victorian factories and engineering works that used to line the banks at this point are gone.

Furthermore, the shores are lined with pretty red-brick, tile-roofed houses, "low and not large, standing back a little way from the river" with a continuous garden in front of them, "going down to the water's edge". Small pleasant homes, sympathetic with Morris's notions of low-key rural socialism.

The homes are still small. I could see them from the Barnes shoreline. Rows of Victorian and Edwardian terraces. But they are not sympathetic with any ideas of equality, by any stretch of the imagination, as I confirmed later in a Google search. The average price of a home in Hammersmith & Fulham is nearly £750,000, the fourth highest in London, only marginally less expensive than the money your average banker would cough up for a bijou pad in Kensington & Chelsea or Westminster or Camden, and certainly dearer than the City of London or Richmond. And that's taking apartments into account. One of those modest terraces would set you back at least a million pounds.

As for Victorian industry, it has largely disappeared as Morris imagined, though some of its ugly remnants remain. At Mortlake, I passed the Victorian malting houses of the Mortlake Brewery which started up in 1869, a high brown-brick warehouse standing forlornly on the river bank. The creek at Ship Lane beside it had flooded on the day I was there, meaning that I had to turn inland onto Mortlake High Street for a while before finding another alleyway back to the river.

Morris was strangely right about the post-industrial approach into Putney, though. William Guest saw great trees rising on the reaches towards the London village as if the river was "a lake with a forest shore". I saw the same thing. About ten years ago, the reservoirs of the old Barn Elms Water Works were converted into the London Wetlands Centre, creating a marsh habitat for all kinds of wildlife right in the heart of London. It made a soothing backdrop to those painful last steps towards my hotel just off Putney High Street.

On the edge of Putney Bridge at the beginning of the high street, there was an important historical landmark: St Mary's Church where, in the autumn of 1647, soldiers and officers of Oliver Cromwell's New Model Army, which by then had the upper hand in the struggle against the Cavaliers in the English Civil War, held discussions over the future constitution of England.

The Putney Debates were a significant landmark in our political past because it was then that the radical Levellers movement headed by Colonel Thomas Rainsborough called for something close to universal manhood suffrage – an idea way ahead of its time, anticipating by a century and a half the French and American revolutions.

It would have been interesting to pop into the church and breathe in some of that revolutionary air, but my suffering feet would have none of it. Moments later, I was falling into my lime green room in a trendy post-industrial hotel, my idea being to descend into some sort of sweet slumber, cradled in the enduring antiquity of London. Round the corner, on Putney High Street, it would be a soft drizzly day in 1863: John Drummond, the tailor at No 46 shutting up shop for the day; James Funston, the tea dealer at 47, closing his accounts book with a weary sigh; while at the big house at No 59, the young children of a British Raj family – Charlotte, Brook and Clarence, all borne in Lahore – would be playing around the dolls' house and the train set in their cavernous attic room. They had filled their dolls' house and railway landscape not only with the imaginative avatars of the characters they knew on Putney High Street – the dour barrister John Osbourne living at No 64, the prim schoolmistress Elizabeth Simpson at No 66 and the cheerful booksellers, John and Ann Robinson, at No 43 – but also with people they knew back in British India: the punctilious station master at Lahore, their watchful ayah.

—⚹—

Incomprehensible as it may seem, though, I was off out again within the hour. Lying flat on the bed with my eyes closed for ten minutes and then taking a shower seemed to restore some feeling to my aching body, and at eight in the evening I was in a London black cab heading for the Bull's Head at Barnes.

I had been very disappointed at missing the street party in Twickenham the day before, not to mention missing the jazz and blues heyday of Eel Pie Island by about half a century, and so I was determined to catch some music at another legendary London institution, the Bull, which has been hosting jazz gigs every week since 1959. I had seen a few Sunday lunchtime concerts there in the 1980s and 1990s when I was living in London, including the famous trumpeter Humphrey Lyttleton; and today I had seen there was something on this June evening.

It was just the same when I got there, the same high Victorian ceilings in the bar, and the same dark music room where the bands played.

The snippets of conversation I overheard were of a different tone, however. "It's closing down next month," said one jazz buff to another. "The new owners, they say it's just for a refurbishment, and they will continue to have music here, but everybody's saying they're going to close down the music room. Going to turn it into a gastropub."

Not even the Bull at Barnes was sacred, it seemed; but now the band was coming on. A good-looking man with long wavy locks sitting down at a piano, a burly mafia-boss type picking up an accordion, a wispy young man with a beard reaching for a clarinet.

The lights went down, except for the few picking out the faces and instruments of the musicians; and the audience settled down to the lyrical French cafe-style music of the David Vaughan Trio.

Their music was almost like the Thames itself. The sharp chords of the piano like the sunlight that flickers on the water, the mellow sounds of the clarinet rippling across the surface.

And then there were the melancholic bellows of the accordion, expanding and contracting like the story of the river. Sometimes a forlorn factory on the riverside, sometimes the venue for radical English ideas; but at other times breaking its banks and spreading across the world. Becoming the red flowers of a Madagascar tree. Becoming the sultry meander of a river in Borneo and the curvaceous sweep of a bay in Sri Lanka. Becoming the shady verandah of a colonial bungalow in Lahore.

XXI

Craven Hill Gardens

"If you look at this map from 1840, and compare it with the 1895 Stanfords map you have in your hands, you can see the difference, can't you?"

The tall angular man in the Wandsworth antiques shop had engaged me in conversation as soon as he had seen me gazing at the collection of Stanfords maps of London through his window on the Old York Road.

"You can see there's nothing in Wandsworth and Putney in 1840, just fields and farms, and a few market gardens here and there. But now look at the same area in 1895, all that grey shading showing that the area is covered in houses."

"Yes, I see what you mean," I said, peering a bit closer.

"It was the railway, you see. All that urban stuff is spanning out from the railway station. The 1890s was the real take off point for this area. It all happened when the railway arrived. Fascinating, really," the antiques dealer – his name was Leslie – enthused.

"It is," I agreed. "Have you heard of the nineteenth century mapmaker, Edward Weller? He drew a lot of maps of London. I've got one of his maps at home, a map of the Thames."

Leslie had heard of him, but wasn't familiar with his work. There were a lot of draughtsmen in the Victorian era, eking out a living from making maps. Weller was just one of many.

"This map is from 1863," I explained further. "So, it's before everything changed. Very like your 1840 map. Nothing much in Wandsworth or Barnes or Wimbledon except a few parks and a few hills. Maybe a few houses but not many."

"Well, the take-off point for Barnes and beyond was actually later than Putney," the antiques expert replied, rifling through another stack of maps standing in the middle of a gallery packed not only with maps, but also with artworks, polished wooden furniture, and various smaller items such as old tea caddies, mirrors and brass candlesticks.

"Look, here's a Stanford's map of Barnes in the 1930s. Part of the suburban sprawl of London, but before that there was very little there."

I really liked this map. It had a real art-deco feel to it. But I couldn't consider buying it with a heavy backpack on my back. "Do you have a card?" I asked.

Leslie handed me one from his desk. "So, what brings you here?" he asked.

"I'm walking the Thames Path."

"Quite a daunting task," Leslie enthused again. "What a mission. How long has it taken you?"

I told him that I was walking it in three stages, following the upper reaches, then the middle and lower ones; but that all in all it had taken me about five weeks so far.

"Actually, I had a father and his son in this shop a few months ago who had done it in three weeks."

"Well, you should have seen me struggling from Richmond to Putney yesterday. Then you would realise why it's taken me five," I laughed.

Leslie smiled. "Well, good luck with it all," he said. "Not far to go now." With that, we shook hands and I stepped out into the bright June day again.

I walked on through the ever changing city. It had actually been a construction site for new riverside apartments that had forced me away from the bankside path and onto the Old York Road in the first place, and it took me a while negotiating a major roundabout in the centre of Wandsworth before I made it back to the river again, just under the arches of Wandsworth Bridge.

There was no bridge here on Edward Weller's chart. That wouldn't arrive for another decade. And there was only a light peppering of buildings on his map; Wandsworth wouldn't fully blossom, if that is the right word for the expansion of Wandsworth, until Leslie's take-off point in the 1890s.

Still, the Red Lion Square cartographer would have recognised my view now of the river's shingle shoreline that had been laid bare by the morning ebb of the tide and all the barges beached on it. He might have known too about the small street I passed on my journey towards Chelsea called Jews Row, which, as the name suggests, denoted a small Jewish quarter in Wandsworth in the eighteenth and nineteenth centuries; and moreover he may have known of St Mary's Church, a Georgian-built place of worship on the Battersea reaches, where William Blake was married and the point from which Turner painted some of his views of the Thames.

—◊—

It was on the shingle beach just below the promontory on which St Mary's stood that I suddenly spotted a young man and woman scouring the shoreline, pacing slowly over the watery margins, heads down, surveying every inch. Sometimes, they would pick something up and examine it carefully before throwing it back into the mud; but, occasionally they would decide to keep whatever it was they had found, sliding into their jacket pockets. My curiosity aroused, I went over to find out what they were doing.

"Found anything interesting?" I asked as nonchalantly as one can when breaking out of the blue into other people's time and space.

"No, not yet." A plumpish American woman looked up as I approached. "We're not that serious, you know. We just come down in our lunchtime to see if we can find things."

"What are you looking for?" I asked.

"Anything that might have fallen from a ship. There have been so many shipwrecks in the Thames estuary over the centuries that you never know. Or anything just thrown in the river around here."

Her companion – a tall young man with a dense mop of hair and a pair of thick-rimmed glasses to match – now looked up. "But all the serious finds are downriver, round the City of London and Southwark. That's where the mud-larks find all sorts of things – Roman coins, pottery, bits of garments from the old Globe theatre, all sorts of things."

"So, have you ever found *anything* precious here?" I asked, remembering that I had seen them pocket a couple of things.

"We found a ring and a love note once, but that was from recent times," the American woman laughed.

"But we did find ...." She looked at her companion as if she was about to spill some great secret. "We did find some bits of Chinese willow pattern porcelain once."

Her admission brought to my mind again the 1863 *Daily Telegraph* article I had read the previous summer when I was trying to find out more about the life and times of Edward Weller. The "old London landmarks of the romantic and the mysterious" had "nearly all disappeared" under all the construction projects going on in the Victorian capital, it had lamented. So much so, that London was no longer a place where you could discover some hidden treasure hiding away in some obscure vault. It was no longer the sort of place where mudlarks could chance upon any "caskets of Oriental Pearl".

I continued my slow hike alongside the luxurious riverside apartments springing up in twenty-first century London. Did that Victorian newspaper article have something to say to us in our own time, I wondered. Everywhere, the precious landmarks of the past seemed to be disappearing. The glory days of Eel Pie Island had long gone, the future of the Bull's Head at Barnes appeared to be under threat. There may be still be mudlarks combing the shore of the Thames, but was there really any chance of a serendipitous discovery of Oriental pearls?

The river suddenly sparkled beside me as if the dazzle of a thousand treasure troves in the hulls of all those sunken shipwrecks had suddenly broken through in a clear patch of water.

But then the sun went in again.

—⟋⟍—

A new vista was now opening up on the horizon, though. One that always filled me with delight when I lived in London in the 1980s and 1990s, and one which always will, I think. It was the wedding-cake pink of Albert Bridge.

For me, I had now reached the heart of the matter. The Thames, which had sauntered all the way from its birthplace near Cirencester like an unstressed vowel, a schwa, threading itself humbly through the punctuated stresses and phonetic spurts of Lechlade, Oxford and Dorchester, the linguistic posturing of Reading and Windsor and the sharp lexical tones of Pangbourne and Maidenhead, had now reached what seemed to me to be the object of its long flowing sentence, the centre of London – the great city created by the river, borne of it. It was to this city that one sweltering day in August 1984 I had come, a naive, fresh-faced 22-year old, to scrabble around for that elusive thing of the early 1980s – a job.

For Plato, a city was where the politics of human relationships were worked out. For the Romans and other ancient cultures, it was the cradle of civilisation; for modern city planners it is the domain of reason where access to food, housing, transportation, water and sanitation is guaranteed and maintained.

But for me, in that first year in the capital city, London was a whole new universe, a heavenly vault of planets, stars and galaxies waiting for me to explore. Every weekend, at the end of a long week in my first job as a 'programme summariser' for a broadcast monitoring company in a dark basement on Grays Inn Road, I would take my celestial chart, the London *A to Z*, and delve into my new-found cosmos.

I would feel its gravitational pull as soon as I stepped out of the white stucco doorway of the Regency terraced house in Paddington in which I eked out an austere existence in a tiny bedsit with the help of a Baby Belling ring. The leafy Holland Park, the defunct Whiteleys department store in Bayswater which had closed its doors a few years before, Khans curry house down the road on Westbourne Grove, a pub near Kensington Church Street – bit by bit I got to know them all.

I kissed a girl in the snow by the Round Pond in Kensington Gardens and I met another at High Street Ken tube station; yet for the most part I was alone, often deep in consultation with the *A to Z*, but sometimes just drifting among the white stuccowork and tarmac and neon signs of London's streets and squares, a wanderer among the constellations of the big city.

The stars of this city were clearly laid out along the colourful lines of the tube map – Marble Arch, Paddington, Shepherd's Bush, Gloucester Road – but by walking most of the time, I got to explore the intergalactic spaces between them too: the shabby curtains in Victorian sash windows in the area rotating around Bayswater, the exhaust-fumed dilapidation of the Edgware Road, the wasted atrophy of the Cromwell Road until it was revived again in the bustle of Earls Court. Even these places, if the zodiacal signs were in their right alignment, if I found the right pub, could take on their own sparkle.

And you know, things hadn't changed nearly thirty years later. I felt the gravitational pull of the London streets again as soon as I saw the icing-sugar hues of the Albert suspension bridge.

Without a second thought, I left the riverside and turned towards the streets of Chelsea.

Edward Weller scrawled the word 'Chelsea' on one of the bends in the river on his 1863 map – a river now curling and coiling dramatically as it made its final serpentine entry into the capital. But like Wandsworth, Barnes and Richmond upstream, his Chelsea didn't amount to much, just a few houses and lanes here and there stretched out on a canvas of fields. In fact, in the middle of the nineteenth century, the borough wasn't much more than a village, growing up as a separate entity to neighbouring Kensington which was emerging at a similar pace on the other side of the Fulham Road. And it would be another 30 years until the 'take-off point', when all the villages would come together to become part of the sprawling London metropolis.

Still, things were changing fast in Weller's time as the Victorian spirit of improvement took hold. The

Metropolitan Board of Works would begin an extension in Chelsea to Joseph Bazalgette's London Embankment and drainage scheme in 1871, completing it in 1874; and plans were firmly on the drawing board in 1863 for the Albert Bridge, named in memory of the Prince Consort, to be thrown across the river to Battersea at the bottom of Oakley Street. Meeting at a local pub in April that year, the Chelsea Parochial Protection Society welcomed the plans as "one of the greatest improvements Chelsea could have", though delays over the Embankment project meant that the bridge took quite a while to come to fruition. Way behind schedule, construction began in 1870 and the bridge finally opened in 1873.

I followed the trajectory of the bridge back onto Oakley Street, following its course into the depths of Chelsea, past the borough's solid Victorian terraces, and into the stately but busy King's Road, pausing momentarily to cross the road near Chelsea's old town hall where in May 1863 the Chelsea Glee and Madrigal Society gave a stirring rendition of *Gloria* from Mozart's *12th Mass in G*.

I then turned up Sydney Street, past the site of Chelsea's Victorian workhouse and past the flying buttresses of St Luke's Church until I reached the rather down-at-heel road junction surrounding South Kensington Underground station. I knew all these streets well because I had a friend in my time in London who lived in a flat on nearby Beaufort Street, and with whom I sometimes met for a drink in the area.

From South Ken, I took another well-trodden route down the side of the V&A Museum and up towards Kensington Gardens.

—⚏—

At the corner of Exhibition Road overlooking Kensington Gardens is the neat red-brick home of the Royal Geographical Society of which Edward Weller was once a prominent member, though in his day the society met in Whitehall Place. As I passed by, I saw a notice advertising a public lecture the following night. 'Discovering Indonesia' it was called, promising that the evening would follow the 'Wallace Line' – that invisible stripe across the Indonesian archipelago discovered by the famous British naturalist which apparently divided one range of animal species from another.

It was an interesting coincidence, which I expect the RGS was aware of, that it was exactly 150 years since Alfred Russel Wallace had given a paper in the RGS lecture theatre about his travels through the Malay archipelago. I wondered whether Weller, who had just produced a beautiful map of the Indonesian archipelago for the *Dispatch Atlas*, had been at the lecture, and perhaps afterwards had stopped Wallace in the hallowed corridors of the RGS to ask him more about his travels.

Perhaps, the shy explorer, whose enthusiasm for collecting specimens of plant and wildlife had persuaded

London scientific circles to send him to the Far East in the first place, regaled Edward Weller with the story of how he had come up with his theory of the line.

It is difficult to say. But maybe he did. Perhaps he told the map engraver how he had sat during the rainy season in a little wooden cottage overlooking the mouth of the Sarawak River in Borneo and pondered a great mystery: the mystery of why palms and orchids in almost every case are confined to one hemisphere; and why the closely-allied species of the brown-backed Trogon bird are all found in the East, but all the green-backed ones are only found in the West.

But then – he might have told Weller – as the rains of the north-east monsoon in Borneo soaked the wooden veranda outside and the outline of the bay disappeared in a steamy grey mist, he began to hit on the answer.

And it was all to do with the changes to Earth's geological history, which had seen, over the span of thousands of years, land sinking beneath the ocean and mountain ranges rising up from it, and islands elevating into continents, while other continents had sunk beneath the waters until they became islands. Animal species, in response to these changes, must have done the same sort of thing: creating themselves, dying out, and then renewing themselves in a different form, perhaps.

And as the monsoon rains began to ebb away at the end of the wet season, and a series of sandy coves on the other side of the bay became slowly visible, so too did his ideas, he had perhaps told Weller. The Galapagos Islands, as Darwin had found, had a whole range of species unique to them – the result of their isolation for a long geological period. Conversely, the islands of Java, Sumatra and Borneo together with the Malay peninsula – separated only by a shallow sea which in earlier times had probably been a continent or large island – had a considerable number of species and closely-allied species in common, the result of a one-time unity.

There it was, he had possibly told Weller. Animals were creatures of their environment, changing themselves, shedding their skin, shedding their spots, evolving, mutating, becoming something else or conversely, staying the same, in a mirror image of the landscape around them. They hadn't been delivered as the finished item in one huge heavenly eruption of divine creationism.

One hundred and fifty years later, I had visited the wooden shack on the edges of the river estuary in Borneo where all this had been decided. I had found the very spot during my visit to the island in 2011, to the Sarawak river and Kuching, the site of the Batu Lintang POW camp which killed many of the soldiers of a Berkshire and Oxfordshire regiment but not their memory, which now hangs as a Union Jack in the abbey at Dorchester on Thames.

Well, anyway, I had been determined to find the Wallace cottage and after a few directions from Mrs Soon in the Chinese convenience store in the local village, I had climbed a hillock wrapped in banana trees and topped with a telegraph mast.

There it was, the place where Wallace had fumbled towards a theory of evolution, echoing the efforts of Charles Darwin sitting seven thousand miles away in his cold study in the Kent village of Downe. Half way up the hill, a large wire fence had been erected, and a large red sign advised: "keep out, protected land".

—⋙—

It was with a similar sense of mission that I now crossed Kensington Gardens, the Serpentine lake snaking to my right towards central London, and ended up on a street called Leinster Gardens spinning northwards off the Bayswater Road.

It had been a long time, but the Leinster Arms was still there – people drinking outside in the intermittent spells of sunshine – as was the Greek restaurant with the rustic wooden facade on the other side of the road which I had often thought of trying but never did. A few steps further on, I slipped down a road called Craven Hill, which, I knew, led eventually into Praed Street and onto Paddington Station.

After about 50 yards, though, I stopped and looked to my left. I was searching for something. Would it, I wondered, still be there?

The garden was there, certainly. And the row of high Regency entranceways. Yes, and the sash windows framed in white stucco.

Yes, I could see it now. Number 35. No 35, Craven Hill Gardens. My first home in London. In Weller's time it had been a grand house owned by an East India Company merchant called Charles Weber, but by 1984 had been carved up into about 20 bedsits. I remember very well the tall ceilings with their ornate covings hovering over the wide staircase I climbed to my third floor retreat, which would once have been tramped by Weber's wife and their nine children and their six servants.

Six servants. Weber was obviously doing very well out of India in the way that the famous ceiling painting of 1778 in East India Company House on Leadenhall Street had envisaged – 'The East Offering its Riches' by an Italian artist called Spiridione Roma depicts a scantily-clad woman representing Calcutta offering up a basket of jewels and pearls to Britannia.

But the writing could have been on the wall for Weber. At 55 he wasn't getting any younger, and by 1863 the East India Company's trading monopoly in the Far East had long gone, symbolised finally by the transfer of all its authority in India following the debacle of the 1857 Mutiny to the British Government. East India House had been sold off in 1861 and the company would be finally dissolved in 1874.

The writing appeared to be on the wall too in 2013. The house was all boarded up. I had read somewhere that it had become a boutique hotel called the Hempel, the 1999 film location for Hugh Grant's and Julia Roberts' wedding reception scene in Notting Hill. But obviously the Hempel had succumbed, like so many other businesses, to the post-2008 Depression.

Still, I had my memories. That hot August day I arrived from Euston Station to take up residence in my cramped bedsit. Cockroaches used to scuttle freely in the communal bathrooms then, and Mrs Smith, the moody landlady living in the basement flat, used to stalk the corridors.

It was where my life in London began. Within a few months, I was catching the Central Line from Lancaster Gate to Chancery Lane to my first job in Grays Inn Road.

It is also where Edward Weller ended the middle reaches of his Thames map. At Lancaster Gate, the pastoral villages of Kensington and Chelsea gave way to the grey blocks of Victorian London. The beginning of the lower reaches.

Before too long, I would be on that last leg of the Thames. But for the moment, I was happy standing here on the tarmac in Craven Hill Gardens, just looking, just remembering.

The Lower Reaches

LONDON, 1863

'Aripo'. 'Chilaw'. 'Manaar'. Edward Weller is inscribing place names on the map of Ceylon and the eastern provinces of India he is drafting out for the *Weekly Dispatch*. It is delicate, painstaking work; but he enjoys it, especially when a place means something to him as it does in this case. It was only the other day that his old friend Theo was telling him about the famous pearl fisheries located in this part of the world – how this usually desolate part of Ceylon's west coast is suddenly filled up with hundreds of sail boats at the end of February each year, ready for the annual harvest of the precious jewel. How a lonely beach on the coast called Sillawatorre suddenly becomes a vast town of tents housing not only the boat crews and their pearl divers, but also traders and pearl merchants, usually of Arab descent, from all over India and the East Indies.

Yes, he likes it when a place means something. Like the chart of a journey through northern China he drew up for an article for the Royal Geographical Society Journal after the explorer Alexander Mitchie had described to him how he had crossed the Yellow River, watching the pagoda of

Lanzhou slowly appear on an isolated hill on the opposite bank. Or all the illustrations he has drawn up of London over the years, opening up this bit of the Thames that he knows so well to scientific scrutiny.

His maps are all around him here in his studio at Red Lion Square. Some he has brought home from his office on Duke Street in Bloomsbury to finish off; others he has started from scratch and completed here in his private dominion. The final draft of his map of the River Thames is here, stacked up in the row of charts assigned to the *Weekly Dispatch*. Next to it is a map of Borneo which he particularly likes. He has been reading in the newspapers how adventurer James Brooke has turned this island in the Orient into a model of British industry. Edward Weller has a hankering to go to Borneo, perhaps to climb the famous Mount 'Kini Baloo' that he etched out so carefully at the top of his map or perhaps to wend his way by boat up the River Rajang into the depths of the steamy equatorial jungle, a jungle that even Brooke cannot tame.

Beside his stack of *Weekly Dispatch* maps, in the corner of the room in front of the potted tropical fern, Weller keeps a Scarborough travelling trunk with leather straps and a great brass lock. Yes, who knows? Maybe one day. Maybe one day, he will be drifting out on the open sea, drifting among the nutmeg rocks and isles of the Orient.

But for now, it is his gas-lit studio that surrounds him – a warm pool of smoky yellow light in the late winter storm that is lashing through London. The gusty squalls that had beset the capital a few days ago – the day he met Theo and Henry in the chop house – have developed into severe gales and heavy rain.

And it is the darkness of the night that surrounds him too. It is late. Way past midnight. Weller retreated to his studio on the first floor of his town house after the dinner party at which his wife, Mary Anne, had worn the pearl filigree pendant he had bought her a few days ago; and at which everybody had had, by all accounts, a lovely time. His fellow members of the Royal Geographical Society had remarked on the saddle of mutton, served up with potatoes and sprouts; and their wives had admired the cut-glass fruit stand depicting a deer standing under palm trees in the middle of the dinner table. Afterwards the gentlemen had retired to Weller's small smoking room to discuss the pros and cons of the newly-opened underground line in London; and the women had withdrawn to the drawing room to discuss the revolutionary wallpapers being produced by William Morris and his firm on the other side of Red Lion Square.

The evening had ended amid the ruby red flock-wall-paper of the Weller drawing room with the dinner guests gathered around the accomplished piano playing of Mrs Weller, who in another age might well have made some sort of career out her talent. Her husband was proud of her. He had thoroughly enjoyed the evening.

But in the end he was still glad to disappear upstairs to his studio for an hour of extra work after all the guests had gone, just to put the finishing touches to 'Ceylon' for the *Weekly Dispatch*. There among his maps, he can dream of other lands far across the sea. His studio is his window on the world.

He hears the deep oaken chime of the hall clock downstairs strike two o'clock. The wind is still raging outside and the rain is still dashing against his window overlooking Red Lion Square.

In Ceylon, though, a tropical sun is rising on a flotilla of boats floating in the calm waters of the Aripo pearl banks. The pearl divers have been at work since first light, and the decks of their boats are awash with the saltwater lustre of Oriental Pearl.

XXII

Red Lion Square

The sound state of William Gladstone's finances at the Exchequer, the forthcoming wedding of the Prince of Wales to Princess Alexandria of Denmark, the building of the Thames Embankment – Edward Weller and his fellow Londoners entered 1863 "without fear for the prosperity, the honour and the greatness of England". That, at least, was the opinion of the *Illustrated London News* in its New Year's Day issue.

These were the boom years of a confident age. The industrial unrest of the first half of the century were long forgotten and the ranks of the middle class – merchants, factory owners, doctors, lawyers, architects and civil engineers – were filling up fast as prosperity grew with the international trade of the world's first superpower. The Thames was full of steamships, clippers and barges bringing in the commodities of Britain's empire – tea, silk and so on – and the international order books of factories and iron works lining the river were running full to bursting.

As a result, the advertising pages of the *Illustrated London News* were full too, marketing everything from Indian shawls and silk scarves to Lea & Perrins Worcester Sauce and the magic lanterns that could be bought or hired at a shop at 39 Albemarle St, just off Piccadilly.

Chances are that the Weller household could afford many of these items if their large house in Red Lion Square with its two servants were anything to go by. Perhaps Mary Weller followed up one of the many adverts for Indian shawls and perhaps Edward Weller hired a magic lantern for the weekend to entertain his children with photographic projections of all those exotic locations depicted in his maps, places like India, China and the Blue Nile. No doubt he wanted to see these places for himself too, see pictures in the flare of the lantern limelight of the distant lands that he had etched out for the Dispatch Atlas. Far-away places were rooted deeply in his psyche, and in the psyche of the nation too – the *Illustrated London News*, like other London papers of the time, did not waste too many column inches on actual London news; it was far more preoccupied, as it was in 1863, with the building of the latest railway in India or with new expeditions, such as the disputed discovery of the source of the Nile by British explorer John Hanning Speke.

Whether Weller attended the reception for Speke and his fellow Nile traveller, Captain James Grant, at the Royal Geographical Society that year, I have no idea; but one thing is fairly certain – the map engraver's business was doing well. His services were much in demand, not only by the Weekly Dispatch Atlas and the RGS, for whom he was the unofficial cartographer, but also by other publishers such as Longman. By 1871, it looks as if he had expanded into publishing because he now described himself in the census as a 'geographical engraver and lithographic printer', and in 1881 he was employing '14 men and four boys'. When he died at Red Lion Square on 17th May 1884, he left an estate worth £7,626, which was a respectable amount for the time.

Things move on, though. By 1871, his sons Edward and Francis had left home and Alfred, it seems, had died; and by 1881, one of his daughters – Margaret – had fled the nest. Only Francis followed him into the mapmaking business in which he worked until his death in 1910.

By that time, No 34 Red Lion Square had been split into three, now being the home of two societies – the National Sunday League and the North London branch of the Independent Order of Odd Fellows – and Emlyn Jones, a singing teacher. Any last remnants of the Weller household's aspidistras and Staffordshire figurines had long gone.

Finally, in 1941, the Victorian house went altogether, wiped off the London map by a German bomb. At the beginning of that year, the building had contained the offices of quantity surveyor PT Walters, two architectural firms May Stanley James and Goldie E & Son as well as the National Sunday League. A year later, they were all gone, lost to the flames of the Blitz, together with all the little businesses at Nos 32, 33, 35 and 36. Only John Andrews, the cash registry representative at No 31 and, perhaps rather appropriately, the lighting conductor experts JW Gray & Son Ltd at No 37, remained of the row of sooty Victorian terraces that once bustled with the industry of Britain's Age of Improvement.

Number 34 reappeared in 1948 as the home once more of the National Sunday League, but the building we see today was almost certainly the work of the architectural firm which moved to the premises in 1961. Richard Seifert & Partners, which was about to ride the wave of the booming 1960s office market with the construction of the soaring 36-storey Centre Point on Oxford Street, designed a jazzy little white pebbledash frontage for itself in Red Lion Square inscribed with a rather unusual icon, which is still there, that looks like a set of measuring dividers: doubtless a key instrument for the architect, but also an accidental homage to Weller, who would have used a similar instrument to calculate distances on his maps.

Seiferts moved out in 1979 and another firm of architects took up residence in the 1980s, but when I arrived one warm afternoon in July 2013 at the modern 1960s block with shaded 70s windows, I found an intercom system on the doorway that signalled that No 34 was now home to several businesses.

As I say, things move on.

From No 34, though, I followed in Edward Weller's footsteps on what I imagined would have been his regular beat to the offices of the *Weekly Dispatch* on Fleet Street, along the north side of Red Lion Square until I arrived at Lamb's Conduit Passage, flanked on the one side by the large mullion windows, curved iron balconies and stone urns of the rather grand Conway Hall built in the 1920s; and on the other side, by the dull brick of a 1950s block of flats.

Conway Hall, which was built as premises for the nonconformist organisation, the South Place Ethical Society, replaced James Perry's ink factory, which had been brewing its dark substances in a dingy Victorian tenement at No

37 since way before Weller's time. The flats, on the other hand, were built as part of a new-look London emerging from the ruins of the Blitz, not so much grand as bright and breezy and modern in a drab post-war sort of way.

In the 1860s, peering up the passage through the foggy gloom, Weller would have just made out the dim gas lights of The Grapes on Red Lion Street. The pub is still there, looking as ornate as it would have done in Weller's time; but it is now called The Enterprise, with a picture of a Victorian sailing ship on its sign outside. On the opposite corner, The Dolphin is still serving beers and hot lunches as it undoubtedly did in Weller's day.

As far as the rest of Red Lion Street is concerned, it is naturally all change, though there is some kind of continuity there too. Where once there were makers of watches and umbrellas and cabinets, there are now kebab houses and Chinese take-aways. The hotel at No 23 which once hosted the killer of William Whiteley is now a trendy maisonette. Yet No 25 still has an Italian connection for an area which in Weller's time was home to London's original Italian quarter: Mr Stoppani's looking glass shop at No 25 is now a stylish Italian restaurant and wine bar serving pappardelle with hare ragu.

But it is definitely all change in Fleet Street, once home to the *Weekly Dispatch.* All the newspapers are long gone, having abandoned it for Docklands in the 1980s. *Bradshaw's British and Continental Guide of Railways* at No 59 has been replaced by a branch of Snappy Snaps. *The*

Sunday Times building at 103 is now a juice bar. As for the *Weekly Dispatch* offices at No 138, they were subsumed by the art-deco columns of Peterborough Court in the late 1920s. The building, which was home to the *Daily Telegraph* for half a century, is now gated up.

Across the street, on the corner of an alleyway called Dorset Rise, is the 1930s Reuters and Press Association building. Reuters said goodbye to it in 2003, moving its headquarters to Canary Wharf, and the building is now decked out in the cool white art-deco of the Conran-designed Lutyens restaurant, named in honour of the building's famous architect.

Look down Dorset Rise and you will find the work of another famous architect. St Bride's Church has been devastated by fire on two occasions during its long history: once in 1666 in the Great Fire of London, after which Sir Christopher Wren rebuilt it, giving it a 234-foot high steeple which was later described by Victorian poet William Henley as "a madrigal in stone"; and a second time on the night of 29 December 1940 when it succumbed to a German bomb, after which it was faithfully restored to Wren's original drawings.

It was the excavating power of the Luftwaffe firebomb that unveiled a secret crypt underneath the church that Edward Weller and his contemporaries would have been unaware of, a chamber containing a mosaic pavement, red-tiled wall and stone foundations belonging to a Roman villa.

The draughtsman is likely to have known, however, that since medieval times St Brides had been the printers' church. William Caxton's apprentice, Wynkyn de Worde, set up England's first printing press with moveable type in 1500 alongside this Fleet Street chapel because the church was, at the time, the industry's main customer. Printers such as Thomas Berthelet and Richard Redman followed in his footsteps, and by the nineteenth century hundreds of publishing houses were clustered around Fleet Street, now serving a new secular priesthood, the growing newspaper industry.

Cassell's lithographic printing works – located only a few steps away on Ludgate Hill – would have been hard at work in 1863 preparing Weller's charts for publication in a one-off volume, the *Dispatch Atlas*. Printing ink from James Perry's factory would have been rolled over his copper plate engravings, seeping through the grooves to the transfer paper below. To the transfer paper, a patcher would have added borders, scales and notes and then set the page for its application to the stone.

The print workers would then have trundled an enormous round piece of limestone weighing at least a ton to the press, where it would have been propelled back and forth under giant rollers. If there were no problems with the first 'pulls', if the pastel shades of brown hugging the coastlines of the Indian archipelago and the shades of pink hugging the River Thames had turned out satisfactorily, then the printing would have gone ahead at full speed.

"In the hands of the printers now", the cartographer might have said to himself as he disappeared down a narrow alleyway to the side of St Brides towards the Thames, for another ramble along the river he loved. I watched him go and then turned up Ludgate Hill towards the great dome of St Paul's Cathedral.

—⁓—

At St Paul's I turned right onto Peter's Hill, which leads down to the Millennium Footbridge spanning the Thames between the cathedral and the old Bankside power station, converted so strikingly into the Tate Modern art gallery a few years back. Nothing stays still in London – a brick-clad electricity plant becomes an exhibition hall, a traditionally Jewish area around Brick Lane in the East End becomes Banglatown, a neighbourhood in south London laid waste in the Blitz becomes home to the Windrush generation. And nowhere was this more apparent on this sunny day in the summer of 2013, or so it seemed to me at the time, than on this pedestrian walkway leading down to the waterfront. An Afro-Caribbean man pushing a pram, a Chinese girl with a pink knapsack, a sharp-suited Indian woman on her mobile: faces, black and white and brown, their many different languages and dialects jostling together to form a diverse stream of humanity flowing down to the river.

And overlooking it all, the Tower of Babel itself, built with the labour of construction workers from as far afield as Brazil, Bulgaria and Australia, standing like a mirage from a futurist utopia, a great spire of glass tapering high into the midday sky. The Shard.

I stood blinking at the newest addition to the London skyline for a while, as so many people do, all 1,017 foot of it, soaring enigmatically above the waterfront, inspired, says its Italian architect, Renzo Piano, by old paintings of ships' masts in the Thames and of the hundreds of church steeples in the city behind.

Presently, though, I moved on, joining the throngs crossing the bridge to the Tate side, stealing past the new Globe theatre, a line of Victorian wharves converted into luxury flats and smart restaurants, and a replica of Sir Francis Drake's Golden Hind, on my way towards London Bridge.

I was definitely in modern London, but in many ways I was just as much in Weller's London. I could almost imagine London Bridge being adorned with the 130 lantern flames on the night of the wedding of the Prince of Wales (the future King Edward VII) to Alexandra, the Danish princess who on her marriage would inherit the famous 'Dagmar' pearl necklace of Denmark's royal family. Illuminations were lit up all over London that evening – 10 March 1863. Perhaps the mapmaker brought his family down to the bank side here to see the lights, though the father of six young children would have been cautious in the thronging crowds. Quite a few Londoners died that night, crushed or suffocated in the mass scrums of people fighting for a view of the lights, and some died afterwards as a result of their injuries, according to the authorities – people like 58-year old Jane Darling from Wapping who died from a heart attack a few days after her arm was broken and she was heavily bruised in the melee.

I was also walking along the Thames Embankment on the south side of the river, built long after the Bazalgette scheme between Victoria and Blackfriars, but still the heir to that original innovation and all the other Victorian improvements underway or opening up in 1863: the railway bridges at Ludgate Hill and Charing Cross, the opening of the Metropolitan underground line and the grand sewerage project over which Bazalgette's embankment was being built.

Moreover, Hays Galleria soon came into view, a redevelopment of the old Hays Wharf which in Weller's time was one of the main docks in London for the tea clippers returning from China and India. In fact, the 1860s were the heyday for these magnificent sailing ships – schooners such as the *Cutty Sark* and the *Flying Spur* – racing across the Indian Ocean, round the Cape of Good Hope and through the Atlantic, arriving in London only a 100 days after they had left Fouchow in China, a trip that had once taken a year or more. The opening of the Suez Canal in 1869 and the growing numbers of steamships eventually led to their demise, but for a brief moment they must have been an impressive sight.

The river was full of ships then, putting down anchor and setting sail from the Pool of London. They were slipping wearily into port after a long stormy journey from Singapore or Sarawak, Shanghai or Madras; or arriving chipper from Palermo and Alexandria ready and willing for the onward journey to New York and Kingston.

Many, however, never made it into port, succumbing to heavy gales in the Mediterranean, or the deadly monsoon squalls in the Bay of Bengal, run ashore, dashed against rocks, washed up on beaches. In January 1863, the Port of London was still waiting for the arrival of The Joseph Fish which had sailed from Rangoon on 20th May the previous year and had not been heard of since. At the same time, a vessel had sunk much closer to home, just half a mile from the lighthouse on Southend Pier in the Thames estuary. Perhaps it had been laden with Oriental pearls from Ceylon. Who knows? A green buoy had been put out to sea to mark the spot for incoming ships.

If your vessel – these were the days of ship-owning families rather than multinational shipping companies – did make it home, though, the chances are that its cargo of wool from Australia or spices and Oriental carpets from Bombay or perhaps timber from Burma would have been transhipped to one of the hundreds of wharfs which lined the Thames in Bermondsey. Soon after passing by Hays Galleria, I was in the area of Shad Thames in Bermondsey and crossing the muddy creek that leads to New Concordia Wharf, the warehouse complex that swept aside the stinking slum of Jacob's Island in Weller's time.

Jacob's Island is now a smart residential complex called Providence Square where a two-bedroom apartment costs more than half a million pounds. It looked like a thriving sort of place.

And so did the Tower Bridge Moorings, a cluster of old Thames lighters, some of which were obviously homes, bobbing up and down in the water to the side of the wharf. A woman in beige dungarees was working on the hull of one of the boats; a couple were sitting on the deck of another with cups of tea.

Apparently, the moorings are owned by the architects Nicholas Lacey & Partners to offer an alternative lifestyle for a community of over a hundred people, living and working there and tending to the communal gardens which straddle the decking between their floating homes. Twice a year, the gardens are thrown open to the public.

It was good to see that the tradition of houseboat living was alive and well here because, as Honor and Helen on their lighter in Richmond had suggested, communities like these are constantly under threat from property developers eyeing up the lucrative real estate opportunities that the Thames offers.

Actually, I had seen a number of examples of the tradition appearing to do well during my five-week stroll: there was the assortment of barges and old motor launches I had glimpsed on my approach into Oxford, their roofs topped with an eclectic mix of vegetable pots, solar panels and the occasional bicycle lying flat on its side; there were the colourful and rather exclusive houseboats of Taggs Island near Hampton Court; and there was the smart red-and-yellow barge I had chanced upon near Teddington Lock, the owner of which was exhibiting on his roof a collection of sculptures he had carved out of river driftwood.

On the other hand, the future of a houseboat community near the derelict Battersea Power Station in London was under threat, I had read recently, from a developer looking to build a swanky new marina and residential complex at Nine Elms Pier.

—◊◊◊—

At Tower Bridge, the walker of the Thames Path has a choice. He or she can either take the south bank through Bermondsey, Rotherhithe and Deptford or they can take the north bank through Wapping, Limehouse and Canary Wharf. More by drift than by design, but possibly because of the lure of the Docklands area, I decided to take the northern route, and from Shad Thames I made my way back across the river again, a short hop that Edward Weller would not have been able to make because Tower Bridge did not appear until 1894.

Dominating the northern shoreline as I jostled with the crowds on the bridge was the Tower of London, which has had a long and varied history as a fortress and a royal palace but is probably best known for the famous historical figures who died there – among them Ann Boleyn, the so-called 'Princes in the Tower' who were allegedly murdered by their dastardly uncle Richard III, and Sir Walter Raleigh.

Unlike the unfortunate wife of Henry VIII and the young princes though, Raleigh had time – about 14 years – to ponder the course of history before he was finally executed. The beginnings of civilisation, he decided in his never completed History of the World written in his cell overlooking the Thames, started with the four great rivers which flowed out of the Garden of Eden. Two of these were the Tigris and the Euphrates which started somewhere in Armenia and flowed through Mesopotamia (modern Iraq); the other two, named in the Bible as Pison and Gehon, were possibly the Ganges or the Indus or even the Nile.

The great mystery of things, or at the very least a great deal of booty, lay at the source of a number of sacred rivers, he believed, and to that end he managed to persuade King James, who had originally clapped him up in the Tower for treason, to send him in search of El Dorado, the golden land which was rumoured to lie somewhere near the source of the Orinoco river in South America. Unfortunately for everyone, himself especially, his mission was a failure and on his return to England the death sentence hanging over him was reinstated. He was executed on 29 October 1618.

But Raleigh is still remembered – mainly because of his earlier success in bringing a bad smoking habit back from the New World to England – as part of England's first great age of exploration, putting him alongside other English maritime heroes such as Sir Francis Drake who returned to Bermondsey from his circumnavigation of the globe with the Golden Hind stuffed full of gold, Hugh Willoughby and Richard Chancellor who set sail from Deptford on their doomed mission to find a northeast passage to China and the Pilgrim Fathers on the Mayflower which sailed for the New World from Rotherhithe. These pioneers all became, in the words of the writer Joseph Conrad centuries later, part of a river "crowded with memories of men and ships".

By Weller's time, the launching pad for England's early explorers and adventurers had become most important port in the world with big impressive docks to match. The West India Docks on the Isle of Dogs had opened in 1802, the London Docks at Wapping in 1805 and St Katherine Docks in 1828. The massive Victoria Dock, which was able to accommodate the newest steamships, followed in 1855 and very soon was handling more than 850,000 tonnes of cargo every year, substantially more than all the others put together.

Around and behind these docks there grew up a maze of streets, filled with ships chandlers, lodging houses, gin shops and brothels, catering for sailors from all over the world holed up in port waiting for their next ship. Some called this area 'Sailortown', others called it 'Tiger Bay'. Nowadays people call it Wapping and it was this district I now turned into as I headed east from the Tower of London.

What is so striking about Wapping is that, in spite of all the changes that have happened in the past thirty years or so – the final demise of London's working docks in the 1960s because they were unable to accommodate the new generation of container ships and the influx of new industries – the neighbourhood still retains a slight whiff of the past. No doubt, this is due to the Victorian warehouses with their high connecting catwalks lying half-derelict along Wapping High Street which runs parallel to the shoreline and because of the historic pubs still tucked in between them. In 1863, this high street was bustling with tradesmen working in one way or another for the Port of London: shipwrights building the ships and the barges; sailors, watermen and lightermen crewing them; and numerous victuallers and ship chandlers supplying them with food and other provisions. They lived on top of one another in suffocating tenement blocks – a lighterman and his family and a coal barge labourer and his family, for example, living above the coffee house at No 125 run by Jane Darling, the woman who tragically died from the effects of injuries sustained during the Royal Wedding light show.

It was in Wapping too – in St John's Churchyard – that I found a plaque dedicated to an important but little known historical figure; someone, in fact, who had cropped up earlier in my travels: Colonel Thomas Rainsborough of Cromwell's New Model Army.

"I think that the poorest hee that is in England hath a life to live as the greatest hee," Rainsborough had told soldiers and officers at discussions on the future constitution of England at St Mary's Church in Putney in 1647. In a speech aimed at hearts and minds, he went on to advocate a universal manhood suffrage that included most male householders.

His words went down well in the neighbourhood of his birth, Wapping, which, as church and state power collapsed during the English Civil War, had become a hotbed of non-conformist and dissenting creeds – from the Quakers and the Baptists who set up their places of worship in Meeting House Alley and the Diggers who wanted to set up a classless, agrarian society to the Adamites who simply liked walking around in the nude.

His words did not go down so well with conservative military officers such as Oliver Cromwell and the other grandees of the Parliamentarian army who wanted the franchise to be restricted solely to property owners; and within a year or so Cromwell and his allies had managed to crush the popular idealism of Rainsborough and the political movement he represented, the Levellers.

Rainsborough himself was murdered by Royalist agents during a siege of Pontefract Castle in October 1648, and the Levellers organised a massive funeral procession for him past St Paul's, the Tower of London and through the East End to the Wapping chapel, where he would be buried beside his sea-captain father. Three thousand men on horseback, and 60 carriages carrying women supporters, plus many more thousands lining the streets wearing ribbons of sea-green, Rainsborough's colour, turned up to bid him farewell.

After it was all over, I expect, everyone piled into the pub seeking some kind of solace as people tend to do after a funeral. For the congregation in Wapping this would have been a local tavern called the Red Cow which had been around since the War of the Roses in the 1460s. The pub was later renamed the Town of Ramsgate after the fishermen of the Kent town began to land their catches at Wapping Old Stairs to avoid the taxes further upriver at Billingsgate fish market. In 1863, incidentally, it was the scene of a coroner's inquiry into the suicide of a local woman called Eliza Smart who had been washed up at the stairs. She had thrown herself off London Bridge after the death of her only child.

The Town of Ramsgate is still there, perching over the river beside the stairs, which are probably most famous for the condemned pirates who were once chained to it, await-ing their fate from the rising tide. I took the old stone steps down to the river. The tide was out again, revealing a stony foreshore, and, remembering the two amateur mudlarks I had met on the line of beach at Battersea, I climbed down to take a look. Sure enough, under the crunch of my shoes, I found a twine of rope, an iron bar, and then something metal and wiry embedded in the sand and mud in between the pebbles as well: it looked like a hat pin.

A pin for the flowery hat of a Sailortown prostitute? Or a left-over from a Boots cosmetics bag accidentally dropped in the river on a drunken night out in 1985? I couldn't tell, but I slipped it into a trouser pocket, nonetheless, and took it on with me along Wapping High Street until I spied the possibility of a late lunch at another riverside pub – the Prospect of Whitby.

The Prospect opened its doors in 1520, and since then has been a regular drinking haunt of everyone from Samuel Pepys and Princess Margaret to the privateer Captain Kidd; as well as the sailor John Westcombe, who apparently brought the fuschia plant to the shores of Britain in 1780 by trading in seedlings he had found in Japan with a local market gardener at the bar for a noggin of rum. I ordered a lime soda and a snack at the same wooden counter, and went outside to the pub's pretty riverside terrace.

Unsurprisingly the prospect out there wasn't of Whitby, but of the Thames waterfront, for the most part lined with expensive-looking riverside apartments. A public notice I had seen earlier, alerting local residents to a proposal to redevelop three of the Wapping wharves – King Henrys, Phoenix and Swan – into 'residential units' had offered the hint, I suppose. And now I saw it, the uniformity closing in on the banks of the old river. The silver chrome taps and sleek wood finishes of well-mannered pieds-à-terre replacing the din of the old shipping warehouses with their cranking chains and creaking cranes. Muted tiles and intercom security systems taking the place of hollering porters and shipwrecked mariners, telling their strange tales of the ocean. Smart motor launches on private moorings instead of that silent coal smuggling boat skulking in the moonlight by the water-stairs. A hot computer line to the office instead of the old Quaker and Baptist meeting houses which once made Wapping a stronghold of dissent, ready when the time came to call for political reform in the English Civil War, or in the 1800s an end to the slave trade or, in the 1930s, to take on Oswald Mosley's Fascist Blackshirts in the Battle of Cable Street.

I remembered again the 1863 *Daily Telegraph* article I had read when I was delving into the world of Edward Weller the summer before. The building boom of 1863 was playing "sad havoc" with the old London landmarks, it had said. "A smirking uniformity" had replaced "the scowling yet picturesque vagabondage of the past."

Was it the same scenario playing out in 2013, I wondered: new technology, the hot money of the property speculators, modernity, sweeping away everything in their path? The old communities, their beliefs and their ideals.

Very soon after I left the Prospect of Whitby, just on the edge of the King Edward Memorial Park, I came across a large banner attached to the embankment fencing. "Save your local park, river path and river front from destruction by the Thames Water Super Sewer", it read.

Proposals for a controversial £4.2 billion upgrade to the 100 miles of London sewers built in the 1860s are well underway. If, as planned, construction begins in 2015, what will be the cost to the local cityscape?

XXIII

The Thames Barrier

From the King Edward Memorial Park, the Thames Path took me quite quickly onto the Limehouse Basin, a district which from the 1860s onwards saw the emergence of a small Chinatown, home to Chinese sailors, who, having reached London, decided for one reason or another to stay on for a while.

It was a hard-working slum neighbourhood bustling with eating houses, grocery stores, laundries and a couple of opium dens, which grew up around the corner from the Strangers' Home for Asiatics, Africans and South Sea Islanders opened by Victorian philanthropic organisations in 1857 for foreign sailors stranded in London while waiting to be recruited by a ship returning East.

And it quickly caught the imagination of London journalists and writers who quickly played the 'moral panic' card over this exotic community emerging in the midst of Imperial London. The *London Standard* salivated over the alleged murder of a Chinese sailor called 'Acqui' by another Chinese sailor called 'Sequi' in March 1863, Sequi apparently pulling out a knife and stabbing his counterpart to death after an argument about opium and money; and later, in 1872, reporter Blanchard Jerrold lingered lovingly on the exotic details of the Limehouse drug dives in his *London pilgrimage.*

Meanwhile, Charles Dickens sent one of his characters to a den in the *Mystery of Edwin Drood* (1870); and in *The Man with the Twisted Lip* (1887), Sherlock Holmes and Dr Watson find themselves in a low-life establishment called the Bar of Gold where the only light is that of the waxing and waning of burning opium in the bowls of the smokers' metal pipes.

The greatest poet of Limehouse, though, was a journalist called Thomas Burke who during the First World War invited the nervous suburban readers of his book *Nights In Town* to escape the "dreary bands playing ragtimes and bilious waltzes in West End beer cellars" and join him on a journey eastwards to the darkness of Limehouse where in the muffled wail of reed instruments playing in the bars, one could hear "the heart-cry of the Orient".

According to Burke – quoted in a 2009 book by London academic Anne Witchard – the scents of "cinnamon and aconite, betel and bhang" forever hanging in the air in Limehouse suggested that the opium dens were never far away, ready to welcome you into their low rooms "sunk in a purple dusk, though here and there a lantern stung the glooms".

When the lights went up at the end of the war, Hollywood picked up on this East End Chinatown, featuring it in a number of films such as *Limehouse Blues* and *Broken Blossoms*, while George Formby with his ukulele gave us a tribute of sorts when he sang about a lovesick Mr Wu in his Limehouse laundry.

Most of Limehouse, however, was destroyed in the Blitz, and in a piece of 1951 journalism Peter Fryer of the Daily Worker found there were only a few Chinese families left in the neighbourhood, many of them relocating to another Chinatown beginning to emerge in Soho at the other end of town.

Only a handful of Chinese restaurants and shops remain in Limehouse. The old landmarks – such as the Quong Yen Sing grocery shop, and the Chee Kong Tong freemason society – are long vanished. I walked on towards the self-satisfied skyscrapers of Canary Wharf on the Isle of Dogs.

—ᴡ—

The Isle of Dogs on Weller's 1863 map of the Thames is a sparsely populated affair with a few notable exceptions. There was the all important West India Dock and a timber dock next to it. There was also a ropery, a police station and the 'Scott Bussels' shipyard; and at the very southern tip of this teardrop peninsula created by a double-back loop of the Thames, the cartographer marked up the ferry over to Greenwich.

It was not a boat that I stepped into in 2013, but a lift which sunk slowly to 50 feet under the ground, despatching a group of cyclists and me into the Greenwich foot tunnel, first opened in 1902. It was a slightly odd experience down there, making my way through a gloomy tunnel lined with ceramic tiles, the voices of pedestrians and cyclists echoing all around me. However, within minutes I was getting out of the lift at the other end and emerging into the bright day again underneath the lofty masts of the *Cutty Sark*. From there I turned towards the magnificent buildings of the Old Royal Naval College.

I was now on the last leg of my long walk from the source of the river, 184 miles away on a barren hillside near Cirencester, to the Thames Barrier, where the Thames Path ends.

And it felt like it. Crossing a couple of hemispheres was about the measure of it, which is what I actually did when I passed the invisible line which runs from the Royal Observatory up on the hill behind the college. From the western to the eastern hemisphere. From the stone villages of Gloucestershire, Wiltshire and Oxfordshire, and the neat red-brick hamlets of Berkshire and Buckinghamshire to the glamorous post-industrial bleakness of the London Docklands. From heavy walking boots and several layers of clothing to walking shoes and a light T-shirt. Those stone villages back at the beginning of my journey felt like a million miles away.

But now I could see the O2 Arena ahead, and from there I knew it was only a couple of miles to the Thames Barrier. I battled on with renewed resolve, past the clanking and drilling of a couple of boatyards still in operation maintaining and mending the passenger and haulage vessels using the London waterway, though one of them at Babcocks Wharf, I had read, was in danger of being replaced by another one of those new residential developments. I reached the O2 Arena and was then on the path beyond it. It would not be long now. It was coming into view. Like a row of silver lotus leaves sitting on the water. The Barrier.

A little later, a signpost confirmed it. "Thames Barrier. 1 m", it read.

I tramped on, past the rumbling conveyor belts of a cement works, and past a desolate-looking pub called the Anchor & Hope where an entertainer was playing 'You are my sunshine, my only sunshine' on a Hammond organ.

And then I reached it. I reached the end of the Thames Path. I was beside the strange contraptions of the Woolwich Barrier, their metallic shields shining silver then gold in the shifting sunlight.

I read a couple of public information notices to prove I had finally arrived. As recently as the 1960s, one said, the riverside here was a busy scene of cable laying boats, small tankers, jute and hemp carriers, and of cable and rope making factories, ship breakers and coal depots, but of all of these only one significant presence still remained after the demise of the London docks and that was the Tate & Lyle refinery which I could see on the opposite shoreline, still the biggest refinery of cane sugar in the world. Except for the working silos and chimneys of this ugly complex, I was standing in the middle of an industrial wasteland.

Henry VIII established his Royal Dockyards near here, another board said. The dockyard built *HMS Beagle*, on which Charles Darwin sailed to the Galapagos Islands and many of the warships that maintained the British Empire's mastery over the seas. By the mid-nineteenth century, however, the docks were beginning to fill up with silt from the river, and after years of gradual decline when the Chatham dockyard on the Thames estuary took over much of the shipbuilding they finally closed down in 1869.

And then the last notice. This commemorated the 2,100 lives in the littoral countries around the North Sea which were lost during the massive storm surge in the early hours of the morning on 31 January 1953, including the 58 people who died on Canvey Island in the Thames estuary when the huge waves breached the sea wall and swept into their homes. Up and down the estuary that night people took refuge in their lofts and on their roofs as the waters swept upriver, cutting down power lines and blowing out windows.

The tragedy finally prompted the authorities to build the Thames Barrier to prevent such a storm surge reaching London. It opened in 1983, but still may be not enough, say some, to protect the capital against the rising sea levels caused by global warming.

The waters looked benign enough today, but the notice board reminded me of the potential power of the Thames. I had tramped through the waterlogged fields surrounding the upper reaches of the river, and had my progress checked by sections of the path which had turned into a muddy swamp. I had heard about the destruction it had wielded in Oxford and on villages upstream of it, and on the businesses and livelihoods of the people who lived in them. I had read all about the floodings of 1947, and the day in 1928 when another tidal surge from the North Sea had sent a wall of water over the London Embankment, drowning 14 people living in basement flats in Pimlico.

The great river had been my best friend on my long walk along its banks, offering up its soft companionship wherever it led me; but on another day, in another time, it might as easily have been my enemy.

—ᴍᴍ—

That evening I caught a ferry back into the centre of London. This meant taking my aching feet for the two miles back to the North Greenwich Pier at the O2 Arena, and, although I broke my journey for a pint at the Anchor & Hope, it was still with great relief that I stepped onto a black-fume belching Thames Clipper from a swaying pontoon and sank into a soft seat heading back to the great metropolis, which was beginning to sink into the shadows of the western dusk.

I watched the landmarks of the day's walk slip past the window – the *Cutty Sark*, an old wherry anchored at Wapping, the names of the Victorian wharfs plastered in huge lettering on their warehouse walls – and mulled over my plan for the evening. A rest at my cheap hotel in Victoria before heading out again for a late dinner? Or another pint near London Bridge underneath the towering gaze of the Shard?

In the end, I opted for the lure of the Shard. It had been with me all day soaring over the skyline if I looked backwards towards central London and now this great splinter of steel and glass was looming above me again: at one moment, above the warehouses and cranes of Bermondsey and Rotherhithe; at another, exploding out of the deck of *HMS Belfast* as if the old warship docked at Tower Bridge had suddenly sprouted another mast; and in one last moment just before we docked at London Bridge, all 72 floors of it shimmering indistinctly in the fading sunlight like an apparition in a Turner or Whistler painting.

I got off at the pier and joined the evening crowds thronging upstream towards the pubs and restaurants of Bankside until up ahead, I saw the homely lamplight of a pub.

As I approached, I noticed the sign outside depicting a young boy by a river with a net in his hand, and then I noticed the livery in gold letters on a black sign above the door. The pub was called The Mudlark. A few minutes later, I was sitting at a table with a pint in my hands, watching in a half-hearted sort of way all the customers around me.

There was a couple making gurgling sort of noises behind me, and then there was a table full of loud City men in pin-striped suits in the middle of the lounge bar vying with each other for the funniest office story of the day. In the far corner, there was an Indian man and a woman, preferring the company of their mobile phones rather than of each other. That was inside. Outside, in the evening light, there were more people having a drink after work, and then there was a table of three older couples, debating the direction of somewhere over an *A to Z*.

Where had all these people come from, I wondered. I guessed a lot of them had walked across the bridge from their offices in the City for a couple of quick ones before they caught that train back home to the cats waiting for them in their Bromley kitchens. Others, I speculated, were staying at a local hotel on a short break in London, seeing the sights. No-one, I surmised, had just completed a 200-mile journey down the River Thames.

Although in the scheme of things, I suppose, 200 miles through the English shires isn't the longest or most difficult journey in the world, it still felt a long way from those early lonely days on the river when there was just a far-off farmhouse or a Second World War pillbox to keep me company to the busy London pub I now found myself in.

Yes, it felt like a long journey. I had walked along lines of crack willow on a bleak winter's day and stayed the night at a pub open again after being destroyed in devastating floods. I had floated through dreamy watercolour meadows on the fringes of Pangbourne before camping out on another meadow near Henley to listen to a ukulele orchestra. I had seen the children of Guernica arrive at Buscot Park, and then peered into the disembodied faces of 13

Roman emperors perched on the gateposts of Oxford's Sheldonian Theatre. In Oxford I had eaten noodles, and in Reading I had eaten lamb thali and then in the 'fairly-like nook' of Sonning I had drunk a bit too much beer.

And that was just the start of it, I felt. I had also stood at the Wittenham Clumps and seen the dormant towers of Didcot Power Station, closed down to try to hold back the tide of climate change; and I had stood on Marlow Bridge, looking over to the Wild Wood. More than this, I had wandered in the footsteps of Edward Weller in 1863 from his home in Red Lion Square to the one-time offices of the Weekly Dispatch in Fleet Street.

Edward Weller's map of 'the River Thames from its source to the sea' had been my starting point. It had offered me a journey away from modern Britain – a country that seems to me in my darkest middle-aged moods as one obsessed with shopping malls and celebrity tittle-tattle – and into something different: an amble downriver exploring an older country lurking beneath the sneer of those malls, a sort of communion with the river's rich and varied past.

And I had found another country, by and large. Well, several other rivers, to be exact. Not only the bustle and business of Weller's Victorian river, but also many other ones. There was the international waterway which had seen wave after wave of migrants settling on its banks and had been the launching pad of the early English explorers, the fleets of the East India Company and a little later on all those Victorian adventurers egged on by the Royal Geographical Society. A waterway too that became the cradle of global cities such as Oxford and, of course, London, where a mapmaker could draw up his maps of Oriental lands, and dream about them too.

And then there was a river of remembrance: a river of benches and statues and flags containing the memories of those departed, the memories of four Maidenhead schoolboys who died in a skiing accident, for instance, and those of the Oxfordshire soldiers who fell in far-away Borneo in the Second World War.

And then there was the soft stream of illusions and dreams: the river of the artists Nash, Spencer and Turner and of writers such as Lewis Carroll. The river, perhaps, of heavenly visitations.

There was the river of dissent, too: not only the struggles for political liberty fought by non-conformists and radicals in the English Civil War and during the Industrial Revolution, but also the voices of William Cobbett, Mary Shelley and George Orwell who had warned us about the industrial machine, the machine which crushed and exploited farm labourers in Cricklade and factory workers in the new brick towns in the early nineteenth century; and made one part of the world indistinguishable from another in the twentieth century. The machine, the Frankenstein, which had started as benign innovation, but now – depending on your point of view – holds us all in its malevolent thrall, deciding the look of the identikit towns we live in, the identikit shops we shop in, and if the algorithmic driven emails we all now receive on a daily basis are anything to go by, is even beginning to know every move we will make in the future.

Yes, Weller's chart had been the starting point; but in the end I had created my own map, adding my own backwaters and meanders, peppering it with what I had seen and what I recalled.

A key feature of my map, as of Weller's in 1863, was the age-old battle between old and new. The Red Lion Square cartographer marked up all the new railways on his illustration, the key agent of change in Victorian Britain, creating new towns and expanding others, and destroying the commercial trade of the Thames in the process. For my part, I had bumped into people trying to preserve things before they were lost: the community in Bourne End fighting for the independence of their local pub, a group in Richmond struggling to save the traditional river industries and communities amid all the new developments being thrown up along the river.

They had been all too aware of this age-old conflict in Weller's time, as much as we are now. I had read about it in the *Daily Telegraph* article from 1863 when I had been delving into all things to do with the mapmaker. Metropolitan improvements sweeping away the old London. A smirking uniformity replacing "the scowling yet picturesque vagabondage of the past".

In a way, this newspaper article had been as much a starting point for me as the tidy Victorian grid of the Thames map. I had wanted to find something more romantic and more mysterious than the modern humdrum of things. Discover the hidden treasure in the subterranean vault that the article had suggested was so elusive, or the casket of Oriental Pearl that the Victorian mudlarks never tired of looking for along the river banks. Something hiding away in the translucence of the map, waiting to be unearthed.

Had I found it? I didn't think so. The map – a guide for a modern mudlark, if you like – had taken me on a wonderful journey, but amid the babble and laughter of The Mudlark tavern, I couldn't help thinking there was something missing, some half-finished business. I fumbled in my trouser pockets for the hat pin that I had found amongst the pebbles of the Wapping foreshore. I examined it and gave it a rub; but it didn't sparkle.

I left my pint half-finished on the table and left.

I joined the crowds again thronging in the alleyways around Southwark Cathedral skulking in the shadows of the gleaming Shard, and down Clink Street. Underneath the railway arches an African saxophone player dressed in grey slacks rolled up to his knees and a smart blue shirt was filling the summer night air with his meandering blue notes.

They still hung in the air, but now joined by the lapping of the sea-salt tides of the river and the clinking of cutlery at the waterside, when I got onto the Bankside walkway.

"Exchange, as you know, is part of our global push," a smart young man said into his mobile next to me.

"She had a tent big enough for all of us," said another man, pushing past.

"They are talking Olympic legacy for things like boxing clubs for young black girls in poor areas like Deptford, yet at the same time they are taking money away from these areas," a sandy-haired woman said to her work colleague as they passed by.

Shards of conversation floating like fine crystals in the air around me as I now continued on towards Charing Cross Bridge, which I would cross to catch a tube from Embankment back to Victoria and my hotel. The Millennium Bridge, the Tate Modern: I passed them as I had done that morning. Then it was the Oxo Tower and theatres and concert halls of the Southbank Centre; all these places were wharves and docks in Weller's day.

I reached the bridge as the sun was going down. My father had come here during the war while on a day trip to the Air Ministry in London to learn more about wireless operations. My mother had crossed the bridge in a flouncy skirt with her friend Pat in the summer of 1951 as they headed for the bright lights of the Festival of Britain on the south bank. Now, the bridge was busy with twenty-first century sort of people – buskers and tramps, tourists and mavericks, executives, me.

But all of us, really, were just a microcosm of the daily cascade who had poured across the bridge since it opened in 1845. Tailors, hairdressers, boot makers; broadcasters heading to the World Service building on the Strand and jazz fans on a Monday night in 1933 on their way to see Duke Ellington play at the Astoria.

And then – in my mind's eye – there was Edward Weller, in 1863, gazing downriver towards the West India and Royal Victoria docks, down Britain's great imperial stream and out onto the wide oceans of Victorian idealism.

XXIV

Southend Pier

A brilliant red sun, I was convinced, was rising somewhere over the Thames estuary in anticipation of my arrival, but inside the tenement courtyard in Victoria everything was grey and silent except for the intermittent humming of an air-conditioning unit and the trickling of water from one of the water pipes that hugged the backs of the terraces opposite my hotel room window. No-one seemed to be getting up for breakfast or taking a shower or wandering blearily into that dining room with the French windows over the way. It seemed a very quiet beginning to my big day, the day I would catch the train to the final point on my journey. I had completed my tramp down the Thames Path, but that had finished at the Thames Barrier in Woolwich. Edward Weller's map, on the other hand, had naturally continued onto the mouth of the river. And at that point, where the Thames meets the sea, he had marked something out very distinctly: Southend Pier.

An hour or so later I was on a train pulling out of Fenchurch Street Station under a milky blue sky on the filigree line that Weller called the London Tilbury and Southend Railway, which nowadays is a route run by a smart green-liveried train company called C2C.

Rows of redbrick council blocks around Limehouse and West Ham slowly gave way to rows of redbrick semi-detached houses in Rainham which, in their turn, petered out into the flat, featureless fields of Essex.

Only a few miles away lay Tilbury docks, which in the 1960s and 1970s took over as the main port of London from the Royal Victoria and Albert docks in London. There was only a glimpse though of the cranes. I had a much better view of the grim tide of lorries lurching from the port towards the M25 orbital.

Somewhere out there, the great river was making its final approach to the sea, carrying with it 300,000 tonnes of sediment that it had picked up from the English shires during its long journey from source to sea. But I could see only a landscape created by the estuary, haunted by it, but offering no views of it.

I had to get back to the river, I decided as we pulled out of East Tilbury, check it was still there, see what it was doing. I had read somewhere that there was a nature reserve on the edges of the river which had just been opened to great fanfare by the TV naturalist, David Attenborough. I got off at the next station.

—⚡︎—

The young woman in the taxi booth in the desultory row of 1950s-era shops in Stanford-le-Hope had never heard of Thurrock Nature Park, but luckily the taxi driver had, and ten minutes later we were on a dirt track driving out to the Mucking Flats with the river slowly coming into view.

It was much wider than I had ever seen it and a little grey perhaps but now with a definite swagger about it. It looked very much like a river that had just broken free of the shackles of the capital city, and was now roaming free, snaking through low hills and mud-flats looking for its final exit.

I walked from the visitor centre down a gentle hill towards a bird hide perched over the waterside. Built on an old landfill site, the nature reserve is now a refuge for all sorts of wildlife, a notice inside told me, particularly wading birds finding easy pickings in the mud-flats and marshes below, birds like plovers, avocets and the distinctive black-and-white oystercatcher. I peered through the viewing gap for a while, hoping to see something, but as the expressions on the faces of the serious bird-watchers already camped out in the hut suggested, I had scared the birds off already by blundering so noisily into the hide in the first place. I had only bashed my rucksack on the door frame and then dropped it onto the bench with a noisy sigh of exhaustion, I thought to myself, a little hurt by all the looks of disapproval, but obviously that had been enough.

Halfway up the path back to the visitor centre about twenty minutes later, I met one of the volunteers who maintain this new attraction. Sweeping the path around me, he was a slight man, a pensioner obviously, with a well-groomed white beard; a man, as it turned out, looking for a chat.

"Sorry, excuse me," he said, as his broom knocked against my feet accidentally. "But got to get this done. Countryfile are arriving on Thursday, you see. You know, the wildlife programme."

"Oh, really," I said. I'm not that interested in wildlife, I have to say, but when Countryfile has been on as I have switched on the television on a Sunday night, I have always succumbed to the latest story about hedgehogs or some similar animal surviving against all the odds.

"Yes, it's David Attenborough who did it. Said a lot of good things about this place and preserving the natural environment of the Thames and all that when he opened it. Now, there's a lot of excitement about it."

The pensioner brushed some bits of soil into his pan, but it wasn't going to stop his flow. "You know this place is built on an old rubbish tip, don't you," he said. "They've done a wonderful job, I think. See the creek down there, they had to dredge all that."

I looked down the hill to the east, and saw the river seeping into a muddy inlet. "And when they dredged it, do you know what they found?" the volunteer continued, now leaning on his broom.

"No."

"They found lots of Roman stuff. Roman artefacts, pottery, that sort of thing. Mind you, the kids around here, they already knew about it. They've been finding Roman bottles and things from Roman galleons for years, and selling them on."

I had to get on now, but wished him well with the Countryfile visit. "Yes, thank you, we are all looking forward to it," the elderly man replied. "Mind you, you know what they're like. They'll turn up, take four hours of footage, and then there'll be 30 seconds of it on TV."

Somehow I rather hoped the 30 seconds would be of him. He had plenty to say, after all. My taxi driver on the way back to Stanford had rather less to say, until, that is, I started asking him about business.

"I guess you get a lot of customers from Tilbury Docks down the road," I said, trying to strike up conversation with the rather serious-looking man sitting at the wheel.

"No, not at all. There's a taxi firm in Tilbury itself. They get all that trade."

For a moment, I thought that would be that as far as conversation was concerned for the rest of the journey to the train station, but suddenly the large man with big shoulders piped up again.

"But when you were at the nature reserve, did you see those cranes by Mucking Creek?" he asked.

"Just downstream from the creek? Yes, I did," I replied.

"Yes, well, they're going to build a super-port there, where the oil refinery used to be. We'll get trade from that, I'm sure."

I suddenly remembered the huge rusting anchor I had seen in the driveway of the visitor centre at the nature park.

On a plaque beside it, the anchor had been dated at around 1841. It could have fallen from a local cutter, brig or even a three-mast schooner and was dredged locally from the Thames, the writing on the plaque said. At the bottom, it was signed off "DP World, London Gateway".

"Yes, it's Dubai Ports who are building it," my driver confirmed. "They are dredging the river so the port will be able to take those huge container ships, you know the ones. And they're going to build Europe's largest logistics park next to it, employing 12,000 people. So it's going to be good for the local economy. They say Marks & Spencer are going to build their major UK hub there."

I had a question. "So did Dubai Ports create the nature reserve as well?"

"Yes."

"So, on the one hand they are saving the environment, and on the other, they are building one great huge dirty, dusty, noisy port."

"Yes," my driver laughed.

The suited railway commuters whispering into their mobile phones or sleeping in front of their laptop on the early rush hour train out to Southend didn't look as if they cared either way as I boarded it late that afternoon. It was the end of a long day in the City of London. They had dealt with that important email, sat pointlessly in front of that powerpoint presentation, pushed that piece of paper; now, all they wanted was Pitsea or Benfleet. It wouldn't be long now.

It would not be long now for me either. I was now truly on the last leg of my journey. After Benfleet, the stopping-off point for Canvey Island, we pushed through the pretty fishing village of Leigh-on-sea. In ten minutes or so I was turning left out of Southend Central, into the sea-salt air, under the squabbling seagulls, then right down the pedestrianised high street and onto the Western Esplanade where a room at the art-deco Palace Hotel, now a 'Park Inn by Radisson', was waiting for me.

In 1863, Southend was being billed as a 'new suburb of London', a place where according to the well-regarded London weekly, *The Era*, those of middle incomes would "find in the handsome range of buildings known as Cliff Town, the opportunity of living within the bracing influences of a marine atmosphere and yet be only one hour and a quarter from the centre of the City" via the Tilbury and Southend Railway.

There were plenty of attractions too for the new resident; not only the magnificent esplanade along the cliffs but also well-appointed shops and for those more sportingly-inclined, the "famous pack of Squire Scratton's fox-hounds", the new swimming baths and, of course, plenty of sailing and boating. Then, at the end of a long day, there was always just the splendid "panorama of the shipping" coming in from the sea, (as well as numerous coal barges from Newcastle that the article forgot to mention). Your eye could follow the line of the famous pier with its "shell-encrusted timbers" into the middle of the Thames estuary and watch "the world's wealth of commerce ever floating upon the waters".

Southend in the nineteenth century was clearly a town on the up. It is probably fair to say that the Southend of the twenty-first century doesn't have quite the same reputation, being usually regarded as a town of tacky amusement arcades, one of those old English seaside resorts that have never quite managed to reinvent themselves. The view out of my bedroom window was of the distinctive dome of the Kursaal, an Edwardian amusement park that closed down long ago, but now houses a bowling alley, a sports bar and a casino.

But the town did have bright lights and a lively atmosphere, and as I was eager to experience it, before long I was stealing out into the night.

I found a Chinese restaurant on the seafront called the Pearl Dragon, where a waiter called Ray, who had just returned to Britain after a ten-year gap in Hong Kong, the place of his birth, berated me for choosing the vegetarian oyster sauce option on the menu rather than the real thing.

"You choose the duck with chilli and black bean sauce, and then you have *vegetarian* oyster sauce," he chided. "I mean, you're obviously not vegetarian. Otherwise, you wouldn't be having duck."

He had a point. I had chosen it to placate my guilt for eating such a sweet bird. It didn't make sense. Ray was right. I relented, and had another beer to make it up to my irascible waiter, and then, after a very tasty meal, headed out again into the bright lights of the sea promenade.

I love the sea, the freedom of it, the smell of it; and I ended my day sitting in the Park Inn hotel's hideous bar – decked out in bright reds and yellows to recreate the lost optimism of the 1960s – peering out of the windows into the night trying to glimpse where the island of Britain finally gave way to water.

Below the windows, the Adventure Island fun park lay dormant, the thunderous, thrilling danger of the roller-coaster, the helter-skelter and the scorpion all closed down for the night. Behind it was a long dark smudge stretching out into the estuary – Southend Pier.

Over on the other side of the black estuary there was the soft outline of the Kent Marshes and the old smuggling harbour of Egypt Bay. To the left of these were the twinkling lights of the Isle of Grain power station. And beyond that, there was a dark smudge of reddish light which, according to Edward Weller's map of the Thames, was the Isle of Sheppey.

—ɯ—

It was in this bar next to the long windows overlooking the estuary that on a cold Monday night in November 1948 my father, Ronald Wilcox, found himself suspended horizontally in mid-air, answering to the name of Hollywood film star Alan Ladd.

After three years as a wireless operator on Ghana's Gold Coast during the war, my father had returned to Britain looking to pick up the threads of his journalistic career. Now he was in another newspaper job and currently under the spell of a spivvy-looking hypnotist with greased-back hair and a pencil-thin moustache called Edwin Heath, who was giving a special display of his powers to the local Press.

"I don't remember much, but, somehow, I can't say I am thoroughly convinced I was hypnotised," my father said afterwards, according to a fellow reporter writing in the *Southend Standard.*

Although he never did quite explain how he came to be suspended above the ground with only his neck and ankles resting on the backs of two chairs, R spilled the beans in his diary a couple of days later. "I pretended," he wrote, "so I could get a story."

He had written a good many stories for the *Southend Standard* since he had arrived in the town with his demob kit bag on Saturday 1 February 1947 and knocked on the door of his lodgings in a little terraced house in Scratton Road near to the railway station.

Writing news items for the *Standard* during the week and features for the *Southend-on-Sea and County Pictorial* at the weekend, these stories were often harder-hitting than the ones he had written for the *Banbury Advertiser* before the war, quite simply because a Southend emerging from the war was a grittier prospect than a rural beat before it. The town had taken its fair share of German bombing, including the infamous V1 and V2 rockets, and, in the aftermath of victory in May 1945, faced a severe housing shortage. As late as 1948, R was still reporting on families forced to live in terrible conditions, setting out one day to visit the Peglers of Ashburnham Road, "a man and his wife who were living and sleeping with their four children in one small back room". One of their daughters, Maureen, had been sent home from school on account of her "verminous state" due, according to her mother, to "the conditions in which they were living".

Food shortages were another problem. In September 1947, as the nation celebrated the seventh anniversary of the Battle of Britain, R visited an agricultural fair to see the farm equipment on offer to Essex farmers now engaged in "an even more intensified Battle for Food".

With tropical fruit still hard to come by in the shops, he also visited Southend banana wholesaler Denman and Archer to see how bunches of green and cold bananas delivered from the ships sailing up the Thames estuary turned yellow in the gas-burner heat of the firm's ripening rooms.

In the tropical humidity of those store rooms, he wrote about a brave new world of abundance waiting for post-war Britain if everybody did their bit.

It was clearly a time of austerity, but slowly the normalcy of peacetime was reasserting itself; and life for my father soon became a routine round of long newsroom shifts and taking young ladies to the pictures. The most serious of these dates was with a brunette called Doreen who, in between flirting with my father's arch-rival – a fellow reporter and arch-villain called Flannery – accompanied my father regularly to the Palace Theatre on the London Road to see the latest film offerings, movies such as *Arsenic and Old Lace* and *Lady from Shanghai.*

Southend was also a seaside town, of course; and very soon, with memories of the war beginning to fade, the day trippers began arriving again from London. On a sunny August bank holiday in 1947, for instance, a steamer arrived at Southend Pier to take a gaggle of holiday-makers on an inaugural day trip to Margate. *The Lady Enchantress* had been a Royal Navy vessel during the war, escorting Allied shipping convoys on the dangerous route from Londonderry to Freetown in West Africa. But now she had shed her war paint and donned a pleasure steamer red and white funnel and creamy-yellow hull.

She was something of a showboat when R boarded her on behalf of the *Southend Standard Pictorial Supplement* with his reporter's notebook and pencil at the ready on that balmy Bank Holiday Monday. The boat was filled with stars from the stage and screen and BBC types, as well as ten 'glamour queens' on their way to a beauty contest in Ramsgate. A band from the Coronation Ballroom in Ramsgate was playing on the sun deck.

As I write this, I can see the beauty queens waving out of the page of the *Pictorial*, pretty faces peering out of a dog-eared newspaper cutting that I found one day in a battered tin chest languishing in the corner of an attic.

—〰—

At breakfast on the last day of my Thames odyssey I had a wonderful view of Southend Pier, a dark appendage of wood and iron extending more than a mile into the silver estuary. The longest in the world, they say. It had to be to provide safe passage over the treacherous Southend mud flats in Weller's time when it doubled up as a lighthouse, and to provide large boats like the *Lady Enchantress* a deep enough berth on which to dock in my father's day.

Sometime that afternoon, I promised myself, I would be out there, at the end of the pier, in the middle of the channel, watching the far-off container ships navigate a course towards Tilbury between the shifting sands of the river mouth. This morning, however, I wanted to visit the old fishing village of Leigh-on-Sea, which had looked so pretty from the train window the evening before.

Leigh's importance as a port began as early as the fourteenth century when it became a safe haven for English merchant ships being preyed on by French and Spanish fleets further out to sea. However, it was the fishing industry which grew rapidly in the eighteenth and nineteenth centuries that really made the town. Oysters had always been picked from the shoreline, but by the eighteenth century they were being cultivated in large numbers, joined by the farming of winkles and mussels shortly afterwards and a shrimping industry that saw the emergence of 'boiler houses' up and down the high street, built to cook the live shrimps brought in on the night catch of the fishing boats.

Until the mid-nineteenth century, the main catch would have been sent onto London by sailing boat or by road; but all that changed in 1856 with the opening of the London Tilbury and Southend Railway, marked up judiciously by Weller on his map. Thereafter, fish and seafood were carried by train up to Billingsgate Market near London Bridge.

I picked up that railway for just one stop from Southend Central, getting off at Leigh to walk via the cockle sheds down to the fishing village. It was mid-week so there were only a few people around: engineers in overalls working on the hull of a fishing boat in a boatyard, amateur sailors painting their dinghies on the small shingle beach and a few families milling around the seafood stalls. Emery's was selling fresh crabs – three for £6 – and Osborne's was doing a good trade in shrimps and cockles. I ordered a plate of cockles, smothered them in vinegar and went to sit on a bench beside the water.

According to the weather forecasters, an area of high pressure was building in the Atlantic – the Azores High – and would be with us by the weekend, but today was quite cloudy with the sun struggling to make an appearance.

There was a warm breeze, however, bringing with it the delicious seaside aromas of mud, slime and seaweed, and gently knocking at the mast of a fishing rig at the quay-side called the Renown, the successor to a rig which was tragically lost in 1940 on its way back from the beaches of Dunkirk. Further out, there were motor launches and yachts stranded on a sandbank unveiled by the receding tide. Beyond them lay the great wide silver-grey estuary itself.

It was a memorable scene. But, after a while I decided I would explore a bit more of the coastline and I headed back alongside the boatyards and the cockle sheds, past the railway station again, and out to Leigh Creek.

The creek is sandwiched between the mainland and Two Tree Island, a wildlife reserve and a haven for birds of every size and description: grey herons, yellow legged gulls and, like the Thurrock Nature Reserve, scores of wading species.

It was a strange landscape of salt marshes and mudflats, littered with the half-submerged wrecks of fishing vessels, rowing sculls and small schooners sitting forlornly in the rough lagoons created by the sandbanks. Gulls had made a home of these rotting boat carcases, balancing on the bulwarks or squabbling on the bows, sleeping in the bilge or in a cabin that had seen better days.

I picked my way through the high grasslands, reedbeds and scrub of this strange land, trying not to stray into the slimy mud that lay all around the paths. Quicksand? It would just be my luck to sink into a deadly bog just when I had finally reached the end of my journey, I thought.

Presently, all the wading birds working industriously in the mud around me began to capture my attention. Fat ones, thin ones, ones with long beaks, all on the look-out for the cockles and mussels and small crabs lurking in the sands. One of them, in particular, a bird of black and white plumage, with distinctive black markings on its crown and tail, caught my eye. A bird with a bright orange-red bill. Was it an oystercatcher? One of the birds I hadn't managed to spot the day before at Thurrock Nature Reserve when I had blundered noisily into the bird hide.

It was wading very close to a bed of high reeds, its eyes fixed on the mud swilling around its clawed feet. Did it ever actually find oysters, I wondered. Or was it always cockles and mussels or worms and insects.

And if it ever found an oyster, did it ever chance upon a pearl? I wasn't sure of that either. After all, it took a very rare set of circumstances for a pearl to grow inside a clam or oyster or any other sort of mollusc, I had read somewhere.

It needed a foreign substance, larvae or a tapeworm or something like that, to slip inside the oyster and splinter the mantle, the substance that produces the shell. The mantle would then, given exactly the right set of lucky chances and conditions, cover the splinter with nacre, also known as 'mother of pearl'. From this point, a pearl would form.

It needed exactly the right alignment of imperfections to create the perfect pearl. It was extremely rare. That's why a casket of pearls would be so coveted.

Oh dear. I was off again. Always thinking about that casket of pearls. Always thinking about the casket of Oriental Pearl, to be precise. The one the Victorians were always looking for. The one that almost every age and culture has looked for. From the Greeks and Romans who believed that pearls were the teardrops of the gods to the Chinese who peppered their temples with images of dragons swirling through the air in pursuit of a mystical pearl.

A casket full of them. The casket of Oriental Pearl. The one I was looking for and hadn't found. It remained elusive. Hiding away somewhere in the mudflats.

And yet. And yet.

And yet, there was something I had been thinking about for quite a while now. Yes, there was something. And it was now bubbling like some rogue current to the surface of the estuary around me.

I turned around and headed back to the railway station.

—⟋⟍—

The peroxide-haired woman at the kiosk looked confused when the man without children brought his ticket for the family attraction of Southend Pier. But it didn't matter. I knew where I was going now.

I headed out towards the middle of the estuary over the wooden boardwalk of a structure opened in 1830, first suspended over shallow waters covering mud and sand and then gradually over the slopes and trenches of the Leigh Channel. High above me, a deep ridge of storm clouds drifted lazily eastwards.

Occasionally, the pier toy train rattled past me; and once or twice I sat down on an iron bench under a Victorian-era shelter; but for the most part, it was just me and the sky and the estuary. Eventually I reached the head of the pier and the pier's cultural centre, a pre-fabricated glass monolith made in Holland the previous year.

I walked on to the very edge.

It was waiting for me, as I knew it would. *The Lady Enchantress*, moored up alongside. On deck, scores of 'New Look' couples were swooning to the saxophones and trumpets of Gordon Homer's big band, the young women's rolls and perms waving in the breeze, the young men standing firm in their V-necks.

Jack Jackson, the band leader, was standing with his baton in front of the band; to his side there was the double bass player and the pianist in sunglasses bashing on the keys of his white piano. At the same time, the beauty queens on their way to Ramsgate were taking their photo call against the bulwarks of the ship. Miss Malvina Scales of Shepherd's Bush (Miss Hammersmith), Miss Maureen Macer of Crouch End (Miss Park Royal) and their six rivals all gave a little wave at the prompting of the news photographer from the *Southend Standard.*

Beside him, the reporter in a trilby hat whom everybody called R stood at the ready with his shorthand notebook and pencil.

R? I had first seen you, hadn't I, when I stumbled upon the bicycle shop of William Morris in Oxford, when I followed you to the grand press visit of the Austin Morris factories in Australia in 1956. I had seen you lighting up a cigarette with your after-dinner liqueur at the farewell dinner in Sydney.

And then I had seen you again applying for that job in Maidenhead after your return from service in Africa in the Second World War.

Oh, yes, of course, then there was the time you held me in your arms on the banks of the Mawddach estuary in Wales and the time we flew kites on the beach nearby, and the time we climbed that mountain to the hidden lake near Grasmere and the time you took me for my first curry at a little place called the Bengal Garden in Birmingham.

But then came the moment, impossible to catch, when you began slipping away from me. I was barely ten when the veil of illness began to shroud you, and bend you over, and haunt you. I could see it unfolding in your eyes.

Slowly, the kites got folded away, the mountain walks stopped and there was no longer the prospect of a shared biriyani. Then, one day, before I had really worked out how to face the world, you were gone, and I was alone.

Of course, I never called you R, did I? To me, you were just my Dad.

—ⱳⱳ—

I watched *The Lady Enchantress* pull away from the pier, the trombones and trumpets now swooning and swelling through Moonlight Serenade. Did you look up at me on the receding jetty and smile? I couldn't tell. Was I that twinkle in your eye, or just a line of shorthand in some future notebook? I couldn't really tell. But I could see you. You were young and happy. The veil of illness that covered you and broke you in later life had been lifted. I could see you properly for the first time for many years. You were lost. But now I had found you.

I had found you like I found the map in the shop off St Martin's Lane. The map that through the valleys and plains of the great river had brought me back to you.

The Lady Enchantress would be chugging out to sea now, out into the Fairway Channel, sketched out by Edward Weller all those years ago. Slowly, after that, you would disappear in a summer haze on the horizon.

But I had caught you before you did.

Beyond that horizon were more coastlines, more bays, more rocky headlands and creeks. Sitting in his studio in Red Lion Square in 1863, the coal in the fireplace crackling, Edward Weller would be examining them all, measuring them with his pair of dividers, beginning to draft them out.

And somewhere downriver, beside the Paris Garden Stairs near Blackfriars, a group of mudlarks had unearthed something in the receding tide.

Slowly, gingerly, they broke open the latch.

9878754R00201

Printed in Great Britain
by Amazon.co.uk, Ltd.,
Marston Gate.